FIRST
TO FIGHT

POLAND'S CONTRIBUTION
TO THE ALLIED VICTORY IN WWII

Published by the Polish Ex-Combatants' Association of Great Britain under licence from MSS Consulting 2009.

www.Polish Forces Memorial.com

ISBN: 978-0-9557824-4-2

Printed in Great Britain by Antony Rowe Ltd., Chippenham and Eastbourne

Acknowledgments:

Photographs and illustrations courtesy of The Polish Underground Movement (1939-1945) Study Trust, London, The Polish Institute and Sikorski Museum, London, Museum of the Polish Army, Warsaw, Anna Branicka-Wolska, Jacek Korzeniowski, Dr. Marek Stella-Sawicki, KM, Dr. Andrzej Meeson-Kielanowski, KM, Robert Małolepszy, Aquila Polonica, Marzenna Schejbal, Jan Żyliński, Mjr. Jan Lissowski, Col. Stanislaw Berkieta, Feliks Keidrowski, Barbara Conway, Winston S. Churchill, Danuta C. Włodarczyk, Wiktor Kunicki, Michał Moszyński, Grzegorz Stachurski, Jacek Zbroja, Marek Fiedler, Teresa Karska, People's Commissariat for Internal Affairs, NKVD, Moscow.

Main articles, historical advice and translations contributed by:

HRH The Duke of Kent, KG, Winston S. Churchill, Jarek Garliński, Dr. Marek Stella-Sawicki, KM, Dr. Andrzej Meeson-Kielanowski, KM, Col. Stanisław Berkieta, Barbara Conway, Dr. Andrzej Formaniak, Jan Żyliński, Danuta C. Wlodarczyk, Teresa Stella-Sawicka, Jacek Korzeniowski, Barbara Korzeniowska, Tomasz Lissowski, Michael Moszyński, Frederick Forsyth, Arkady Fiedler, Stefan Mucha, Dr. Wacław Hubert Zawadzki, Andrzej Suchcitz, Zbigniew Jasiński, Jan Lechoń, Jacek Bernasiński, Ewa Cieplińska-Bertini, Rudolf Falkowski.

Supporting contributions by:

HRH The Duke of Gloucester, KG, GCVO, Major General The Duke of Westminster, KG, CB, OBE, TD, CD, DL, General The Lord Guthrie of Craigiebank, GCB, LVO, OBE, DL, Dr. Andrzej Meeson-Kielanowski, KM, President Ryszard Kaczorowski, Krzysztof Barbarski, Dr. Krzysztof Stoliński, Chez Maryszczak, Col. Andrzej F.K. Jeziorski, Marzenna Schejbal, Col. Stanislaw Berkieta, Stanislaw Komorowski, Undersecretary of State for Defence Policy, Warsaw, HE Barbara Tuge-Erecińska, Ambassador of Poland, London, Richard LeBaron, Chargé d'Affaires, Embassy of the United States of America, London, John Dauth, Australian High Commissioner, London, Lt. Col. J.P.E. van Tilburg, Deputy Defence, Military and Air Attaché, Embassy of the Netherlands, London, Col. Robert Vágner, Defence Attaché, Embassy of the Czech Republic, London, Brigadier W. J. Whiting, Defence Adviser, New Zealand Defence Force, London, Brigadier B C Jackman OBE MC, Chairman, The Sirmoor Rifles Association (The Sirmoor Club).

With special thanks to:

George (Jurek) A. Coelho for his help and generosity

also:

Prof. Andrzej Ciechanowiecki, Prof. Janusz Cisek, Wojciech J. Fudakowski, Barbara Kaczmarowska-Hamilton, Teresa Stella-Sawicka, Col. Andrzej F.K. Jeziorski, Col. Stanisław Berkieta, Col. Krzysztof Szymański, Tadeusz Juhre, President Ryszard Kaczorowski, Jacek Korzeniowski, Zbigniew Lis, Chez Maryszczak, Michał Moszyński, Barbara Orłowska, Gienia Marzec, Celina Kumorek, Tomasz Lissowski, Tadeusz Melka, Stefan Mucha, Teresa Potocka, Michael Moszyński, Marzenna Szejbal, Robert Sobociński, Jarek Garliński, Dr. Krzysztof Stoliński, Krzysztof Barbarski, Dr. Andrzej Formaniak, Andrzej Rumun, Rear Admiral Adam Mazurek PLN, DCOS, NATO, Andrzej Morawicz, Dr. Jan Tarczyński, Jacek Winnicki, Robert Nowakowski, Alicja Potocka, Ewa Kwaśniewska, Konstanty Zabłocki, Charles Bagot-Jewitt, Paul Kennedy, John Bryan, Marc D'hondt. *The Polish Daily* and *Soldiers' Daily, Cooltura Polish Weekly Magazine*, Marysia Maryniak.

Publisher's Note:

FREEDOM CUT FROM BLOODIED HANDS,

YET NO HOMELAND IN WHICH TO REST HIS SOUL

JAN LECHOŃ

Contents

CONTENTS

FOREWORD

BY

HRH THE DUKE OF KENT, KG

I feel deeply honoured to have been asked to unveil the Polish War Memorial on September 19th, and thus to pay tribute to the gallant Polish men and women, both civilian and military, who gave their lives in World War II in the cause of freedom.

Poland was the first State to defy Hitler. The Invasion of Poland, by the combination of German air command and modern armour, was overwhelming for the Polish defences and yet they were able to resist the invading forces with determination for six weeks until the Russian army attacked Poland from the East.

When their country was overrun, they continued their fight for freedom on many fronts. During the Battle of Britain, for example, Polish fighter squadrons destroyed many enemy aircraft and Polish air crews became renowned for their fighting prowess. On land, Polish soldiers evacuated from France formed the first Polish Corps, while troops of the Carpathian Brigade fought with the British 8th Army in the Western Desert.

The Second Polish Corps, under General Anders, fought throughout the campaign in Italy and achieved its greatest success at Monte Cassino in May 1944 when, at heavy cost, it captured the monastery. Field Marshal Alexander later described the Second Polish Corps as "one of the outstanding formations of the British 8th Army. The Poles played a part which gained the admiration of their comrades and the respect of their enemies.".

In addition, the Polish Independent Parachute Brigade fought gallantly at Arnhem in September 1944, whIch General Maczek's First Polish Armoured Division served under General Montgomery in North West Europe after D-Day. At sea, warships under the Polish flag, including 2 cruisers, 10 destroyers and 5 submarines, carried out numerous patrols and escort duties and sank much enemy shipping.

Aside from these military operations, Poles also played a vital role in the gathering of intelligence, especially regarding the German VI and V2 missile programmes, and are remembered particularly for their work in cracking the German Enigma code, which was to prove invaluable to allied code breakers.

On 3rd May 1941 Winston Churchill said, in an address sent to the Polish people on Polish National Day: "The fortunes of war have brought to these shores many thousands of brave Polish soldiers, airmen, sailors and merchant seamen. Their bearing has won them universal admiration in this country and cast further lustre, if that were possible, upon the proud, heroic traditions of Poland".

As we commemorate the 70th anniversary of the outbreak of WWII, we remember the sacrifices made by Poland, whose defiant spirit in the face of terrible suffering remains an inspiration to all humanity.

HRH The Duke of Kent, KG

Introduction

Winston S. Churchill

The Polish people and nation will forever hold a warm place in British hearts. It was in defence of Poland's freedom and independence that Great Britain drew the sword against Nazi Germany on 3 September 1939, within 48 hours of the German invasion of Polish territory.

The 145 Polish pilots named in the RAF *Roll of Honour* for the Battle of Britain constituted the largest non-British contingent engaged. They formed 5% of the RAF's front-line strength in the Battle and provided its most battle-hardened pilots. No. 303 Kosciuszko Squadron claimed the highest number of 'kills' (126) of all the squadrons engaged in the battle. Given the knife-edge on which its outcome depended, it could be argued that the Poles played a key role in turning the tide of Victory when the fate, not just of Britain, but of the world, hung in the balance.

In the field of Intelligence Poland made an immense contribution to the Allies' ultimate Victory by sharing with Britain and France on 25 July 1939 — just one week before the outbreak of War —their six and a half years' work in cracking the German military *Enigma* code. This enabled the code-breakers at Bletchley Park, at a very early stage in the War, to provide my Grandfather with the *Ultra* decrypts—undoubtedly the most important single source of real-time intelligence available to the Prime Minister and the British Chiefs of Staff — which played a crucial part in the successful prosecution of the war, and in ending it earlier than would otherwise have been the case.

After the dismemberment of Poland by the Nazis and the Soviets acting in concert, the Polish Resistance came into being, numbering 200-300,000 soldiers & many more civilian sympathizers. In the wider field of Intelligence, 43% of all reports received by the British secret service from continental Europe during the war originated from the Polish Home Army, which furthermore provided the key intelligence that pinpointed and made possible the destruction of the *Peenemunde* V-2 Rocket launch-site by the RAF on the night of 17/18 August 1943.

On land Polish ground-forces, allied to the British (General Anders' Army) or serving under British command, numbered 142,000 by war's end. Meanwhile the Soviets recruited a Polish People's Army numbering 200,000 under their command. Among the key battles in which Polish ground-forces took part were Warsaw (1939), France (1940), Narvik (1940), Tobruk (1941), Normandy (1944), Monte Cassino (1944), Arnhem (1944) and Berlin (1945).

In the air, by the end of the war, there were 14,000 Polish airmen serving in 15 RAF squadrons or with the US Army Air Forces. Losses of Polish aircrew serving with RAF Bomber Command amounted to 929. Meanwhile at sea, 4,000 Polish seamen served with the Royal Navy, of whom 450 perished, most in the Battle of the Atlantic.

My Grandfather, Winston Churchill, was always a great admirer of the Polish nation and staunch defender of their national sovereignty. After the Great War Winston Churchill, on 29 August 1920, echoing William Pitt in 1805, declared: '*Poland has saved herself by her exertions and will I trust save Europe by her example*'.

A generation on, following the outbreak of World War II, in a BBC Broadcast of 1 October 1939 he avowed: '*Poland has been again overrun by two of the great powers which held her in bondage for 150 years, but were unable to quench the spirit of the Polish nation. The heroic defence of Warsaw shows that the soul of Poland is indestructible, and that she will rise again like a rock, which may for a spell be submerged by a tidal wave, but which remains a rock*'.

In a Broadcast to the Polish people on 3 May 1941 he paid this tribute: '*When the call came Poland did not hesitate to risk all the progress she had made rather than compromise her national honour, and she showed in the spontaneous response of her sons and daughters that spirit of national unity and self-sacrifice which has maintained her among the great nations of Europe through all her many trials and tribulations*'.

On 22 February 1944 he declared: '*I took occasion to raise personally with Marshal Stalin the question of the future of Poland. I pointed out that it was in fulfillment of our guarantee to Poland that Great Britain declared war upon Nazi Germany; that we had never weakened in our resolve, even in the period when we were all alone; and that the fate of the Polish nation holds a prime place in the thoughts and policies of His Majesty's Government and of the British Parliament*'.

On 1 August 1944, with the Soviet *Red Army* on the banks of the River Vistula just 60 miles from Warsaw, General Bor-Komorowski, Commander of the Polish Home Army—following repeated calls by Radio Moscow—ordered a general uprising against the Nazi occupying forces. But it was nothing but a cynical ploy by Stalin who—though nominally Poland's ally—was determined to see the destruction, at the hands of the Nazis, of the patriotic Polish forces allied to the West, so as to install in power in post-War Poland a Communist puppet regime.

For my friend & comrade General Sikorski
from Winston Churchill
January 31st, 1942

Sir Winston Churchill with General
Władysław Sikorski at Downing Street

Sir Winston Churchill with Mrs Helena
Sikorska, General Sikorski's wife

Winston S. Churchill, grandson of
Sir Winston Churchill

Accordingly, while the Nazis concentrated in Warsaw 5 Divisions of troops—including no fewer than 3 SS Divisions—to quell the uprising, Stalin ordered the *Red Army*, which had swept Westwards 400 kms in the previous month, to stand fast on the Vistula, arms-folded—a shameful betrayal of an ally, which permitted the Nazis to destroy the Polish Home Army, together with the patriotic forces allied to them. For 63 days the battle raged in the streets of Warsaw—and in the sewers beneath.

Desperate appeals flowed into London and Washington from the beleaguered Polish fighters, requesting urgent airdrops of weapons, ammunition and supplies. But Warsaw was at the extremity of the range of the RAF's planes and Stalin refused to allow Allied transport aircraft, after dropping supplies to the embattled Poles, to land and refuel in Soviet-liberated territory just 100 kms to the East.

Churchill, determined to help our valiant Polish allies in any way that he could, was outraged. He promptly proposed to Roosevelt that Great Britain and the United States threaten to jointly suspend the convoys to Murmansk and Archangel, delivering aircraft, tanks and war materiel to the Soviets, until Stalin agreed to allow our transport aircraft to land and refuel.

Tragically Roosevelt, valuing his relationship with Soviets above his alliance with Poland and fearful of offending his new found 'friend', Marshal Stalin, was content to leave the patriotic Poles to their fate. He replied to the Prime Minister on 26 August: '*I do not consider it advantageous to the long-range general war prospect for me to join you*'. Without US support, the proposal had to be abandoned and the Poles were left to fight on with minimal outside support against impossible odds.

Speaking a month later, on 26 September, the Prime Minister said: '*I welcome this opportunity of paying tribute to the heroism and tenacity of the Polish Home Army and the population of Warsaw, who, after five years of oppression have yet fought for nearly two months to contribute all in their power to the expulsion of the Germans from the capital of Poland*'.

Just a week later the valiant, but forlorn, Polish resistance came to an end. A further 3 months were to ensue before the Soviet advance was resumed and Warsaw 'liberated' by the *Red Army* on 17 January 1945.

It is frequently alleged that Churchill and Roosevelt 'gave away' Poland at Yalta (4-11 February 1945). But the reality was that her fate had already been sealed by the fact that the Soviet *Red Army* was by then already at the heart—and indeed at the throat —of Europe. Short of declaring war on the Soviets, which neither Britain after 6 years of World war, nor the United States was in a position to do, there was nothing that could be done to save our gallant Polish allies, to whom so much was owed.

Given Poland's important, indeed heroic, contribution to the Allied Victory of 1945, and the fact that it was in defence of Polish sovereignty and independence that Great Britain had drawn the sword against Nazi Germany in 1939, I can say without hesitation that it was Winston Churchill's greatest disappointment of the war that Poland, in the very hour of her Liberation, was to discover that 5 years of Nazi slavery was instantly replaced by a Soviet slavery that would endure for a further 45 years, until the end of the Cold war and the demise of the Soviet Union.

Tragically Stalin's imperialist intent towards Europe was something that President Roosevelt utterly failed to foresee, let alone made any effort to forestall.

Winston S. Churchill

Editor's Preface

Poland's contribution to the defeat of Germany as part of the Allied Forces is well-known. As we commemorate the 70th anniversary of the start of WW2 on the 1st September 1939, when Nazi Germany attacked and 17 days later Soviet Russia invaded Poland from the East, it is important to remember the sacrifice, on many fronts, of Polish soldiers, sailors, airmen and resistance fighters.

With Poland's territory overrun, Polish Forces escaped to join their Allies in France until the signing of the Armistice. Later, as part of the Allied Forces, they fought in Norway, Italy, North Africa and also took part in the Battle of Britain, the Normandy Landings, the Battle of the North Atlantic.

As the war came to an end, the Allies met at the Teheran and Yalta conferences where they took the unfortunate decision to appease Stalin at the expense of Poland's freedom. Half of Poland's pre-war territory was then ceded to Russia against the Polish Government's wishes.

Consequently, many Polish soldiers of the 4th largest allied army, despite winning the war, lost their homeland and found themselves unable to return home and, despite the promise of democratic free elections, the country remained under the yoke of communism.

In 2009, there are few Polish veterans left; however, their children and grandchildren live to tell the tale of their bravery. This book contains both historical facts and personal memories of their experiences written by veterans and their children. Throughout this project the support of the British community has been overwhelming and much appreciated.

As Chairman of the Polish Armed Forces War Memorial Committee and on behalf of all the committee members, we are honoured to be able to put that history into stone to commemorate this bravery for many generations to come.

Dr. Marek A. Stella-Sawicki

Chairman
Polish Armed Forces War Memorial Committee

Dr. Marek A. Stella-Sawicki with Mrs Irena Anders,
the widow of General Władysław Anders,
Commander of the Second Polish Corps

SECTION ONE

Prologue

The Second World War did not erupt from a cloudless sky. The 1930s had been a time of growing political tension caused mainly by Germany's attempts to redress what it saw as the wrongs done to it at the Versailles Peace Treaty at the end of the First World War.

Given their precarious geographical location between the two totalitarian dictatorships of Nazi Germany and the Soviet Union, the Poles attempted with varying degrees of success to create a network of alliances in the years preceding the outbreak of the Second World War. Looking to France as a major source of support they signed a treaty with Paris as early as 1921. That same year they also signed the Treaty of Riga with Bolshevik Russia bringing to a formal end the Russo-Polish War of 1919-1920. This they followed up a few years later by signing a non-aggression pact with the USSR in 1932 and renewing it in 1934 for eleven years. These attempts to shore up Poland's eastern border were accompanied by a similar effort in the west, leading to the signing of a non-aggression pact with Nazi Germany in 1934. In the south, a military treaty was signed with Romania in 1921, and it was automatically renewed for a further five years in 1926, 1931 and 1936. However, Poland's unfortunate decision to benefit from the dismemberment of Czechoslovakia and occupy the disputed Teschen area, hard on the heels of the Munich Agreement of September 1938, did not help the Poles' cause in the broader international community.

Great Britain had traditionally stayed aloof from Central and Eastern Europe, not seeing the region as vital to its strategic interests. Nevertheless, Hitler's flouting of the spirit and the letter of the Munich Agreement led to a major policy re-appraisal in London, which resulted at the end of March 1939 in the British most unusually offering the Poles a guarantee of support, as part of a wider effort to attempt to deter German expansionism in the region. This led to Hitler unilaterally abrogating the Polish-German pact the following month.

The British and French now both worked at varying speeds to reach additional agreements with the Poles. The terms of a British-Polish mutual

1

assistance pact were agreed in April; they were, however, very general in nature. In May, the Poles and the French signed a military protocol which stated that, in the event of Germany attacking Poland, France would commence limited offensive ground operations against the Germans on the third day after mobilisation and then commit its main forces on the fifteenth day after mobilisation. There was also talk of an undertaking to launch an air offensive and the French were considering flying 'shuttle' missions from Polish airfields. However, the protocol was dependent on a political one, which the French signed only on the 4th of September.

The British conducted military staff talks with the Poles in May 1939, largely at the request of the Poles, and in July despatched a very senior general (a future CIGS) to Poland partly to reassure Warsaw. Unfortunately, the Poles saw these talks and the visit as more important than they in fact were and a confirmation of British intentions to come immediately to their assistance, which they really were not. This unfortunate misunderstanding was to lead to many subsequent recriminations.

Nor were the Poles aware that during military staff talks in May between the British the French it had been agreed that little could be done to help Poland in the event of a German attack on her. Furthermore, the French had stated that they would not launch military operations on the western front, but would prepare for an offensive against Italy.

The reality was that Britain's guarantee to Poland, and the subsequent five-year assistance pact signed on the 25th of August, were more of a vain attempt to deter Germany than to provide the Poles with concrete military assistance, and both British politicians and the military were only too aware that there was little that they could actually do to help Poland in the event of German aggression. Indeed it had been for this very reason that the British Chiefs of Staff had opposed the March guarantee and they were to cling to the conviction that only by ultimately defeating Germany would they be able to help Poland. In other words, they anticipated a long-drawn-out affair. At this stage no-one foresaw the effectiveness of German *blitzkrieg* tactics and there was a general belief that any future war would be essentially static, along the lines of World War One.

Neither the French nor the British provided the Poles with much in the way of military supplies in the months leading up to the outbreak of war in September, the British in particular being unwilling to divert resources from their own crash re-armament programme. Indeed as late as June 1939, Poland was in ninth place out of eleven on the British priority list for overseas military aid, despite the Foreign Office's objections. Defence of major lines of communications with the Empire were seen to be more important.

During 1939 tension in the region grew, especially over the status of the Free City of Danzig (Gdańsk), while the Germans also stridently accused the Poles of mistreating the German minority in Poland. The Germans wanted to annexe Danzig and to gain access to East Prussia, which was physically cut off from the German Reich, by means of an extra-territorial road and rail link over the so-called 'Polish corridor' in Polish Pomerania. In return, the Germans offered to guarantee Poland's western border. The Poles were not prepared to accede to these demands.

However, everyone's calculations were thrown into confusion by the quite unexpected announcement on the 23rd of August 1939 that a non-aggression pact between Nazi Germany and the USSR had been signed by their respective Foreign Ministers, Ribbentrop and Molotov. Britain and France, which had themselves been trying in a rather desultory fashion to form an alliance with the Soviet Union, were taken by surprise. The way was now open for Hitler to move against Poland and he was not deterred by the Anglo-Polish mutual assistance pact signed hastily two days later.

Thus it was that Nazi Germany's unprovoked and unannounced attack on Poland on the 1st of September 1939 unleashed the Second World War, since two days later, invoking the terms of their agreements with Poland, France and Great Britain declared war on Nazi Germany. Over the next six long years the Poles put their heart and soul into fighting the Germans at every turn, being in essence Britain's only major combatant ally between the Fall of France in June 1940 and the German attack on the USSR in June 1941.

Twice, after September 1939 and again after the Fall of France, the Poles had to re-build their Army and Air Force. Twice they succeeded in creating effective fighting forces. Indeed, in the case of the Air Force, they did more than that and Polish pilots shot down nearly 10% of all the German aircraft destroyed during the Battle of Britain, with Polish 303 Squadron being the most successful squadron in RAF Fighter Command. The Polish Navy fought alongside the Royal Navy from early September 1939 until the end of the war in Europe. Polish Intelligence provided a very significant proportion of top-grade intelligence product for the Allies, while the breaking of the German Enigma coding machine in the 1930s by the Poles turned out to be crucial.

The underground Polish Home Army, the *Armia Krajowa*, was one of the largest such organisations in Occupied Europe, which was remarkable, given the technical problems and distance involved in supplying Poland from the West. Illustrative of this is the fact that during the war the Poles received only 600 tons of supplies through British Special Operations Executive (SOE), whereas Greece received 5,796 tons and France and Yugoslavia, 10,000 tons each. Indeed, some reports suggest that Yugoslavia received as much as 18,000 tons. The Soviet Union, for its part, supplied only the Communist underground forces in Poland.

Polish forces were to be found in all European theatres of war fighting along-side all the major Allied combatants. Individuals, mainly airmen, were also to be found in the Pacific theatre.

Soviet Foreign Minister Molotov signs the German-Soviet Non-Aggression Pact in Moscow, August 23, 1939. Stalin (second from right) stands behind him.

BALTIC
SEA

LITHUANIA

EAST
PRUSSIA

Danzig
(Gdańsk)

Wilno

Minsk

Brześć nad
Bugiem
(Brest-Litovsk)

Pińsk

Poznań
(Posen)

Warsaw

GERMANY

Lublin

Przemyśl

Lwów

© Aquila Polonica

SLOVAKIA

HUNGARY

– – – – – – – – – – – – – German-Soviet Demarcation Line

The German-Soviet partition of Poland, September 1939

This volume attempts to present, primarily for the non-Polish reader, an overview of Poland's contribution to the European war against Nazi Germany. Among the smaller European members of the United Nations alliance, Poland's military effort was arguably the most significant. Yet, when it was all over, the Poles were not to savour true victory. Describing the summer of 1945 a few years after the end of the War, Winston Churchill wrote: 'So far only dust and ashes had been gathered and these are all that remain to us to-day of Polish national freedom.' Thus for 45 years the Polish nation was forced to endure an alien Communist political system with its accompanying apparatus of repression. Indeed a cogent case could be made that the Second World War ended for Poland only with the fall of Communism and when the Polish People's Republic was replaced by the Polish Republic, later the III Republic, on the 29th of December 1989.

The Polish 1939 Campaign

*Polish Army
cap badge 1939*

When Nazi Germany attacked in the small hours of the 1st of September 1939, Poland stood little chance: she was a poor, mainly agricultural country which was simply outgunned. Furthermore, the Polish army was somewhat unprepared for the scale and swiftness of the attack, and since it had always viewed war with the Soviet Union as more likely, it had spent less time developing plans to deal with a full-scale German assault.

The Poles' strategic objective was to hold out for at least a fortnight when, so they had been led to believe, the French Army would honour an agreement with them to attack Germany in the West. They also somewhat mistakenly understood that the Royal Air Force would commence offensive operations against German targets, once it had been established that the Germans were carrying out aerial attacks on civilians in Poland. Indeed the Poles saw themselves as very much part of an allied military coalition with the British and the French. Nevertheless, the controversial decision to deploy along the frontier was partly motivated by a secret fear that the Western Allies might be tempted to accept a Munich-style agreement, should the Germans seize those parts of Western Poland which had been in dispute after the end of the First World War and then propose some kind of arbitration.

The Poles were able to field about 1 million men in 37 infantry divisions, 11 cavalry brigades, 2 mechanised brigades (one of them incomplete) and over a dozen lightly armed National Defence battalions. The Frontier Defence Corps, deployed along the Soviet, Lithuanian and Latvian borders, represented a further 3 divisions. However, confusion over mobilisation orders, which had

1ST SEPTEMBER, 1939

'GERMANY HAS TREACHEROUSLY ATTACKED POLAND'

Soldiers of the German *Wehrmacht* break
into a Polish house in September 1939.

Stuka dive-bombers bomb civilian
and military targets

1939, German soldiers destroying a Polish frontier barrier

been rescinded at the last minute at the request of the French and the British so as not to 'provoke' Hitler and then re-issued, meant that many units were not at full strength. As an illustration, 'Łódź' Army was supposed to have 54 infantry battalions, 45 cavalry squadrons and 316 guns; in fact only 34 battalions, 29 squadrons and 168 gun were in the field on the 1st of September 1939.

The invaders' forces, including 6 panzer divisions, were divided into two army groups: 'North' and 'South'. Army Group 'North', with about 630,000 men, was to join East Prussia to the Reich as speedily as possible and then to advance south in order to link up with the German forces coming from that direction. The task of Army Group 'South', with about 866,000 men, was to attack from Silesia and to advance on Warsaw, destroy the Polish forces defending the city, cross the Vistula to the north and south of the capital and to link up with the northern forces.

The Germans were able to attack from three sides where the Poles had no natural defensible frontiers. The Poles deployed their forces in six field armies under the direct command of the Supreme Commander, Marshal Edward Śmigly-Rydz, with a number of reserve formations. The Germans had roughly a 5:1 superiority in aircraft, most of which outperformed their Polish counterparts. They also had an overall 1.5:1 superiority in manpower, 2.8:1 in artillery and 4.1:1 in armour, with often greater local superiority along specific axes of advance. Furthermore, German units deployed greater firepower, their equipment was more modern and their 'blitzkrieg' tactics combining air power with ground forces, especially armour, more effective.

The Poles, though poorly mechanised, did have more than 300 light and medium tanks which were deployed primarily in the mechanised brigades and they had 500 reconnaissance tankettes, deployed at divisional and brigade level. They also used 10 armoured trains and 100 armoured cars. Of the 4,000 guns which the Poles possessed, only 1,154 were deployed in the field, the rest defended fixed strong points or were attached to the Frontier Defence Corps. The Air Force had 43 combat flights, 16 bomber flights and 27 fighter flights, and there were also 12 independent communications flights. Altogether this represented about 400 front-line aircraft, but only the 36 Polish-made Łoś planes were comparable to the more modern German ones. The Navy had 4 destroyers, 5 submarines and 6 minesweepers/minelayers, which saw little action against the Germans at this stage.

The Polish Air Force was not, contrary to myth, destroyed on the ground in the first 24 hours, but dispersed to grass airstrips from which it attempted to harass the *Luftwaffe* and to carry out interdiction missions against the advancing German armoured columns. The Polish cavalry's primary role was not, contrary to myth, to launch suicidal charges against enemy armour, but to provide a mobile, albeit lightly armed, force. However, the speed of the Germans' advance took the Poles by surprise, just as it was to take the British and French by surprise a year later in France.

The Poles defended fiercely their small Baltic coastline. Although encircled, the port of Gdynia fought on as did the Hel Peninsula, now quite cut off from the mainland. The garrison of only 5 officers and 182 soldiers on Westerplatte, a small Polish enclave in the port of Danzig (Gdańsk), offered stubborn resistance for 7 days. The German battleship *Schleswig-Holstein*, which had entered the port before the outbreak of war supposedly on a courtesy visit, poured fire from her main armament onto the weak Polish emplacements, while from the land the Germans attacked with infantry, supported by artillery and dive-bombers. The Poles also continued to defend the main post office in Danzig, which had a symbolic value for them.

By the end of the first week, the situation on all sectors was very bad: Częstochowa fell on the 3rd of September, Grudziądz on the 4th, Bydgoszcz and Piotrków Trybunalski on the 5th, Kraków on the 6th. The 'Łódź' Army sector crumbled completely, Army HQ lost touch with its subordinate formations and Warsaw was now threatened. The roads were clogged with refugees and troops, which the *Luftwaffe* was able to strafe more or less with impunity.

While able to put up a stout defence and even counter-attack in a number of places such as on the Bzura, the Poles were rapidly encircled and forced to withdraw towards Warsaw and later the Romanian border. Unfortunately, any idea they had of organising a long-term defensive perimeter in the south-east of the country, with supplies arriving from the West through Romania, was shattered by the arrival of the Soviet Red Army on the 17th of September invoking secret terms of the Molotov-Ribbentrop agreement of the 23rd of August. No large-scale resistance was offered to the new invaders, who swiftly proceeded to divide up the country with their Nazi allies.

The Poles had rejected the idea of declaring Warsaw an open city in order to try to spare it destruction for two reasons: firstly, they had decided to fight for every line of defence and every town and secondly, the intention was to slow the Germans at all costs, for the Poles still believed that every day they held out gave the Western Allies more time to prepare their offensive.

On the 17th of September, upon the arrival of the Red Army, the President, the Government and the Supreme Commander crossed into Romania where they were unexpectedly interned. Warsaw fell on the 27th, but fighting continued in the Kock area until as late as the 6th of October. Meanwhile a new Government under General Władysław Sikorski, who had been appointed Prime Minister on the 30th of September, had been formed in Paris. The General would also be appointed Supreme Commander. Britain and France, while declaring war on the 3rd of September, had failed to make any major military move against Germany, having really made no advance preparations to do so, even in the event of an attack on Poland.

The German battleship *Schleswig-Holstein* firing at the Polish Military
Transit Warehouse at Westerplatte on the 1st of September 1939

German forces lay siege to Warsaw

Following page:
1939, Polish forces in action

A Polish cavalry unit during the counter-attack on the Bzura carried out by
'Poznań' and 'Pomorze' armies under the command of General Tadeusz Kutrzeba

Polish P.23 Karaś bomber-reconnaissance aircraft on a field airstrip
in the Warsaw region

1939, Polish infantry in action | The graves of Polish soldiers

Polish cavalry on the move in September 1939

Jan Stella-Sawicki, Polish 5th Lancers in 1939

The final Polish formation in action was Operational Group 'Polesie' under the command of General Franciszek Kleeberg, which fought the Battle of Kock between the 2nd and the 5th of October 1939

Carte D'identité Polish Army June 1940, Antoni R. Witczak who escaped from
Poland to join the Polish army regrouping in France

It appears that Poland lost around 200,000 men during the September Campaign, of whom about 68,000 were killed. As far as Polish equipment was concerned, 100 or so front-line aircraft managed to reach Romania where they were interned, while the remaining 300 were destroyed in the fighting. Almost all the tanks were destroyed, with the exception of a small number which, as part of the 10th Mechanised Brigade, made it to Hungary. A certain amount of small arms were buried, how much it is impossible to tell; the rest were destroyed.

The Germans took over 400,000 prisoners, the Soviets around 200,000 and another 85,000 Polish soldiers were interned in Romania, Hungary, Lithuania and Latvia. Many of the internees made it to France quite quickly, and a small number, mainly airmen and other specialists, headed straight for Great Britain by a variety of creative and circuitous routes, many of them through the Mediterranean.

The Germans lost about 16,000 men killed and over 30,000 wounded. According to Polish calculations, the Germans lost in action 993 tanks and armoured cars, about 300 aircraft (150 shot down in combat and 150 due to AA fire), 370 field guns and mortars and about 11,000 vehicles, including motorcycles. German figures were lower.

We do not know how many Polish soldiers died fighting the Red Army and Soviet figures for their own losses vary from 737 killed and 1,862 wounded to 996 killed and 2,383 wounded. Sadly and tragically, the highest Soviet government authorities decided in 1940 that most of the Polish officer prisoners of war, many of them reservists and professional men in their own right, represented a threat to the Soviet Union and decided to have as many as 21,000 of them shot in cold blood at Katyń, Kharkov and other sites. The Russians continued to deny this until both Mikhail Gorbachev and Boris Yeltsin eventually apologised to the Poles for this crime in the 1990s.

Given the subsequent lacklustre performance of the British and French armies in 1940, the Polish defence in 1939 was more than creditable and no cause for shame.

The Polish Underground State 1939-1945

During the Second World War Poland, although under foreign military occupation, developed an extensive civil and military underground organisation. This included, in addition to armed forces and their attendant training establishments, governmental structures, primary and secondary schools, several university departments, an extensive underground press, a legal system, underground theatre and musical concerts and even some limited arms manufacturing. There were also organisations to safeguard national treasures and works of art. In many respects this represented an underground state:

the largest of its kind in Europe. All of this, it must be remembered, had to be conducted in the greatest secrecy, while those who became involved did so at great personal risk to themselves, to their families and friends.

Between September 1939 and the Nazi attack on the Soviet Union in June 1941, Poland was divided into three political zones: the western part of the country which the German Reich annexed, the central German-controlled *Generalgouvernement* and the eastern lands which had been absorbed into the western republics of the USSR. The Germans also co-operated closely with the Soviet authorities in their new zone of influence in what had been Eastern Poland. While conditions were different in each of these zones, organising underground work was uniformly difficult and dangerous. A number of older Poles though had already gained some practical experience in underground work from the days of Partition before and during the First World War, which helped them in the initial stages.

It would be wrong to assume that there was an immediate general unanimity of outlook throughout the country. While everyone agreed that the occupiers had to be resisted, there was a plethora of organisations with different political platforms all jockeying to position themselves for the post-war peace, it being widely expected that France and Great Britain would overcome Germany in short order. After the 1939 defeat, up and down the country several dozen groups, most of them military, began spontaneously to organise resistance to the German and Soviet Occupiers. Indeed, it was this initial military impetus which led to the development of the Underground State.

The political parties also started to develop their own military wings, an example of which would be the Peasant Party's Peasant Battalions. The Polish Government-in-Exile began working immediately to weld these groups into a single organisation, which, after being known as 'Serving Poland's Victory' and the Union for Armed Combat, eventually became the Home Army (*Armia Krajowa*—AK) in February 1942. By then the Nazis were the sole enemy, the Poles and the Soviets having re-established diplomatic relations in July 1941. However, unity was still elusive and some underground organisations, such as the Nationalist Party's armed formations, the National Armed Forces, continued in some parts of the country to operate independently of the AK, while the Communists with their armed forces always stayed aloof, refusing to recognise the legitimacy of the Government-in-Exile.

The Home Army, with its secret High Command in Warsaw, was eventually to become one of the largest such clandestine military organisations in Europe with over 350,000 sworn-in members. The AK's field structure had the country divided into military districts, somewhat along peace-time lines, with the basic combat formation being a platoon of about 60 men, of which by 1944 there were somewhere around 6,000. Starting in 1942, the AK also organised itself into

Partisans and soldiers of the Home Army (*Armia Krajowa*—AK) and other underground resistance organisations. The Home Army was eventually to become one of the largest such clandestine military organisations in Europe with over 350,000 sworn-in members 'divisions', adopting the name of pre-war formations, but much smaller in size than a regular division.

The Home Army carried out extensive intelligence-gathering and military and industrial sabotage against the Germans and their lines of communication. It succeeded in disrupting German rail and road communications on numerous occasions, thus tying down large numbers of German forces, possibly as many as 150,000 at one time. The AK also liquidated informers and collaborators and those members of the occupying forces, whose brutality and behaviour were egregious, but since the Germans always carried out savage reprisals against the civilian population, attacks on individuals were rare and could be undertaken only after sentence had been passed by an underground court. Any

The Anchor (Kotwica) *was the emblem of the Polish Secret State and* Armia Krajowa *(Home Army, or AK)*

armed attack on German forces also had to be planned and carried out with great care. The Home Army, therefore, had a Counter-Intelligence division to try to protect itself against penetration by German agents, as well as its own military and field police.

In General Stefan Rowecki the Home Army was blessed with an able and energetic commander, until his arrest by the *Gestapo* in June 1943. He was later shot in Sachsenhausen on Himmler's personal orders on the outbreak of the Warsaw Uprising. He built up the Home Army so effectively that, for instance, by the summer of 1944, AK High Command had developed an elaborate command structure with almost 4,000 people working in it.

The Poles always hoped to use the Home Army as a military force in a country-wide rising against the Germans when the latter were visibly weakening, and it was hoped that when the time came, elements of the Polish armed forces in the West, notably the Parachute Brigade and the Air Force, would be able to join forces with the Home Army in Poland. However, a propitious moment never arrived and the Home Army's largest single operation was to be the Warsaw Uprising in 1944. At no time moreover was it ever fully armed, since military supplies parachuted in from the West could never keep pace with the growth of such an extensive organisation.

Every attempt was made to develop a legal underground political structure embodying constitutional continuity. Both the Polish Government-in-Exile, first in France then in London, and the underground political authorities in Poland derived their legitimacy from the 1935 Constitution, and were based on those pre-war political parties which had been in opposition to the ruling *Sanacja* political group, heavily influenced by Marshal Józef Piłsudski, which had governed Poland from 1926 to 1939. The main parties were the 'Big Four'—the

Socialist Party, the Peasant Party, the Nationalist Party and the Labour Party. However, there were also a number of smaller ones.

A Political Consultative Committee was formed in February 1940, followed in July by the creation of a Government Delegacy (*Delegatura Rządu*)—the official representation in Occupied Poland of the Government-in-Exile in the West. A conscious effort was made to balance the political and the military aspects of the Polish underground structures, given that many of the underground military leaders were former professional army officers, members of the *Sanacja* faction and unused to working with civilian political entities. The first Government Delegate was appointed in December 1940, but this did not signal the end of inter-party disagreements or activity which continued throughout the war. Despite concerted efforts, the *Sanacja* faction never regained its pre-war dominance.

Nevertheless, a reasonably viable structure was eventually achieved. The Delegacy proceeded to set up a quasi governmental apparatus with departments, which more or less corresponded to pre-war government ministries. There were between 18 and 20 such departments. Some of them, such as internal affairs, information and records, education, finance, control, justice and the Directorate of Civil Resistance, later to become the Directorate of Underground Resistance, handled current matters, whereas others, such as industry and trade, agriculture, public works, posts and telegraph, focused on the post-war period and also on documenting the Occupiers' behaviour. The Delegacy had its own press, producing the official fortnightly Polish Republic (*Rzeczpospolita Polska*), and ran a number of underground cultural activities, mainly through the Department of Education.

A wide range of publications was produced. The official political and military organisations were not alone in having their own press outlets, every secret group, every organisation, every political party aspired to produced its own magazine, which was proof of its existence and an opportunity to present its views. There were ideological, political, military, social, philosophical, literary, boy scout, instructional, women's and humourous publications, as well as simple news sheets. The largest number were produced centrally, but there were also local ones printed in small towns. The underground press not only provided news about current affairs throughout the world, but also raised spirits and helped people to survive; it instructed, educated and published scientific and literary work; it even ran competitions. The underground authorities also used the underground press to publish proclamations, orders and commendations, as well as death sentences passed by the Special Military Courts. In 1943 and 1944, the Home Army's regularly published *Information Bulletin* (*Biuletyn Informacyjny*) had several print runs of over 40,000 copies.

During the whole German Occupation, 1,075 books and pamphlets were published, every one of them in difficult clandestine conditions. Altogether,

Partisans of the Home Army controlled large areas of the heavily forested regions in Occupied Poland

Following page:

Major Jan 'Ponury' Piwnik a *cichociemny* and commander of Home Army partisan group 'Ponury'

there were probably around 1,400 magazines and newspapers published and overall, the number of copies of all publications produced ran into the millions. The best known underground publication, which was a reprint of a book published in London, and which connected the Homeland with its fighting men in the West, was Arkady Fiedler's *303 Squadron* (*Dywizjon 303*) published in 4,000 copies.

In April 1941, the Government Delegate set up the Directorate of Civil Resistance. The idea was to co-ordinate all efforts directed against the Occupiers which did not involve the use of weapons. These included: ignoring official decrees, avoiding all contact with the Germans, refusing to volunteer for forced labour in the Reich (volunteers were allowed to take their families), carrying out acts of 'minor sabotage' such as tearing down posters, writing slogans on walls, posting flyers, tapping into the street speaker system, or boycotting the cinema. The Directorate was based on political and community organisations, with strong participation from members of the scouting movement, the so-called 'Grey Ranks' (*Szare Szeregi*), and a Central Committee for Civil Resistance was set up in Warsaw. There was also a psychological warfare programme, 'Operation N', which produced publications written in perfect German purporting to come from the German authorities and intended to sow confusion in the enemy's ranks.

The increase in partisan activities, which was quite independent of plans for a general rising and preparations for it, not to mention a number of political issues, forced AK High Command to set up in 1943 a special entity, called the Directorate of Clandestine Resistance. It was headed by the Home Army Commander-in-Chief, with the High Command's Chief of Staff serving as his deputy and as chief of staff to the new organisation. The new entity's basic aim was to combine command and control of current operations with other armed initiatives.

As the Soviet Red Army advanced through Poland in 1944 the Home Army was able to organise short-term local tactical co-operation under the auspices of Operation 'Tempest'. However, in every case, this interlude ended in the arrest and sometimes execution of the local Home Army commanders. The AK rank and file were then either deported deep into the USSR or forcibly conscripted into the Polish Communist Army. After the spring of 1943, the Soviets refused to recognise the authority of the Polish Government-in-Exile, breaking off diplomatic relations with it over the issue of Katyń, and the Western Allies, unwilling to jeopardise the anti-Nazi alliance, did not exert any pressure on the Soviets to reverse their decision.

Yet during and after D-Day in June 1944, the Western Allies were keen to have as many German forces as possible tied up in the East and prevented from transferring to Normandy. They were, therefore, less than pleased at the Red

Army's failure to take advantage of the co-operation offered by the Poles, which, so it was felt in some British quarters, slowed the Soviet advance.

The failure of the Warsaw Uprising spelled the beginning of the end for the Home Army. It was formally dissolved in January 1945 by its final commander, General Leopold Okulicki, who would die the following year in a Soviet gaol, in unexplained circumstances. In March 1945, he, together with fourteen other leaders of the Polish Underground and their interpreter were tricked into giving themselves up to the Red Army, whereupon, despite promises of safe conduct given both to them and to the British, they were whisked off to Moscow. There they were put through a staged 'show trial' in June to demonstrate to the world that the Polish Underground had been working against the interests of the Soviet Union.

Late in the war, in January 1944 to be precise, the Government Delegate called into life the Council of National Unity. This underground quasi-parliament consisted of 17 people with delegates representing the main political groupings. In March 1944, it issued a declaration called 'Why the Polish Nation is Fighting' and it followed this up in July 1945 with a manifesto, called 'Fighting Poland's Testament' calling on the world to ensure that Poland's freedoms were protected. After issuing the Manifesto, the Council unanimously resolved to dissolve the Government Delegacy and then itself. This was the final formal act of the Polish Underground State.

The Warsaw Ghetto Uprising—April 1943

At the start of the war, Poland had the largest Jewish population in Europe. The longer the German Occupation lasted, the more the Jews' situation deteriorated. The Nazis had forced them to move into ghettos, which in the lands annexed by the Reich had been created in the spring of 1940 and in the *Generalgouvernement* in the autumn of the same year. They were stripped of their property, denied the freedom to move freely, ordered to wear yellow stars, forced to do manual labour and subjected to starvation rations, despite retaining a semblance of self-government.

The largest concentration of Jews, numbering about 450,000, was to be found in the Warsaw Ghetto, followed by the Łódź Ghetto with 160,000. Ghettos were set up in Sosnowiec, Będzin, Częstochowa, Piotrków, Przemyśl, Radom and many other towns. After June 1941, further ghettos were set up beyond the Bug and San rivers in Wilno, Lida, Grodno, Lwów, Stanisławów, Tarnopol, Kołomyja, Równe, Dubno, Borysław, Drohobycz and a number of other smaller towns

In July 1942, the Germans began an operation to liquidate the Warsaw Ghetto, dispelling any lingering hopes that some Jews harboured of surviving. The only source of help was the Polish Underground, so the Socialist-Zionist Fighting Organisation made contact with the Home Army and received a

April 1943, during the Warsaw Gehtto Uprising 6,000 Jews perished, many of them burned alive in buildings and bunkers

The Germans captured 56,065 people, of whom they killed 7,000 on the spot and the rest ...

... were sent to the death camps.

promise of assistance. The Ghetto leaders, however, were still hoping that a final liquidation might be avoided and only asked at this stage that the Poles issue an appeal to the allied nations, which they did.

The predominantly Roman Catholic Polish population did not remain indifferent to the fate of its countrymen who were being mercilessly slaughtered. Jews were taken into many private homes in the cities, towns and the countryside. This was no easy achievement in a country such as Poland, which was already on short commons and strictly policed. The Germans had introduced the most draconian laws in Occupied Europe under which anyone harbouring or helping a Jew was put to death, as were their immediate family and often their neighbours. Moreover, food and shelter by themselves were not enough, for medical assistance and some sanitary arrangements were also necessary. For understandable reasons, the situation became even more fraught when babies and very small children were involved. It has been calculated that it took the combined efforts of about 10 people to hide a single Jew.

The alarm, now raised, contributed greatly to increasing the amount of help offered the Jews. Private citizens, among whom the intelligentsia and families in the country led the way, helped. Perhaps one of the most famous of these people was Irena Sendler, who is credited with saving around 2,500 Jewish children in Warsaw. A number of organisations also played a major part; some, such as the Polish Red Cross, the Central Welfare Council, hospitals, orphanages, religious houses and shelters, already in the business of providing relief, were better placed to help and to do so with fewer risks.

Intense efforts were made to set up a permanent organisation to help the Jews, and on the 4th of December 1942, the Government Delegacy's Council of Assistance to the Jews—*Żegota*, was formed. The Council was composed of representatives of the democratic political parties and two inhabitants of the Warsaw Ghetto.

The extermination operation grew and daily 10,000 people were taken to their deaths. Those in the Ghetto who dreamed of fighting started to plan. On the 2nd of December 1942, the Jewish Combat Organisation (*Żydowska Organizacja Bojowa*—ŻOB) was formed, its aim being to obtain weapons and explosives, train a nucleus of fighters, begin appropriate propaganda and take a stand against further deportations to the death camps. Contact was made with the AK whose commander General Stefan Rowecki recognised the ŻOB as a paramilitary organisation and promised assistance in the form of training and weapons.

At the beginning of January 1943, there was a meeting between ŻOB representatives and officers from AK Warsaw District, at which details of co-operation were agreed, in the event that a last stand had to be made. It was recognised that the only real help would be to blow a breach in the wall surrounding the Ghetto, thus allowing a number of people to get away. The AK assigned a special detachment to this operation.

On the 9th of January 1943, the Head of the SS, Heinrich Himmler, paid a surprise visit to the Warsaw Ghetto. By this time its population had fallen to 70,000, although it was supposed to have been no more than 35,000. Therefore, immediate orders were given to step up the deliveries to the death camps. On the 18th of January, German police units entered the Ghetto to be met for the first time with armed resistance. Shots were fired by the Jews and although the Germans killed several hundred people and shipped out more than 6,000, they had been taken by surprise and temporarily abandoned the operation.

This initial success by the ŻOB made an immediate impact on the AK, which now provided 100 further pistols and ammunition, over 500 grenades and a great deal of explosive materials. Representatives from the Ghetto got out over the wall to buy cement in order to build underground bunkers, as well as all kinds of weapons and AK instructors taught the Jews how to make explosives and Molotov cocktails.

On the 19th of April 1943, the Germans at last moved in to finish off the Ghetto. They were reluctant to risk their men and so they began to shell buildings from a distance, later setting fire to them. The Jews took the fight to the Germans with grenades and Molotov cocktails and managed to set one of the tanks on fire and killed a number of the attackers. The AK kept its promise and on the first day of the fighting attacked the Ghetto wall, but the attack unfortunately failed, owing to the Germans' superior strength. The next day an active duty patrol of the Communist People's Guard knocked out the crew of a German machine gun. Later, Home Army detachments made three separate attacks on the Ghetto's walls and one of them actually had a firefight with the Germans inside the Jewish district and assisted by Jewish fighters.

The fighting in the Ghetto, lasting twenty-seven days, was reported to London by the Government Delegacy and AK High Command. An appeal to the Jewish members of the National Council in London was also sent by representatives of the fighting Jews. Unfortunately, the Polish authorities in London could only make fruitless appeals to the outside world, while the Germans proceeded to liquidate the Ghetto and its remaining inhabitants with the same ruthlessness that they employed in the death camps.

The Jews fighting in the Ghetto had no hope of success; at issue though were honour and dignity. The underground bunkers held out the longest and the Germans attacked them by setting fire to the buildings above and throwing flammable materials into the hatches and down the air vents. Only a few dozen fighters, helped by the Home Army and the People's Guard, made it through the sewers to the 'Aryan' side and survived. On the 8th of May, the Leader of the ŻOB, Mordechai Anielewicz, took his own life in the command bunker on Miła Street together with some of his closest colleagues. Fighting continued until the 16th, when the last remaining fighters fell and the Germans blew up the Great Synagogue.

In addition to those who got out through the sewers, a further few dozen defenders of the Ghetto survived, hidden deep underground in the ruins. The Germans captured 56,065 people, of whom they killed 7,000 on the spot and the rest were sent to the death camps. During the fighting, 6,000 Jews perished, many of them burned alive in buildings and bunkers, and supposedly only a little over a dozen Germans were killed and around 100 wounded. The whole Ghetto was then turned into a wasteland of rubble. Nevertheless, a line had been drawn in the sand and a statement had been made.

The Warsaw Uprising August-October 1944

Crudely stamped tin cap badge worn by some units of the AK during the Warsaw Uprising

The Warsaw Uprising was a tragic failure. The Polish Home Army's leadership had always planned to mount a nation-wide rising against the Germans which would be co-ordinated with the Allies. As 1943 lengthened into 1944, it became clear that Poland would be liberated by the Red Army not the Western Allies and that the Soviets were unwilling to work with the Poles on a large-scale against the Germans. Indeed, rolling up the Home Army and any other non-communist groups in Poland was clearly very high on the Red Army's 'to-do' list.

For the Poles, however, their capital was a symbol of their struggle against the Nazi invader and they wanted to repay him in kind for all the damage and pain he had caused. They also wanted to be able to greet the Red Army as masters in their own house and to disprove the Soviet line that the Home Army was reluctant to take on the Germans. As Soviet forces approached in the summer of 1944 there was a feeling in the capital that something was about to happen.

At the same time, throughout the country and especially in Warsaw, a noisy Communist propaganda campaign began. Using journals and leaflets, it attacked the Polish Government in London, as well as the underground authorities in Warsaw, accusing them of passivity towards the Germans and encouraging Home Army soldiers to desert to the Communist People's Army by promising all manner of opportunities to fight the Germans. In mid-July, Soviet radio chimed in using its Polish-language station *Radio Kościuszko* to call on the population of Warsaw to take up arms against the Germans.. This propaganda campaign grew daily and by the end of July had become exceptionally strident.

Since beginning his latest offensive on the 23rd of June, the senior Soviet commander in the area, Marshal Konstantin Rokossovsky, himself of Polish origin, had broken the German line. Soviet forces, together with the Polish Communist First Army, had taken Lublin and Łuków and on the 26th of July they crossed the Vistula near Puławy and, further to the north, reached Garwolin and they crossed the Vistula again by the confluence of the Pilica near Magnuszew. It appeared as if the capital was to be encircled from the south. Indeed, the German authorities had started evacuating non-essential personnel from the city.

On the 25th of July, the Polish Government-in-Exile, recognising the capital's mood, gave the men on the spot full authority to take their own decisions. During the last days of July, the AK detachments in the city were partially mobilised at secret locations and the High Command, meeting daily, followed developments at the front. Soviet armoured units were threatening Warsaw from the south-east, while Soviet aircraft circled the city. On the 31st of July, the Commander of AK Warsaw City District, Colonel Antoni Chruściel, brought information that Soviet armour had already taken Radzymin about 25 km (15 miles) away. A few hours earlier, German HQ had issued a communiqué that the Soviets had begun a general advance on Warsaw from the south-east and the Home Army commander, General Tadeusz Bór-Komorowski, had also received a cable from London that Prime Minister Stanisław Mikołajczyk had left for Moscow to meet with Stalin. This opened the possibility of reaching an agreement with the Soviets and of co-ordinating AK operations in Warsaw with the Red Army, and so the decision was taken to launch a rising at 5.00 pm on the 1st of August. The Government Delegate endorsed the decision.

Even assuming that the Red Army was willing to take advantage of an uprising and would hasten to take the city, the insurgents' means were inadequate, since they only had enough arms and ammunition for a few days' fighting. Altogether, Colonel Chruściel had around 20,000 soldiers in Warsaw and a further 10,000 in the neighbouring sector. The majority of them belonged to the AK, supported by 800 men from the Nationalist Party's armed formations and 500 from the Communist People's Army, plus a few minor groups. Their arms, few in number, dated from September 1939, from parachute drops, or had been captured or bought from the enemy; some of them were even home-made.

The German forces at one stage reached 40,000 men distributed as follows: 8,000 police, 2,000 men in Nazi Party units (*SA*, *SD* and *SS*), 5,000 *Waffen SS*, 6,000 men from the *Luftwaffe*, 4,000 Soviets serving with the Germans, 15,000 men from *Wehrmacht* security detachments, training battalions, vehicle park personnel and reserve units. They were all well armed, and had artillery, armour and air power, and the Waffen SS, Air Force, police and Party units were well known for their determination.

The Government Delegate, together with General Komorowski immediately sent a cable to London on the 1st of August informing the Government of the start of the Uprising, followed the same day by one to the Prime Minister and the

German *Sturmpanzer* tanks are used against the
lightly-armed insurgents

One German, one bullet! *We demand ammunition!*

Many fine buildings are destroyed by German shelling and bombardment

Altar boys during the Warsaw Uprising

Members of AK battalion 'Gurt' honour a fallen comrade-in-arms

Young soldiers of AK battalion 'Gurt' armed with captured German hand grenades

Street-to-street, house-to-house and often hand-to-hand
the fighting rages across Warsaw

Cichociemny Captain Stanisław Jankowski 'Agaton' leads his company
'Agaton' of 'Pięść' battalion through the streets of Warsaw where
Polish national flags are seen on many buildings

Supreme Commander (who was in Italy at the time) asking them to ensure an immediate Soviet attack on the city. They asked also for the Polish Parachute Brigade to be sent to Warsaw, together with elements of the Polish Air Force, and for the German airfields in the area to be bombed. However, even before the cable was sent the situation outside Warsaw had changed: Soviet guns had fallen silent and Soviet aircraft had disappeared from the skies above the city. There was an ominous silence in the east. There was no communication with the Red Army and there were no diplomatic relations with the Soviet Union, which had been broken off the previous year. Prime Minister Mikołajczyk had only just arrived in Moscow and the Western Allies had not been forewarned of the Rising.

Unfortunately, General Komorowski was unaware that it was technically impossible to fly the Parachute Brigade to Warsaw, not to mention the fact that, at the beginning of June, the Polish authorities in London had put the Brigade at the disposal of the British authorities for Operation 'Overlord'. The Polish Air Force, moreover had only the one unit, Special Duties Flight 1586, stationed at Brindisi in Italy, which was physically able to reach and help Warsaw.

Thanks to the element of surprise, the insurgents succeeded in retaining the initiative for the first few days. However, the Germans managed to hold all the barracks, headquarters and command centres, which had been guarded by the army. As early as the 4th of August, the insurgents' pressure began to slacken and their commanders ordered them to adopt a defensive posture, while the Germans, bringing in armour and air power, began offensive operations aimed at controlling the main east-west arteries. They quickly overcame the weak insurgent efforts in Praga, and took Wola after a few days, while in Ochota only a small area remained in AK hands for a fortnight. The Kierbedź Bridge and its approach roads were taken by the Germans, although they were unable throughout the Rising to control a passage along the Aleje Jerozolimskie to the Poniatowski Bridge, which they had held from the first days' fighting. In Wola and Ochota, German units, together with men from General Vlasov's Russian Army, quickly demonstrated the fate awaiting the city and its inhabitants: rapes, shootings, driving people in front of tanks and burning down houses. This led to widespread panic and an exodus from these districts into the city centre.

The second half of August saw a German assault on the Old Town turning it into rubble. On the 1st of September, it passed into German hands, its Polish defenders escaping to the City Centre through the sewers. The loss of this sector and German control of the Ghetto's ruins created a breach in the Polish defensive lines and the Germans were able to apply greater pressure on the City Centre, as well as on the Żoliborz and Mokotów districts. By now the battle had reached its third phase, which consisted of defending to the very last ounce of energy. AK High Command still had hopes of a Soviet attack and sought a means of communicating with the Red Army, refusing to consider capitulation. The Germans also had to take into account the possibility of a Soviet attack and thus, during the first days of September, they captured the Powiśle area, between the Kierbedź and Poniatowski Bridges. The Red Army, however, did not move.

Unfortunately, Prime Minister Mikołajczyk's trip to Moscow, achieved nothing for Warsaw, for the Red Army did not receive any orders at this stage to go out of its way to help the insurgents. In fact, Poland's only diplomatic success was on the 30th of August, when the Governments of the United States and Great Britain recognised the Polish Home Army as a combatant entity and an integral part of the Polish Armed Forces. The Soviets, however, declined to join them in this statement. The Western Allies went on to state that the Geneva Conventions applied to members of the AK, thus putting the Germans on notice. Since the German military commander, *Obergruppenführer SS* Erich von dem Bach-(Zelewski), had on the 18th of August proposed capitulation terms, with a guarantee of respecting the AK's combatant status, thoughts in Warsaw now turned to ending the bloodshed.

On the 8th of September, initial contact was made with the Germans, who agreed to evacuate those civilians who wished to leave the city. Von dem Bach repeated his proposal of an honourable capitulation, but before it could be considered, the city heard the sounds of fighting coming from the direction of Praga. The Red Army, despite considerable German ground pressure, had now launched an attack in Praga on the 10th of September, which lasted until the 15th and the Soviets succeeded in taking the whole district. Furthermore, during the night of the 13th/14th of September, the first Soviet drops of weapons and food were made. Two days later, on the 16th, an infantry battalion of the Polish Communist First Army landed in Czerniaków, near the Poniatowski Bridge, followed on the next day by a further landing by a small infantry unit. Given that there now appeared a real possibility of Soviet help, the idea of capitulation was temporarily shelved.

Meanwhile the British had been doing their level best to send in airborne supplies dropped by parachute. Unfortunately, these had to be flown from Italy, since Stalin had refused point-blank several requests from the British and the Americans to carry out 'shuttle' missions using Soviet airfields, which would have made the Western Allies' task immeasurably easier. This decision did not sit well, particularly with the British.

The night flights to the fighting city, carried out by British, South African and Polish aircrews, were a saga of heroism, technical problems and shabby Soviet intransigence. Even Polish aircrews recognised the missions to be almost suicidal and, given that the insurgents held only various pockets in the city, that accurate delivery of supplies was to all intents and purposes a hit or miss affair. Despite this, the Polish airmen insisted on continuing their missions with but little to show for them.

Repeated Polish requests to send the Polish Parachute Brigade or even elements of it to Warsaw were unrealistic. Given that the Western Allies did

A Warsaw sign—'Looters will be shot!'

Under almost continuous heavy bombardment Warsaw
is covered by a blanket of choking smoke

In a deadly game of cat-and-mouse Varsovians
have to constantly dodge German sniper fire

Insurgents celebrate after the American supply drop, although
much of it fell on German-held positions

After 63 days of fighting Warsaw
lies in ruins

Across Warsaw hundreds upon hundreds
of graves line the streets

After 63 days of heroic struggle the human cost of the
Uprising is immense and forces the AK to capitulate

October 1944, all surviving civilians and AK soldiers are expelled
from Warsaw after the collapse of the Uprising

not have local air superiority and without Soviet co-operation would be unable to achieve it, trying to drop paratroopers into an urban combat zone possibly at night would have been suicidal. Put simply, very few of them would have made it to the ground alive. Furthermore, an adequate number of specially adapted Liberators suitable to the task of getting the men to Warsaw did not exist, and the large numbers of slow aircraft would have been sitting ducks. Trying to send Polish fighter aircraft little sense, since the AK simply did not have the ground maintenance and re-supply facilities needed to keep them operational, even assuming that the aircraft could reach Warsaw unscathed.

After repeated Western pressure, the Soviets eventually relented on the 12th of September, allowing the Americans to fly a 'shuttle' mission to bases which they had on Soviet territory. Bad weather then prevented the Americans from flying until the 18th, when 110 aircraft took off from 4 airfields in Great Britain. Three of the aircraft had to turn back, but the remainder, escorted for part of the way by fighters, took a heading for Southern Denmark where they turned south across the Baltic towards Warsaw. The capital was barely hanging on, the last supply drop it had received had been 34 days earlier and hopes of any more had evaporated, so the arrival of the mighty aerial armada produced an indescribable wave of emotion. Two days earlier, in the Powiśle district of the city, men from the Polish First Army had crossed the river and for several days Soviet supply drops had been arriving and now the Americans had come.

Unfortunately, the pockets where the insurgents were still holding out were so scattered that the great American effort produced a rather modest result. The *Flying Fortresses* dropped their loads from about 5,000 metres (15,000 feet), leading to a huge spread on the ground, with the insurgents getting their hands on no more than 228 containers. Only the City Centre and Mokotów came out of it quite well, but most of the arms, ammunition and medical supplies fell into German hands. Furthermore, hopes had been prematurely raised by the landing by men of the Polish First Army in Powiśle. The bridgehead there had to be liquidated after several days' fierce fighting owing to a lack of support, while Soviet supplies of food and ammunition were dropped without using parachutes and were thus for the most part useless.

Conditions for the civilian population had become truly frightful, given the lack of food and medical supplies. What medical staff remained struggled to cope with the injured, gamely assisted by the clergy and members of religious orders whose devotion to their fellow man set an example for all. Thus capitulation talks re-started on the 28th and after 63 days of very heavy fighting, indeed some of the fiercest of the war, marked by exceptional German brutality, Warsaw had no option but to lay down its arms. The act of capitulation, signed on the 2nd of October, provided for the soldiers of the AK and all subordinate organisations to be afforded the protection of the Geneva Conventions. It provided too for the complete evacuation of the entire civilian population from the city. After which, on Hitler's orders, German troops proceeded to raze to the ground what was left of the Polish capital.

The decision to start the Uprising was based on two fatally flawed premises: that the Soviet Union would come to the Poles' aid and that the Western Allies would be able to provide extensive airborne support. Tragically for the Poles, Stalin was quite prepared to have his forces sit by and watch the Germans tear the heart out of the Polish Home Army. The Home Army lost about 18,000 fighters, a number which was dwarfed by the civilian death toll, which was nearer to 200,000.

Nevertheless, while it is not unreasonable to assume that the decision to fight for Warsaw would have been taken, even if the underground leaders in Poland had been aware of the broader political picture, it appears that neither the Polish Government and the Polish Supreme Commander in London, nor the Polish Section of SOE had taken it upon themselves to keep Warsaw fully informed of political and military realities and of the limitations of Western air power. The Home Army Commander's requests for the Polish Parachute Brigade and Air Force to be deployed immediately to Warsaw at the outbreak of the Uprising revealed a lack of knowledge of the larger picture, which was, however, somewhat understandable given that he was working in dangerous and secret conditions in an occupied country and that he was not an airman.

Ultimately, the Warsaw Uprising was a clear statement to the world that Poland was fighting for her freedom. It was also an attempt to arouse the conscience of the world. In this it was partially successful, since the Western leaders, especially Winston Churchill, were genuinely moved and for the first time lost patience with Stalin. Furthermore, the American decision to help the Uprising, when hitherto only the British had carried supplies and parachutists to Poland from the West, was a significant change of policy. For many, the Warsaw Uprising was one of the first episodes of the subsequent Cold War.

Breaking the Enigma Code

Arguably Poland's greatest contribution to the Allied war effort was made quietly in the 1930s, several years before the first shot had even been fired. In 1932, a team of Polish cryptanalysts, working for Polish Military Intelligence, including the mathematician Marian Rejewski and his colleagues Henryk Zygalski and Jerzy Różycki, succeeded in breaking the German Enigma electromechanical coding machine, which had hitherto defied the best efforts of British and French cryptanalysts. Enigma was eventually to be widely used by the German armed forces, the *SS*, the *SD* and German Intelligence, the *Abwehr*. Even German railways, *Deutsche Reichsbahn*, were to use it.

The Enigma machine had been developed at the end of the First World War by a German engineer, Arthur Scherbius. Looking like a rather complicated typewriter, it was based on a combination of electrical and mechanical systems with keys, rotors, a plugboard and electrical connexions, which together produced an astronomical number of permutations. It was initially available commercially for German businesses and was later adopted by the German armed forces: the *Reichsmarine* in 1926, the Reischwehr in 1928 and the *Luftwaffe* in 1935. At the time it was considered to be unbreakable, and indeed the Germans continued to believe until the end of the war that the Allies had not succeeded in breaking it.

By the start of the 1930s, the Poles had been working for some time on breaking German codes, approaching the problem from its mathematical side. Earlier than most, the Polish Intelligence Service had recognised the need to employ mathematicians and engineers, as opposed, for instance, to classicists or linguists, in their code-breaking organisations. Fortuitously, French Intelligence had already supplied the Poles with a great deal of useful information on Enigma, some of it coming from a German agent, Hans-Thilo Schmidt, who worked in the *Reichswehr* cipher bureau and who was the younger brother of a general in the German Army. Schmidt would eventually be shot in 1943. The French had also provided copies of intercepted German messages which they themselves had been unable to break. With this information in hand, the Poles obtained a commercial Enigma machine and set about understanding its more complex military version and establishing its daily settings.

By November 1932, Rejewski's team, by now transferred from Poznań to Warsaw, had mathematically established the internal connexions of the machine's rotors. Now the team had to solve the problems of the plug connexions and the key to each individual signal. Over Christmas 1932, Rejewski was finally able to decipher a complete signal sent by the *Reichswehr* using Enigma. This theoretical work provided enough information for the Polish AVA electrical firm to start producing several replicas of a military Enigma in the greatest secrecy.

However, given the regular changes of setting that the Germans made, this did not mean that henceforth the Poles were able to read all German encoded radio traffic within a reasonable period of time. Far from it. Speed was of the essence, since if it took so long to break the code that the information gleaned was no longer relevant, then the effort would have been in vain. Hence, the years leading up to the start of the war were devoted to grappling with the machine's innumerable permutations and daily settings, since the Germans were continually adding refinements.

In late 1938, the Polish team came up with the idea of mechanising the process by creating an electro-mechanical device, that they called a 'bombe' (bomba)—supposedly after an ice cream bombe—which was in essence the equivalent of six Enigma machines connected in pairs in order to speed up the laborious process of examining every permutation of the rotors.

An Enigma cipher machine

1932, Marian Rejewski reconstructed the Enigma's internal connections

Henryk Zygalski, worked with Rejewski's team at the Cipher Bureau which opened in the utmost secrecy in Poznań

Jerzy Różycki, also with Rejewski's team at the Cipher Bureau in Poznań

The Poles' greatest problem was their lack of financial resources to develop the specialist equipment necessary for this task. Paradoxically, this may well have contributed to maintaining the secret of their success, for when the Germans invaded Poland in 1939, they found none of the sophisticated code-breaking machinery that the Poles might otherwise have built. Indeed, they found very little, since the Head of the Polish Cipher Bureau, scooping up everything, had headed in the direction of the Bulgarian frontier and had ended up burying 10 Polish-made Enigmas in a field.

In July 1939, a British and French team of specialists visited the Polish cryptanalytical centre at Pyry outside Warsaw. Interestingly enough, the meeting was conducted in German—the participants' only common language. The British, who had themselves been working to break the German secret were, after initial scepticism, deeply impressed by what they were shown. The Poles then proceeded selflessly to hand over to the British and the French the fruits of their labours: two reconstructed Enigma machines with supporting technical documentation.

The British swiftly proceeded to set up a top secret cryptanalytical centre at the Government Code and Cipher School at Bletchley Park. Their greater technical and human resources, supported by the Americans, allowed them eventually to read relatively quickly a high proportion of German encoded radio traffic, this intelligence product coming to be known as 'Ultra' or 'ULTRA'.

The Polish team made it to France after the September defeat with French help. It then worked fruitfully with Bletchley Park, albeit at a distance, until the Fall of France. Indeed the Poles were remarkably effective between January and June 1940. Thereafter, the French refused to allow the Poles to go to England and sadly, owing to turf battles between the French and the British, the Poles' talents were subsequently never fully employed during the war. Furthermore, the Polish émigré authorities seemed unaware of the extraordinary trump card that they had in their hand and they too failed to take full advantage of the cryptanalytical team's skills.

The Polish team remained hidden in Vichy France and continued to work on breaking German codes. However, the Bletchley Park boffins, with Alan Turing as their star, as well as the Americans and their superior financial and technical resources, were now making all the running. They were, for instance, able to produce extensive numbers of 'bombes', which were a more sophisticated version of the earlier Polish version. When the Poles did eventually reach England in 1943, they were not invited to work at Bletchley Park and spent the rest of the war breaking relatively low-level German codes.

It is safe to say that 'Ultra' contributed greatly to the Allied victories in the Battle of the Atlantic, the Mediterranean, North Africa and elsewhere, thereby probably shortening the war. However, it was the initial Polish breakthrough at the heart of these achievements that is still considered to be one of the great feats of cryptanalytical history. Rejewski's work in particular, has been seen as seminal.

Interestingly enough, neither the existence of Bletchley Park nor the Poles' role in breaking the Enigma machine came to light until the 1970s, so well had the secret been kept by all those involved. Hence, Winston Churchill's memorable description of the codebreakers as 'the geese that laid the golden eggs, but never cackled'.

The Polish Intelligence Service 1939-1945

During the inter-war years, the Poles developed an extensive intelligence network to monitor their two large and potentially dangerous neighbours. By 1939 Poland's Intelligence Service, Department II as it was known, employed 250 military and 450 civilian personnel.

Over the course of the war the Service, the so-called 'silent front', provided the Allies with several major streams of vital information: on German deployments and order of battle in the east, on German military production, especially within the Reich itself, and on the effects of the allied bombing campaign. Polish agents also operated throughout occupied Europe providing information on every aspect of German military and industrial activity. At its wartime peak in May 1944, Polish Intelligence had 8 stations, 2 independent intelligence cells and 33 intelligence cells; 2 stations and 8 cells were in enemy territory with the remainder located in neutral or allied countries. Polish Intelligence resources covered all the current major theatres of war running, for instance, the only Allied intelligence network in North Africa, thus making a valuable contribution to the Operation 'Torch' landings in 1942.

Reports on dispositions of German forces prior to the attack on the USSR in June 1941 and on general German military preparations were extremely valuable. Indeed, the Poles as often as not provided intelligence product in response to specific British requests. Thanks to these reports, Churchill was able to warn Stalin on more than one occasion in 1941 about the impending German attack; warnings which Stalin chose to ignore. Then, in 1942, it was Polish Intelligence which provided the Soviet High Command with invaluable information that the Germans were in fact aiming their major thrust that summer towards the south and the Caucasus rather than towards Moscow, as expected.

Polish parachutists were dropped by British Special Operations Executive (SOE) into occupied Albania, France, Greece, Italy and Yugoslavia on special missions. There were also various Polish operations planned by SOE in the Pas de Calais region of France, as well as others to coincide with the D-Day invasion, using Poles resident in the area, as well as men from the Polish Army who had remained after 1940. The Poles too were involved in Operation 'Fortitude', whose aim was to feed the Germans disinformation on the exact location of the D-Day invasion.

A well organised network of couriers and good radio communications ensured the reports' speedy arrival in the West, thus increasing their value. Indeed, it has been estimated that Polish Intelligence provided over 45% of all British European Intelligence during the war: an extraordinary achievement, given the circumstances.

The Underground in Poland set up its own Department II with three principal sections: Offensive Intelligence, Defensive Intelligence, in other words Counter-Intelligence, and Research, which conducted analysis of intelligence received. Offensive and Defensive Intelligence sections were organised at regional, district and sector levels.

Offensive Intelligence set up a foreign division, code-named 'Stragan' ('Market Stall'), which had four sections:

'West' — covering operations within the German Reich itself;

'North' — covering Pomerania and East Prussia;

'South' — covering the area to the south of Warsaw and extending as far as Vienna;

'East' — covering the area to the east of Warsaw.

This structure survived until mid-1942 when German Counter-Intelligence managed partially to roll it up. The division was then re-organised into three autonomous sections which lasted until the Warsaw Rising:

'52-kk', later 'Arkadiusz'—covering the *Generalgouvernement;*

'East', code-name 'WW-72', later 'Pralnia' ('Laundry')—covering the East;

'West', code-name 'Lombard' ('Pawnshop')—covering the German Reich and other countries allied with Nazi Germany.

The Poles, it should be noted, also set up an effective Counter-Intelligence organisation, which carried on a protracted and very dangerous cat and mouse game with the Germans throughout the war.

They sent extensive reports on the Nazi death camps on Polish soil and provided the first details of the Holocaust to an incredulous and disbelieving West. They continued to provide military information on the eastern front, but as the Soviet Union advanced westwards, it became less important. However, information on German war production, and especially on the V-1 flying bomb and the V-2 rocket, continued to be critical.

Home Army Intelligence became expert in obtaining information on German industrial production, transport and the effects of the allied strategic bombing

Previous page:
V-2 rocket launch

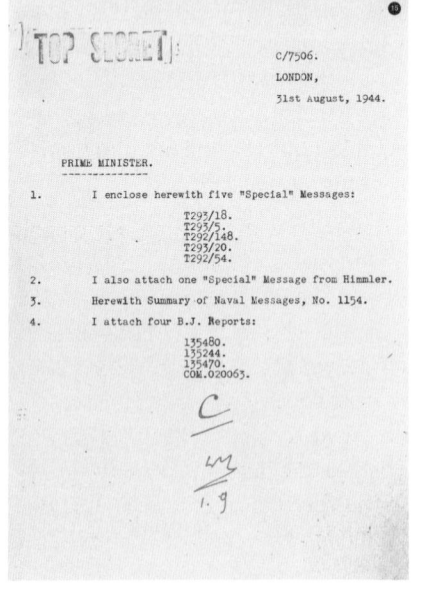

V-1 missile

Top Secret file—Decrypted Enigma traffic, August 1944

3-Rotor German *Enigma* Cipher Machine

campaign, developing a sophisticated intelligence gathering and research operation. The general shortage of manpower meant that the Germans had deported about 2,000,000 foreign workers to the Reich and employed them everywhere, including in the vicinity of high security facilities. Some of the Polish workers had received a certain amount of prior intelligence training from Home Army Intelligence enabling them to obtain much valuable information, which couriers then took to Warsaw, where two expert teams, the Office of Economic Studies and the Economic Council, analysed the material and prepared summary reports. These reports were then sent by radio to London at least once a month, while urgent information, often raw data, was sent more frequently, sometimes even daily.

Some of the Polish workers ended up in an international labour camp on the Island of Uznam, not far from Peenemünde, where the Germans were experimenting with the V-1 flying bombs and V-2 rockets, about which the British still had very little concrete information. Foreigners were not allowed into the actual plant, but the Poles, some of whom had received the intelligence training, had seen flying objects leaving behind a trail of flame and had sent this information to AK Intelligence contacts, who then urgently sent it on to London.

The British had a special scientific section which concentrated on German secret experiments and there began an immediate exchange of cables between Warsaw and London, for the British called for additional details as a matter of some urgency. These arrived from Poland in April 1943 in the form of a report, brought over by courier, which included a diagram of the Island of Uznam with Peenemünde clearly marked, a description of a flying bomb, its launch vehicle, as well as of the extensive German security in the area. This report was at once handed over to the British and became an important part of the big picture that the British were assembling from a variety of sources.

Using the information received from the Poles, British Intelligence was able to establish what part Peenemünde played in the development of the V-1. Information gathered from other sources allowed the British to make a similar determination about the even more dangerous V-2. This led to a major British bombing raid on the eastern part of Peenemünde, where trials were taking place on the V-2. This night-time operation was carried out on the night of the 17th/18th of August 1943 and caused a great deal of damage killing several hundred technical personnel, while the British lost 40 aircraft. After this, the Germans moved their V-2 trials to Poland to the confluence of the Vistula and San rivers, near the village of Blizna, which at that time was still beyond the range of allied aircraft.

After the V-2 trials had been moved to Poland, the Germans quickly developed a test firing range in the forest surrounding Blizna. Towards the end of 1943, local AK Intelligence observed the first firings and subsequent explosions, informing Warsaw which immediately contacted London. AK

Intelligence increased its efforts in the Blizna area, trying to get as close as possible to the launch sites near Częstochowa, Końskie and Rejowiec, while as far north as the Bug it tried to get its hands on pieces of these secret exploding devices.

In London, British scientific intelligence took these German experiments very seriously, for there was no defence against ballistic missiles flying above the stratosphere at an altitude of 90 km (50 miles). It continued to be unclear just how large they were and what was the size of their warhead, with some specialists suggesting that their payload might be as much as 10 tons, thus greater than the heaviest flying bombs. However, there was a faction, which included Churchill's scientific advisor, the eminent physicist Lord Cherwell, which downplayed the whole issue, maintaining that the rockets were a myth, since the Germans could not possibly have developed a powerful enough liquid propellant and that the launching sites were dummies. Therefore, getting hold of a rocket, or at least parts of it, was of enormous importance.

Motivated by this task, AK Intelligence worked up a number of schemes to wrest the Germans' secret from them. A partisan attack on the range at Blizna was considered, as was an attack on a train carrying a rocket, when quite unexpectedly fate intervened. On the 10th of May 1944, one of the rockets crashed on the marshy left bank of the Bug without exploding. A local AK patrol got there first, camouflaged the rocket, mounted a guard and sent an urgent message to London.

A specialist team rapidly reached the Bug and set about dismantling the complex rocket. This entire treasure-trove was brought to Warsaw, where a Scientific Commission together with the Economic Council prepared a report, which included 80 photographs, 12 diagrams, a sketch of the range at Blizna and a list of observed launches. It was supplemented by 8 original parts of the rocket and three appendices.

This report, together with the rocket parts, was to have been sent immediately to London, but there was a delay, since a very difficult operation, code-named 'Bridge', which involved a *Dakota* transport aircraft flying in from Brindisi in Italy and landing on Polish soil, had to be mounted. Only on the 25th of July were all the necessary elements in place—good weather, a secret landing-site and a protection detail—and the operation was carried out that night. In addition to several other people, a courier of AK Intelligence accompanied the report and a bag containing the rocket's key parts. On landing at Hendon in London on the 28th, the courier steadfastly refused to hand over the precious V-2 parts until a Polish officer turned up. Short of shooting him, there was no way to part him from his precious load. In the meantime a great many Whitehall technical types were kept standing around outside. After a considerable time, a senior Polish general arrived and the V-2 rocket materials were eventually handed over to the British.

It so happened that the a couple of weeks earlier the British had received some important parts from a V-2, which had been launched from Peenemünde and had crashed on the 13th of June in Southern Sweden and then ended up in Allied hands. The value of the Polish find was the radio set, which showed that the Germans were unable to steer the rocket in flight, and a comparison of the two rockets allowed the British to make an accurate assessment of the V-2's capabilities.

After the breaking of the Enigma coding machine, this was one of the Poles' greatest contributions to the Allied cause. In May 1945, Winston Churchill requested a report summing up the achievements of the Polish Intelligence Service throughout the war years. It showed that between the 3rd of September 1939 and the 8th of May 1945, 45,770 reports had been generated by British Intelligence, of which 22,047 (48%) had come from Polish sources covering a wide range of enemy activities. This information came into the public domain only in 2005.

Writing in 1945, Commander Wilfred Dunderdale of the British Secret Intelligence Service stated: 'Polish agents worked unceasingly and well in Europe during the last five years and they provided, often at great danger to themselves and to their relatives, a vast amount of material of all kinds on a wide range of subjects. The Polish Intelligence Service made an invaluable contribution to the planning and the successful execution of the invasion of Europe and to the ultimate victory of the Allied forces in Europe.'

At the end of the war, the Polish Department II was wound up. It burned some of its files for fear that they might end up in the hands of the new Communist regime in Warsaw and handed others over to the British for safe keeping. Many, if not most, of these were subsequently destroyed by the British for reasons, which to this day remain unclear.

The French and Norwegian Campaigns 1940

The French Campaign

At the beginning of May 1940, the German forces poised to attack in the West consisted of 114 infantry divisions, 10 panzer divisions, 6 mechanised divisions (2 of them SS), 1 cavalry division and 1 parachute division. They assembled 2,700 tanks and 3,800 aircraft. These forces were divided into 3 Army Groups: Army Group B in the North, in the centre was Army Group A, and in the south, Army Group C.

The Polish Armed Forces had been working hard to re-form in France, an effort which the French authorities had supported, but without noticeable enthusiasm, thus leaving many of the 84,000 or so Poles without proper equipment. While the Highland Rifle Brigade was seeing action in Narvik, the Polish order of battle in France was as follows:

> The 1st Grenadier Division, commanded by Colonel (later General) Bronisław Duch, of about 16,000 men;

> The 2nd Rifle Division, commanded by General Bronisław Prugar-Ketling, of about 16,000 men;

> The 10th Armoured Cavalry (Mechanised) Brigade, commanded by General Stanisław Maczek, of about 5,000 men, of whom 2,000 were fully trained;

> The 3rd Infantry Division, commanded by Colonel Tadeusz Zieleniewski, of about 8,000 men as yet without uniforms or weapons;

> The 4th Infantry Division, commanded by General Rudolf Dreszer, of about 3,000 men, and still in the early stages of formation.

The Polish Air Force in France, based on a nucleus of men evacuated from Romania and Hungary, began to form at the start of 1940 and was trained on French aircraft at the Polish Air Force Training Centre at Lyon-Bron, as well as at a number of other French locations. The whole Air Force, together with anti-aircraft artillery was commanded by General Józef Zając and had 1,449 officers, 2,836 NCOs and 2,578 other ranks. In May 1940 its order of battle was as follows:

> No. 1/145 Warsaw Squadron, combat-ready and equipped with 34 *Morane-Saulnier* MS-406 and *Caudron* C-714 *Cyclone* aircraft and in June, *Bloch* MB-152s;

> No. 2 Kraków-Poznań Squadron, half of which was called the 'Montpellier Flight' and was combat-ready with *Morane-Saulnier* and *Curtiss*-75 aircraft; the other half was trained, but was awaiting its aircraft;

> No. 3 Squadron had barely begun flight training;

> No. 4 Squadron had begun flight training on French equipment;

> The fighters also had five flights, called 'chimneys', of on average 7 aircraft each, guarding key positions;

> Reconnaissance and bomber formations had not yet been trained. Altogether, Poland had 86 aircraft.

Polish forces did not take part in the initial phase of operations in the West. They were deployed further south and only when the Germans attacked the French defensive line on the Somme and the Aisne on the 5th of June did their short period of combat begin.

The agreement between the Polish Supreme Commander General Sikorski and the French Commander-in-Chief General Maurice Gamelin had envisaged the Poles forming their own corps and fighting as a single formation, but

The Polish 2nd Rifle Division, on parade in France

1940, the Highland Brigade training in France

May 1940, the Polish Pomeranian Heavy Artillery regiment and 1st Grenadier Division, on parade in France

1940, General Sikorski and journalists
with Polish troops in France

June 1940, tanks of the Polish 10th
Armoured Cavalry Brigade fighting
in Champagne, France

1940, Polish *Morane-Saulnier* MS-406 aircraft in France

circumstances dictated otherwise. The Germans rapidly broke through the French defences and it transpired that the French commanders had prepared no reinforcements; thus units, whether ready or not, were thrown into battle.

Two Polish divisions were available: the 1st Grenadiers under General Duch and the 2nd Rifles under General Prugar-Ketling. Part of General Maczek's 10th Armoured Cavalry Brigade was also available and 8 Polish infantry companies and 2 anti-tank batteries had been integrated into French regiments. Finally the 3rd Division, not yet combat-ready, and 2 battalions from the training depot at Coëtquidan could be used at a pinch. Altogether, this represented 40,000 men: admittedly a small force, but one determined to defend every position to the last.

The 1st Grenadiers were deployed to the south-west of Nancy as part of French XX Corps, whose responsibility was the defence of the Maginot Line near the river Saar. Even before the German attack south, the French Corps Commander had withdrawn the Division's artillery, followed by its anti-tank batteries and a battalion of engineers, thus weakening it considerably. The Division's involvement in heavy defensive fighting began on the 14th of June and lasted only a week, during which it suffered 35% casualties. It enjoyed a major success at the two-day battle of Lagarde, on the 17th/18th of June, but to little effect, since the withdrawal of neighbouring French units caused the Division to relinquish its position. On the 17th the new French Premier, Marshal Pétain, contacted the Germans with a proposal for a cease-fire and it was clear that the fighting was drawing to a close.

On the 19th of June, General Sikorski made a radio broadcast stating that Poland would continue to fight as an ally of Great Britain and ordering all Polish units to get to ports in the South of France or to cross the Swiss frontier. The following day, General Duch called an officers' meeting and informed everyone that they needed to follow the Supreme Commander's instructions. On the 21st, the Division disbanded, its equipment was either destroyed or buried, and its men were ordered to break out to the south in small groups.

June found the 2nd Rifles in the area of Belfort, not far from the Swiss frontier, and as part of French XLV Corps. The Germans were expected to attack from the north, but they unexpectedly appeared from the west heading for the Swiss frontier, so the Division was ordered to attack in the direction of Besançon. Speed was of the essence, since the Germans were attempting an encirclement thus the Division headed towards Pontarlier. The approach of German mechanised units forced the Division to halt and take up defensive positions on the heights at Clos-du-Doubs. The ensuing battle lasted two days with the Germans were unable to break through the Polish positions, but the men were tiring, ammunition and food were running low and Franco-German cease-fire negotiations were already underway. Thus General Prugar-Ketling gave the order to cross the Swiss frontier. This took place during the night of the

19th/20th of June when the Division marched over in close ranks, fully armed and with bayonets fixed. It was then interned.

The 10th Armoured Cavalry was still not ready to take its position in the line, so General Maczek formed a unit of 102 officers and 607 other ranks which went up to the front as part of French VII Corps. This unit fought from the 13th to the 16th of June in the area of Champaubert and Montbard where, during the night, seeing no chance to continue fighting, it destroyed its equipment and filtered south in small groups. General Maczek, after a 17-day march on foot, reached Clermont-Ferrand where he reported to General Maxime Weygand, the new French Commander-in-Chief, on the 4th of July.

The fate of Polish anti-tank batteries, scattered throughout French units, was similar. Everywhere the Polish troops wanted to fight, but they encountered only inertia, confusion and the French people's and their army's apathy.

Of the Polish Air Force only No. 1/145 Warsaw Squadron saw any action as a unit, as did 6 three-plane flights of the 'Montpellier Wing', and a further 6 in various French squadrons, as well as 5 of the so-called 'chimneys' protecting airfields and factories (hence the name 'chimney'), scattered all over France. At the moment of the German attack the Squadron was in the Lyon area and later it was transferred to an airfield at Mions, and on the 6th of June it joined French No. 42 Fighter Group and was tasked to cover the stretch of the Seine between Vernon and Menton. From the 8th to the 10th, the Squadron was engaged aginst German fighters and bombers over Rouen and Dreux, with 11 confirmed 'kills'. After a few days at Semaise where the pilots were trained on *Blochs*, the Squadron was moved by road on the 13th to Châteauroux where it was to defend the airfield. On the 19th, during flight operations when one enemy was shot down, the Squadron picked up the Supreme Commander's order to make a speedy evacuation. The airmen set off for the port of La Rochelle and left for Great Britain by sea the following day.

Formations from the 'Montpellier Wing' saw action in a number of areas and as part of various French units. They shot down 25 enemy aircraft, for the loss of only 3 pilots. After the cease-fire, the formations from the South of France, mainly from Perpignan, flew across the Mediterranean to North Africa and a number of the airmen made their way straight to Great Britain via Gibraltar. The 6 other such formations, scattered throughout the country, shot down 5 enemy aircraft. The 'chimneys' also gave a good account of themselves, chalking up 11 confirmed 'kills'. Altogether, Polish fighter aircraft shot down 52 German aircraft in France, with 3 unconfirmed and 6 damaged, for the loss of 11 pilots. A further 15 airmen were killed on the ground.

In Poland the fall of France was greeted with incredulity and some despair. For centuries the two countries had been linked by political and cultural ties, the First World War had bred faith in French arms and the Maginot Line had been

1940, men of the Polish Highland Brigade in Norway

Opposite page:
Polish sappers training in Scotland

Polish sappers in Scotland

1942, Polish *Valentine* MkIII tank of the
16th Tank Brigade

Polish Independent Paratroop Brigade on exercise in Scotland, 1942-43

1941, King George VI and Queen Elizabeth
visit Polish troops in Scotland

1939, General Sikorski, the Duke of Kent and the Polish Ambassador,
Count Edward Raczyński

seen as a symbol of French military might. Now, idealised and heroic France had fallen: worse, she had capitulated almost without a fight.

Altogether, about 20,000 Polish soldiers made it across the English Channel. Some 1,400 had been killed defending France and 4,500 wounded.

The Norwegian campaign

As the fighting continued in France, the Polish Highland Brigade went to Norway as part of the Anglo-French expeditionary corps sent there in April 1940. The expeditionary force's task was to support the Norwegians in stopping the German invasion of their country. It then planned to take Narvik to the north of the Arctic Circle and destroy the port and the railway lines, the aim being to prevent the Germans bringing out ore from the Kiruna-Gällivare iron ore fields in Northern Sweden through Narvik.

The Highland Brigade had been given two objectives: to capture the town of Ankenes across the fjord from Narvik, as well as the small town of Beisfjord further up the fjord and it achieved both on the 27th and 28th of May. On the evening of the 29th, the Germans pulled out of Narvik which was then entered by a battalion of Norwegian infantry , the Poles having greatly contributed to this success.

However, overall German resistance turned to be too strong, while the Allies were so sluggish and poorly co-ordinated, and the news from France so bad, that allied plans were changed. A few days later, an evacuation began and the Brigade left Norway between the 3rd and the 8th of June, together with the other allied units. The Norwegian King and Government also left for Great Britain. The Brigade left behind 2 Polish officers and 95 other ranks in a field cemetery near the town of Meiri. The Poles also lost the destroyer *Grom*, which was sunk by German aircraft, and the troop-carrying liner *Chrobry*.

A convoy then carried the Brigade to the Scottish port of Greenock whence, on the 13th, it set off for France in several ships in the hope that it still might play a part in the fighting there. A day later, it landed in Brest only to have almost immediately to find a way to get back to Great Britain. Most of its members did make it across the Channel. However, the whole Norwegian venture had been a failure, although the Poles had put up a good show.

The Polish First Corps

Upon its arrival in Britain after the Fall of France, the Polish Army was deployed to the East of Scotland where it was assigned to defend a 100-km (60-mile) stretch of coast from the Firth of Forth to Montrose, with the city of Perth more or less in the middle, against a possible German invasion. On the 5th of July 1940, a Polish headquarters was set up in Eastend near Lanark.

In addition to the British-Polish pact of the 25th of August 1939, two others had been signed covering military matters: the Polish Naval Agreement of the 18th of November 1939 and the Polish Air Force Agreement of the 11th of June 1940. However, the new situation with foreign troops actually stationed on British soil required further legislation. Therefore, on the 5th of August 1940, the British-Polish Military Agreement was signed, governing the formation of Polish armed forces in Britain, and adapting all Polish regulations and standing orders to local laws and practices.

Two rifle brigades were hastily formed in Scotland; they were almost entirely mechanised and had their own armour, artillery, engineers, signals and other supporting arms. Given a great preponderance of officers, eventually five other cadre brigades were formed, but with a full complement of officers and very few other ranks. In addition, four armoured-train columns were formed, with three trains to a column, manned almost entirely by officers (each train having 47 officers and 5 soldiers!).

In late 1940, work was begun on forming Polish First Corps in Scotland, which included, in addition to a wide range of support units, the 1st Rifle Brigade, the 2nd Rifle Brigade, which was turned into the 10th Mechanised Brigade and its two battalions re-designated as regiments and named after cavalry regiments which had been part of the Brigade during the September Campaign, the 24th Uhlan Regiment and the 10th Regiment of Mounted Rifles, and several skeleton rifle brigades. The 4th Rifle Brigade would later become the 1st Independent Parachute Brigade. General Kukiel, hitherto commander of Polish camps in Britain, was now appointed to command the Polish First Corps. Later, the 4th Infantry Division and the 16th Independent Armoured Brigade would also be raised.

The Corps never became a field formation and was remain in Scotland for the duration of the war providing rear echelon support, which included hospitals and training establishments.

The Polish Carpathian Rifle Brigade

One of the truly outstanding combat formations raised abroad by the Poles during the war was the Independent Carpathian Rifle Brigade named after a unit which had fought in the 1939 Campaign. It would later become one of the famous 'Rats of Tobruk' for having taken part in the defence of that city.

General Sikorski, believing that 'all roads lead to Poland' and wanting to be as helpful as possible towards his Allies on whom Poland's fate ultimately depended, agreed early on to the formation of a unit in the French Army of the Levant. It fitted into a strategic vision of launching a campaign through the Balkans from the Middle East.

The Brigade, commanded by one of Poland's ablest senior officers, Colonel (later General) Stanisław Kopański, who having escaped internment in Romania had then been sent from Paris, was formed in December 1939 in Syria under French command. It was made up of men who had managed to get away from Poland and Romania in 1939, many of them by way of the Middle East. Other Poles, who had left Poland under their own steam, volunteered for the Brigade, as did a great many others who lived overseas and who wanted to fight for Poland and for whom Syria was closer than France. In May 1940, the Brigade was not fully ready, but already numbered around 4,000 men.

Badge of the Carpathian Rifle Brigade

The Fall of France dramatically affected the fortunes of the Carpathian Brigade stationed in Syria. The local French commanders who now came under the new Vichy Government ordered the Poles to lay down their arms, but General Kopański defied them and succeeded in withdrawing the whole Brigade, with its weapons, to Palestine, where it was warmly greeted by the British ,and on the 2nd of July came under British command. At the beginning of October, the Brigade, now almost 5,000-strong, was transferred to Egypt, where it was entrusted with the defence of an area on the outskirts of Alexandria.

Meanwhile on the 9th of December, General Sir Archibald Wavell began an unexpected offensive in North Africa. Hence the British, who had appeared to have used all their forces preventing an invasion, in fact still had enough reserves to be able to equip and prepare an army in Egypt capable of offensive action. While it had barely 30,000 men, albeit with modern equipment, within a few weeks it had broken an extensive Italian army of over 200,000 men. Starting from Sidi Barrani in Egypt, Wavell captured Tobruk after a 24-hour siege and reached Benghazi in Cyrenaica, covering almost 900 km (500 miles) and capturing about 150,000 prisoners and a large amount of equipment.

The Carpathian Brigade did not take part in this successful offensive since Poland was not formally at war with Italy, having merely broken off diplomatic relations, the Poles still harbouring the illusion that together with Italy they might be able to dominate the Balkans after the war. The British were aware of this position and respected it, thus the Brigade remained in its defensive positions near Alexandria. However, new instructions from General Sikorski dispelled any confusion and Kopański's intention to mechanise the Brigade was accepted and began to be implemented in mid-January 1941. The Brigade's re-organisation called for the creation of three independent battalions, a heavy machine gun battalion, an artillery regiment, a reconnaissance regiment (the Carpathian Uhlans), two anti-tank companies, detachments of sappers and signallers, as well as supporting transport, supply, medical, provost and anti-gas units. Altogether, 348 officers and 5,326 other ranks.

Polish troops fighting in North Africa during the Western Desert Camapign

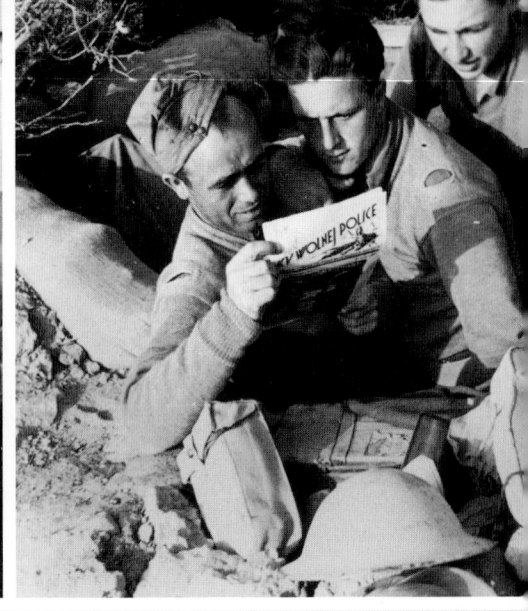

Generals Sikorski, Kopański and Klimecki with Polish troops in the Western Desert

1942, men of the Carpathian Rifle Brigade in Gazala

Polish troops parading in the Middle East before Generals Auchinleck and Ritchie

The Brigade was to have been part of the British expeditionary corps in Greece. Indeed, it had already been equipped and trained for mountain warfare and some units had even already embarked, when at the last minute its orders were changed and it was returned to Alexandria, owing to General Erwin Rommel's rapid offensive, which changed the balance of forces in the region. German tanks were now at the gates of Egypt and would probably have continued to advance had it not been for the fortress of Tobruk, which was still in British hands. It was defended by the 9th Australian Infantry Division, together with a Bengali mechanised cavalry regiment, as well as some British artillery and the 32nd Tank Brigade.

Meanwhile, the Carpathian Brigade was stationed at the fortified camp of Marsa-Matruh protecting the approaches to the Nile Delta, from which General Kopański was summoned in mid-August by the new British GOC, General Sir Claude Auchinleck. Kopański now learned that General Sikorski had agreed to the Brigade being moved to Tobruk in order to relieve the Australians. Therefore, after hurried preparations, the Brigade was shipped by sea into Tobruk between the 18th and 28th of August 1941 under cover of darkness and without loss. The Brigade's strength was now 288 officers and 4,777 other ranks.

The Brigade itself, although a relatively small unit, was an élite formation of exceptionally well-qualified men. They were either volunteers from all quarters of the globe, eager to see action, or they were experienced soldiers who had fought in the September Campaign. Recent re-equipping and re-organisation had turned the Brigade into a powerful unit able to take on even the best equipped enemy. Furthermore, it was an exceptionally well-knit formation in which a bond of mutual respect led to a high degree of self-discipline and battlefield competence, and thus it made a great deal of sense to deploy it on such a challenging assignment in an unaccustomed climate as was the defence of Tobruk. Indeed at the time the Brigade was the only unit of the Polish Army in action against the enemy, which laid an almost symbolic responsibility on the shoulders of these 5,000 men.

After a short period in reserve, the Brigade took over a stretch of the Western perimeter of about 20 km (12 miles). It was, however, too small for such an extensive sector and so it received a Czechoslovak battalion and an Australian battalion, which remained in the fortress. This was a difficult sector to defend, for elements of the German division, which, together with three Italian divisions, was besieging Tobruk, had broken through the first defensive line in May. A breach had been made opposite Medauar Hill and an enemy attack was expected there, thus the Poles needed to display constant vigilance. They laid down harassing fire, patrolled, carried out raids, cleared mines and laid mines of their own.

As a result of taking over the sector from the Australians and then having an attached Australian battalion, a close Polish-Australian bond was forged. There were in fact a number of Poles who spoke English and this helped the Polish unit, which no longer felt quite so isolated. Relations with the British also became very good. In mid-November 1941, General Sikorski arrived to inspect the Brigade, which helped to raise morale. The Poles now began to shine and elements of the Brigade remained for a full 10 weeks in the most exposed part of the line, which even hardy Australian units had found hard to hold for more than 30 days.

Operation 'Crusader' began on the 18th of November with the objective of pushing the Germans to the west and relieving Tobruk. Some initial progress was made and on the 21st the garrison, including elements of the Polish Brigade, made a serious foray. The fighting raged about 16 km (10 miles) from the defensive perimeter, but a German counter-attack bit deeply. However, the second phase of the battle, lasting from the beginning of December to the 5th of January 1942, brought victory. The Carpathian Brigade captured Medauar Hill on the 10th of December leading to the end of the siege and then it took part in the Battle of Gazala where it broke through enemy lines.

After March 1942, the Brigade was withdrawn to Egypt and then Palestine where it was reorganised into a division, the 3rd Carpathian Rifle Division, which came to form a key component of Polish Second Corps. Hence it did not take part in the critical battle of El Alamein in October 1942.

The Polish Second Corps

Despite their manpower shortages, the Poles were able to put one major formation in the field in the West. This was Polish Second Corps, commanded by Poland's most effective senior battlefield commander, General Władysław Anders.

The roots of this powerful formation go back to the summer of 1941 when, after the Nazi attack, the Soviet Union found itself, whether it wanted to or not, a member of the anti-Hitler alliance. The Polish-Soviet agreement (the so-called Sikorski-Maisky pact) of the 30th of July 1941 called for an 'amnesty' for the million and half or so Poles who had been deported into the depths of the USSR in 1940 in three great waves from the eastern Polish lands, which had been incorporated into the

Commemorative breast badge of the Polish Second Corps

USSR on the basis of rigged plebiscites, after the September Campaign. There were also those POWs, mainly other ranks, whom the Red Army had captured in 1939 and who had not, like their officers, been subsequently murdered at Katyń and elsewhere in 1940.

It was agreed to raise a Polish army, which would join the fight against Nazi Germany alongside the Red Army. The Soviet authorities accepted General Anders's nomination as Commander of this force and he was immediately released from the Lubyanka prison in Moscow. The town of Buzuluk, to the east of Kuybyshev (now Samara) on the Samara River, was designated as his headquarters.

The larger units were to be formed at Totsk, about 40 km (25 miles) south-east of Buzuluk and at Tatishchevo, north-east of Saratov. However, raising the Polish units was exceptionally difficult and took place in conditions which were a far cry from those the Poles had encountered in France, not to mention in Great Britain. The Soviet authorities almost immediately started putting obstacle after obstacle in the Poles' way. Only during the first few weeks was there any evidence of a real spirit of co-operation and already by the beginning of

December 1941, Generals Sikorski and Anders visiting troops of the Polish Army in the USSR

December 1941, General Sikorski with Polish soldiers in the USSR

Opposite page:

1942, Polish army in Buzuluk, USSR

September things had changed. The recruits arrived, many with their families who needed food, often having covered hundreds of miles with the greatest difficulty, but the Soviets did not even provide enough supplies for the agreed-upon military units, let alone their dependants. Autumn was approaching, and the soldiers were living in tents, had no boots and were still wearing their camp rags, the 'amnesty' was not being honestly implemented and weapons were promised for only one division.

Thus, in three-way discussions with the British and the Soviets, it was eventually decided to evacuate the whole force, with as many accompanying dependants as possible to Iran to serve under the British. The evacuation began in March 1942 and altogether around 114,000 souls were allowed to leave the Soviet Union. The British were deeply shocked at these people's deplorable physical condition and set about helping them recover. Many of the dependants were therefore moved to other parts of the British Empire, while the approximately 70,000 men of fighting age were given military training and became part of the Polish Army of the East.

Polish Second Corps (2 Polcorps as the British called it) was formally formed in July 1943 in Iraq and it was decided that it would join the Allied order of battle in Italy as part of British Eighth Army. It consisted of two infantry divisions, with two brigades apiece, an armoured brigade and full supporting units, including a company of commandos. In mid-December 1943, the process of moving Second Corps to Italy began. The transfer was carried out by the British with the help of a number of Polish ships, the last troops arriving in April 1944. In order to avoid losing the whole Corps, its transit to Italy had been carried out using different routes and ports and in smaller convoys, hence the time involved. However, the whole operation went off without a hitch.

After re-grouping, the Corps's units began to move out into their operational areas. The 3rd Division, which had been the first to arrive in Italy, took over from a British unit on the Sangro River along a 40-km (25-mile) front as early as the 2nd of February. The 5th Division did likewise on the 8th of March, replacing a French Moroccan division along a 13-km (8-mile) front. The Corps joined the line at the juncture of the American Fifth and the British Eighth Armies with the task of holding a string of hills and ensuring communications between the two armies. The weather at that time of year did not help, there were still snowdrifts on the ground, the mountain roads were well nigh impassable and operations were restricted to patrolling, with a major focus on training, road-clearance and improving defensive positions. In mid-April the Corps was relieved.

In Italy, things were not going as well as expected. The road to Rome was blocked by the Gustav Line, which in its central sector contained a mountain range with the 7th century Benedictine monastery of Monte Cassino atop one of its high points.

After a number of failed assaults on Monte Cassino, it fell to the British Eighth Army to finish the task. General Sir Oliver Leese, GOC Eighth Army, asked General Anders if the Polish Corps would be willing to take up the challenge. After a few moments' thought, Anders agreed, knowing the very great importance of his decision for the Polish cause.

The General's reply followed the guidelines for using the Polish Armed Forces abroad. They clearly could not play a major role, nor influence the final outcome, but the Poles needed a success, if only to refute Soviet accusations of passivity, or worse.

General Anders was only too conscious that his two divisions, the 3rd Carpathian and the 5th Eastern Lands, each had only two undermanned brigades each and major losses could prevent the Corps playing any further part in the fighting Thus the assault needed to be planned with precision. The Germans had established extensive defences and had brought in two additional battalions. Anders decided to attack the two neighbouring hilltops, Hill 593 and San Angelo. The 3rd Division would attack Hill 593 and the 5th Division, San Angelo. Every available man was used leaving no reserves. The 11th of May 1944 was chosen to launch the attack and the Polish divisions moved forward at 1.00 am following a general allied bombardment. After very heavy fighting, the initial assault failed and the Poles retired on the 13th having none the less managed to tie down part of the enemy's forces, thus allowing adjacent allied units to advance.

Meanwhile General Leese started to move British XIII Corps along the valley of the River Liri, with the aim of engaging part of the enemy's reserves and artillery fire. If closely co-ordinated with Second Corps, this move would give the Poles a chance to break through. On the 17th and the 18th, the Poles stuck tenaciously to their task and the Germans began to fall back. Finally, at 10.20 am on the 18th, a patrol of the 12th Uhlan Regiment raised the Polish flag over the ruins of the monastery.

The Second Corps sustained heavy losses: the 3rd Carpathian Rifle Division had lost 1,571 men, of whom over 20% were killed; the 5th Eastern Lands Division had lost even more at 2,174, of whom 22% were killed. 72 officers were killed, including a brigade commander and two battalion commanders, and 209 were wounded. However, the military and propaganda success of the operation was considerable. News of it soon reached Poland where it was greeted with great pride. In later years, the Battle of Monte Cassino became a symbolic Polish feat of arms and when General Anders died in 1970, he was, at his own request, buried in the Polish war cemetery there.

After the heavy fighting, the Poles needed time to recuperate and repair their equipment. Unfortunately, although the Corps had no reserves of manpower, the theatre commander, Field Marshal Sir Harold Alexander, was unconvinced that

Polish troops from Second Corps attacking
Monte Cassino

Opposite page:

A Polish machine-gun postion manned by
the crew of a knocked-out *Sherman* tank
on the slopes of Monte Cassino

Following page:
The Polish flag flying over the ruins of
Monte Cassino

A Polish *Sherman* tank destroyed in the
battle for Monte Cassino

A stretcher party on Monte Cassino

Poles who had been forcibly conscripted into the Wehrmacht and who were now allied prisoners, could fill the gaps. He wanted to turn the Corps into a single infantry division with supporting armoured units. General Anders strongly opposed this idea and stuck to his guns, believing that he needed to be able to operate independently.

Towards the end of May, Second Corps received new orders. The Indian divisions which had hitherto been fighting on the Adriatic sector needed to be moved to the central sector and the Poles were to replace them. On the 15th of June, the move began and two days later General Anders assumed command of the whole sector in the area of Pescara, with not only his own corps under command, but also two British artillery regiments, an armoured regiment, a great number of engineer, signals and anti-aircraft units, not to mention a whole Italian corps. The Italians were at full strength, but poorly equipped, especially in the transport department.

The initial mission was to gain control of a long stretch of the road linking Pescara to L'Aquila. However, before this could be done, there was a change of plan. The new orders called for a pursuit of the retreating Germans and a dash to seize the port of Ancona, which was vital to the Allies who had moved far to the north of the southern ports of Taranto, Bari and Naples. Now they needed the ports of Ancona on the Adriatic and Leghorn (Livorno) on the other side of the Italian peninsula.

The change in its orders did not come at the best of times for the Corps, since it still needed rest and time for re-organisation and it also lacked adequate transport to move men and supplies. There was a problem too with sappers, who had been moved to the Rome sector, and the terrain to be crossed was difficult, the retreating Germans having blown all the bridges and mined the roads. However, progress was made and after about a fortnight's contested advance, the River Musone was reached on the 1st of July. After the river was crossed, the eight-day battle for Loreto began. Success in this operation allowed suitable positions to be taken for an attack on Ancona.

The attack went in early on the 17th of July and, after a day's fighting, success was within reach. Only the Polish 6th Rifle Brigade, having some difficult terrain to cross including the River Musone, was late in coming in from the north, thus allowing the Germans to withdraw part of their forces. In the afternoon of the 18th, the Carpathian Uhlan Regiment entered Ancona, whose port had been undamaged. Almost 3,000 Germans were taken prisoner and a great deal of equipment fell into allied hands. However, Polish losses had been quite considerable: 34 officers and 150 other ranks had been killed and a further 116 officers and 1,850 other ranks wounded.

After the capture of Ancona, Second Corps had a moment of respite. However, it was soon faced with a number of new tasks. The Allies now decided to break through the German Gothic Line, and the Poles were tasked with conducting operations on the Adriatic coast, giving the impression that the main thrust would come there, when in fact it would come nearer Florence.

The central thrust failed and it was decided to shift the axis of advance to the Adriatic side of the country, where the terrain was flatter and with the port of Ancona providing a gateway for re-supply. Second Corps's task now changed to pushing the Germans back over the River Metauro and preparing the ground for an advance by the British and the Canadians. Between the 19th and the 22nd of August, the mission was accomplished to the accompaniment of some heavy fighting.

The Corps now had to reach the River Foglia, by-pass to the west German defensive positions at Pesaro and capture the high ground to the north-west of the city. Fighting began on the 23rd of August and ended on the 2nd of September, when the Gothic Line was finally breached and Second Corps ended its three-month campaign fighting the Germans along the Adriatic. It had lost 288 officers and 3,303 other ranks killed or wounded.

After a good rest, the Polish Corps was moved to the western flank of Eighth Army, to a mountainous and trackless area where it was to advance along the axis Santa Sofia-Galatea-Forli. The fighting was hard, but progress was steady and by the middle of December Eighth Army had reached the River Senio and Second Corps had taken Faeza. The losses, however, were mounting: 43 officers and 627 other ranks had been killed, 184 officers and 2,630 other ranks wounded, with 33 men missing.

News of the decisions taken at the Yalta Conference in February 1945 was received badly by Second Corps, most of whose men came from those parts of pre-war Poland, which had now been formally absorbed into the USSR with Western blessing.

In the spring, the Allies began a new offensive in Italy with Second Corps serving as part of Eighth Army. Owing to his new responsibilities as Acting Supreme Commander, General Anders was now in London, but on the 6th of April he arrived to lead the Corps in its final combat operations. It had been reinforced with a British armoured brigade and a number of other units and, together with its two new infantry brigades, formed from Poles who had been POWs, was now an extremely powerful formation. The offensive began on the 9th of April and, after heavy fighting, the Corps's lead battalion entered Bologna on the 21st. With their resistance weakening all along the line, the Germans surrendered in Italy on the 28th . Second Corps's successful war was over.

After the end of hostilities in Europe and with the major powers beginning to demobilise, Second Corps grew rather than shrank. Recruits flocked to it from Germany, France and Switzerland, having been released from POW, internment and concentration camps, some even coming from Poland. The Corps remained

The damaged Benedictine abbey at Monte Cassino

The Polish and British flags flying over Monte Cassino

General Anders congratulates his troops

![A Polish tank drives through liberated Ancona to the cheers of the townsfolk]

A Polish tank drives through liberated Ancona to the cheers of the townsfolk

King George VI and General Anders

April 1945, Polish troops in liberated Bologna

in Italy, with its headquarters at Ancona, and rapidly grew to 112,000, which led to supply problems. There now began a new phase in the Corps's life: work was done on military cemeteries, elementary and secondary schools were set up, Poles studied at Italian universities, newspapers and magazines were started, there was a first-class theatre, and sports teams were formed. A little Poland had been created.

The Corps was finally demobilised by the British in 1946 when most of its men decided to remain in Britain.

The Polish Navy

Cap badge of
the Polish Navy

Between the wars Poland had only a very short coastline and the economy was such that the country could not afford a large navy. Nevertheless, in the weeks leading up to September 1939, discussions were held with the British with a view to safeguarding the small Polish fleet and bringing it to British ports. As early as May of 1939, an appropriate agreement was reached and in late August three Polish destroyers, *Błyskawica*, *Burza* and *Grom* (the fourth, the *Wicher*, would be sunk in September off the Hel Peninsula) left the Polish naval port of Oksywie in Gdynia and by the 1st of September they were in the Scottish port of Rosyth. After the commencement of hostilities, they were joined there by the submarines *Wilk* and a little later *Orzeł*, the latter having made a daring escape from the Estonian port of Tallinn, where, on German insistence, she had been interned. Sailing for over 1,600 kilometres (1,000 miles), across the Baltic and the North Sea, without navigational instruments and with charts drawn from memory, she successfully avoided pursuit by the German Navy and reached Scotland on the 14th of October. The three remaining submarines, *Ryś*, *Sęp* and *Żbik*, sailed to Swedish ports where they were interned. Almost the whole Polish merchant fleet, with a total tonnage of around 140,000 tons, left the Baltic as early as August.

Unlike the RAF's initially reserved attitude towards the Poles, the Royal Navy's was positive and welcoming and the Polish vessels were immediately put to good use, a Polish Naval Agreement being speedily signed in November. All the Polish ships were to carry a British signals officer in charge of the code books, they would all come under British operational command, but the Poles would retain their own uniforms, badges of rank, flags and ship's standing orders, and come under the command of Admiral Świrski. By the 6th of September, the three destroyers were already taking part in patrols as integral units in the Royal Navy. They then moved to Plymouth, followed by Harwich in November.

On the 8th of April 1940, the Orzeł torpedoed and sank the German troopship Rio de Janeiro with about 500 German troops on their way to Norway. This was the first information that the Allies received of German designs on Norway. Tragically, the *Orzeł* never returned from her next patrol in May/June off the Norwegian coast, going down with 6 officers and 49 sailors on the 5th of June. The Polish destroyers, *Błyskawica* and *Grom* took part in the battle for Narvik from the 19th of April and were joined by the *Burza* on the 30th. Unfortunately the *Grom* was sunk by German aircraft on the 4th of May, losing a large part of her crew.

The *Błyskawica* and *Burza* were recalled from Narvik on the 10th of May to assist in the evacuation of the British Expeditionary Force at the end of the month from Dunkirk, where the *Burza* was badly damaged by two bombs. They were joined there by the destroyer *Garland,* the first of several ships lent by the United Kingdom to the Polish Navy for the duration of the war in Europe.

Recognising the fighting spirit and good seamanship of the Polish crews, the Admiralty lent the Polish Navy during the war a number of vessels which fought under the Polish flag and with Polish commanding officers. Also France, before its fall in June 1940, lent several ships to the Polish Navy, but while these vessels could be used only for training and support operations and were based in France, the British ships were all fighting vessels based in the United Kingdom.

The Polish Navy was strengthened by the arrival from the British of the destroyers *Piorun*, commissioned on 5.11.1940, *Krakowiak* and *Kujawiak*, commissioned on 30.05.1941, *Ślązak*, commissioned on 14.04.1942 and *Orkan*, commissioned on 18.11.1942. They were joined by the submarines: Sokół, commissioned on 19.01.1941, *Jastrząb*, commissioned on 4.11.1941 and *Dzik*, commissioned on 11.10.1942, and later, in 1944, by the light cruisers *Dragon* and *Conrad* (the two largest ships the Polish Navy ever possessed) and a flotilla of fast patrol craft.

The destroyers operated mainly in the North Atlantic, especially during the Battle of the Atlantic, and escorted convoys of military supplies to the Soviet Union in the Arctic Ocean. The *Piorun* earned fame for taking part in the sinking of the German battleship *Bismarck*, sunk in the Atlantic in May 1941. She also escorted British aircraft carriers in their unsuccessful attempts to sink the *Bismark's* sister ship the *Tirpitz*. The *Orkan* took part in 18 anti-submarine operations and a similar number of engagements with enemy aircraft, and escorted 20 convoys. She was in service for only 13 months, since on the 8th of October 1943, while escorting an eastbound convoy, she was hit by a torpedo and sank with heavy loss of life. Her fate was shared by the *Kujawiak* in the Mediterranean, where she was escorting a convoy to Malta and on the 16th of June 1942 struck a mine in Valetta harbour. The *Ślązak* took part in the unsuccessful British raid on Dieppe during the night of the 18th/19th of August 1942. *Garland* escorted a number of convoys in the North Atlantic and the

Opposite page:
1944, Polish submarine *Sokół* at Gibraltar

September 1939, Polish destroyers
en route for Rosyth, Scotland

Polish and British seamen

The *Piorun,* which shadowed the
German battleship *Bismarck*

Polish submarine *Orzeł*

March 1942, Polish destroyer *Blyskawica*
outside Plymouth, England

A parade by the Polish Navy in Portsmouth, England

Captain Bogusław Krawczyk of the *Wilk* meets
King George VI and Queen Elizabeth

Mediterranean and also took part in an expedition to Spitzbergen, where an attempt was made to set up a naval base. The *Krakowiak*, in addition to escorting a number of North Atlantic convoys, operated, along with the Ślązak, for the most part in the English Channel. The destroyers *Burza* and *Garland* did sterling work in convoy protection during the Battle of the Atlantic. By October 1943, they were in the Mediterranean, while the *Garland*, operating even further south, crossed the Equator for the first time in February 1944.

Polish passenger and cargo ships, which after the fall of France had been in British ports, also took part in convoys. Of the three large Polish ocean liners, the largest the *Piłsudski* went down as early as the 26th of November 1939, and the two remaining ones—the *Batory* and the *Sobieski*—served as troop ships, on a number of occasions sailing to Norway, to Great Britain from France, from Australia and New Zealand to Europe and North Africa. The cargo vessels were used above all on the North Atlantic convoys and later on the Arctic convoys to the USSR. They included the *Bałtyk, Białystok, Borysław, Cieszyn, Chrobry, Częstochowa, Kielce, Kolno, Kowel, Kromań, Krosno, Kutno, Lwów, Modlin, Narwik, Paderewski, Poznań, Puck, Rozewie, Tobruk, Warszawa*. Others, like the *Lechistan, Morska Wola* and *Wisła*, carried Polish Lend-Lease supplies from the US to Great Britain. The heavy losses in the Atlantic also affected the Poles, and they lost to torpedoes, bombs and mines 17 ships, among these being the submarine *Jastrząb*, which, six months after entering service and while operating in Norwegian waters, was sunk in error on the 2nd of May 1942 by an Allied convoy escort.

The destroyers, *Błyskawica* and *Piorun*, as well as *Krakowiak* and *Ślązak*, operating from British ports, fought in Norwegian waters until in June 1943 when they were all moved into the Mediterranean and in July took part in the invasions of Sicily and the Italian peninsula. The *Piorun* was deployed as one of the destroyers in 'Force H', which consisted of British battleships, aircraft carriers, cruisers and destroyers supporting the American and British landings in Sicily and mainland Italy.

Two Polish submarines, the 'terrible twins' *Dzik* and *Sokół*, also operated in the Mediterranean, where they too took part in the invasion of Sicily and later of the Italian peninsula. They achieved impressive results, the *Dzik* sinking 50,000 tons of enemy shipping and the *Sokół*, 25,000 tons. In the spring of 1944, the *Sokół* returned to Great Britain for a major overhaul lasting until September, while the *Dzik* followed soon thereafter to drop anchor in Plymouth.

During the invasion of the European mainland in June 1944, most of the Polish ships, alongside the British and other Allied navies, were given the task of defending the invasion force from possible attacks by German naval vessels and aircraft coming from either end of the English Channel. The *Piorun* and the *Błyskawica* were stationed at the western end. The *Ślązak*, the *Krakowiak* and the flotilla of fast patrol craft had a similar task at the eastern end of the

Channel, while the light cruiser *Dragon* was in the centre with the main Allied fleet. During the night of the 8/9th of June, 4 German destroyers, trying at the very least to reach Cherbourg, slipped their moorings in Brest. Aerial reconnaissance picked them up and the British Tenth Destroyer Flotilla, based at Plymouth, headed out to meet them. The Flotilla had two divisions, 19 and 20; the latter, led by *Błyskawica*, also included *Piorun*. The action began with the German vessels launching a salvo of torpedoes, which the Allied vessels avoided and then opened fire. At some stage German coastal artillery joined the fray. The Allied flotilla engaged the enemy, with *Błyskawica* hitting the leading German vessel a number of times. A British ship then finally sank her with a torpedo. At least two German vessels were sunk and the remaining two, badly damaged, escaped under the cover of darkness. All Allied vessels returned to Plymouth with one badly damaged, but still under her own steam. This engagement became known as the Battle of Ushant.

On the 13th of June, the *Piorun*, together with HMS *Ashanti*, patrolling between the island of Jersey and the Cherbourg Peninsula, made contact with seven minesweepers. Although the Allied ships were larger, faster and had heavier guns, the enemy had more guns and outnumbered the Allies. In addition, the German ships were again supported at some stage by German shore batteries on the Island of Jersey. In the end, possibly five German ships were sunk and the remaining two were left burning under the protection of the shore batteries. The *Piorun* and the *Ashanti* returned to Plymouth with slight damage and seven wounded Polish sailors, all of whom later recovered. This became known as the Battle of Jersey and these two battles were the final gasp of German naval operations in French northern waters.

The approaching end of the war in Europe also limited operations by the small Polish naval force. Its main task was now to escort the large transatlantic liners serving as troopships as they entered or left port, clearing Allied and German minefields and dealing with small German vessels which continued to fight, even after they had been ordered to surrender on the 8th of May 1945.

Altogether, throughout the course of the war, not counting operations in the Baltic during the first month of the war, the Polish Navy covered over 1,210,000 nautical miles, carried out 1,162 patrols and operations, escorted 787 convoys, was involved in 73 surface engagements, 211 engagements against enemy submarines, over 50 with shore batteries and over 400 with enemy aircraft. Indeed the Polish Navy was involved in combat operations from the first to the last day of the war in Europe. The Poles sank 7 surface vessels and damaged a further 11, sank 2 submarines and damaged a further 9, sank 41 cargo vessels representing over 80,000 tons deadweight and shot down 17 enemy aircraft. In the West, the Polish Navy lost two submarines, the *Jastrząb* and the *Orzeł*, the destroyers *Grom* and *Orkan* and the cruiser *Dragon*. In the first month of war, in the Baltic Sea, the Poles lost 16 small craft sunk, 3 submarines interned in Sweden and 4 minelayers incorporated into the German *Kriegsmarine*. Polish naval personnel received 1,171 Polish military awards and 83 British, 15 French and a number of American ones. Over the course of the war, the Polish merchant fleet carried nearly 5 million tons of supplies.

The Polish Air Force (PAF)

Cap badge of the Polish Air Force (PAF)

Perhaps the best known of the Polish armed services in the West was the Air Force, since Polish fighter squadrons at one stage formed about 10% of RAF Fighter Command. As early as October 1939, in other words just after the September Campaign, Polish diplomatic officials in the Romanian capital Bucharest approached the British with a suggestion that Polish Air Force personnel interned in Romania be spirited out to Great Britain as soon as possible. Eventually, the British and the French, on whose territory the Polish land forces were being rebuilt, agreed to share these Polish airmen equally between them.

The Polish Air Force saw action in the defence of France 1940, shooting down 52 German aircraft, but that country's collapse brought matters to a head and ensured that henceforth the Poles would rebuild their Air Force entirely in Great Britain. Indeed, they had had to abandon all their equipment in France and air and ground crews had had to get out as best they could.

Polish airmen began arriving at RAF Eastchurch in late December 1939, the British having earlier agreed to allow the Poles to form two active and two reserve light bomber squadrons with *Fairey Battles*, but had been unwilling to let them raise their own fighter squadrons. The first Polish fighter pilots, who arrived in Britain in early 1940 and were considered to be proficient in English, were posted to RAF squadrons. Initially, there were about 40 of them, their number later rising to 81.

However, the perilous circumstances of the summer of 1940 caused the British to rethink their position on Polish fighter squadrons; they signed the Polish Air Force Agreement on the 11th of June under which the Poles had their own Air Force, which was integrated into the RAF operational structure.

The first entirely Polish fighter squadron in Great Britain was formed on the 22nd of July at RAF Leconfield. It was 302 (Polish) City of Poznań Squadron, based on personnel from No. 1/145 Squadron who had been evacuated from France. On the 27th, it received an allocation of *Hurricanes* and became operational on the 15th of August. The next squadron to form was 303 (Polish) Warsaw

Kościuszko Squadron at RAF Northolt on the 2nd of August. That year, additional squadrons were formed: 306, 307 (night fighters) and 308 fighter squadrons, and 300, 301, 304 and 305 bomber squadrons, as well as 309 Army Co-operation Squadron, but they did not become operational that year. In early 1941, three more squadrons were formed: 315, 316 and 317.

The Polish squadrons were in the British chain of command in terms of organisation, operations, training, equipment, supply, personnel and discipline, but a Polish Air Force Inspectorate was formed in October 1940 to act as a liaison with the British Air Ministry and commanded by General Stanisław Ujejski with the functional RAF rank of Air Vice-Marshal. The Inspectorate worked with the British on personnel issues and had the authority to visit the Polish squadrons. The British were soon to appreciate the Poles' true value during the Battle of Britain.

About 1,500 RAF pilots took part in the Battle of Britain, with 151 Poles in the Polish Air Force—the largest foreign contingent, representing about 10% of the total. There were 81 Poles serving in British squadrons, while the remaining 70 manned two Polish squadrons: 302 and 303. 302 Squadron saw combat for the first time on the 15th of August and 6 days later it shot down its first Junkers. 303 Squadron became operational on the 30th in a most unorthodox manner: during a training sortie Lieutenant Ludwik Paszkiewicz shot down a *Dornier* without orders.

Despite conflicting reports and post-war re-assessments, it appears that the RAF shot down some 1,733 German aircraft during the period from the 10th of July to the end of October and damaged a further 643. This figure includes the 203 aircraft shot down by the Poles: 302 Squadron—16, 303 Squadron—110, and Poles serving in British squadrons—77. The British lost 914 *Spitfires* and *Hurricanes*, with a further 450 damaged; 481 pilots were lost and 422 wounded. The Poles lost 33: 302 Squadron—7, 303 Squadron—6 and 13 of those serving in British squadrons; 7 later died of their wounds. In fact, 303 Squadron was credited with being the most successful squadron in RAF Fighter Command during the Battle of Britain and 9 of its 34 pilots qualified as 'aces', in other words pilots with five or more 'kills' to their credit.

After the Battle of Britain during which the Poles had so distinguished themselves, there was an understandable drive to build up the Polish Air force, a move now supported by the British, especially since they badly needed the Polish bomber squadrons too. Indeed, the fighter pilots have overshadowed the less glamourous, but no less dangerous work of the bomber crews flying over Occupied Europe night after night. However, it turned out to be difficult to expand the Polish Air Force, the single most critical problem being a lack of personnel, as it was for all the Polish armed services in the West. After the evacuation from France, the Polish Air Force had numbered 8,384 officers and men and towards the end of 1940 this number had dropped by 700, not only as a

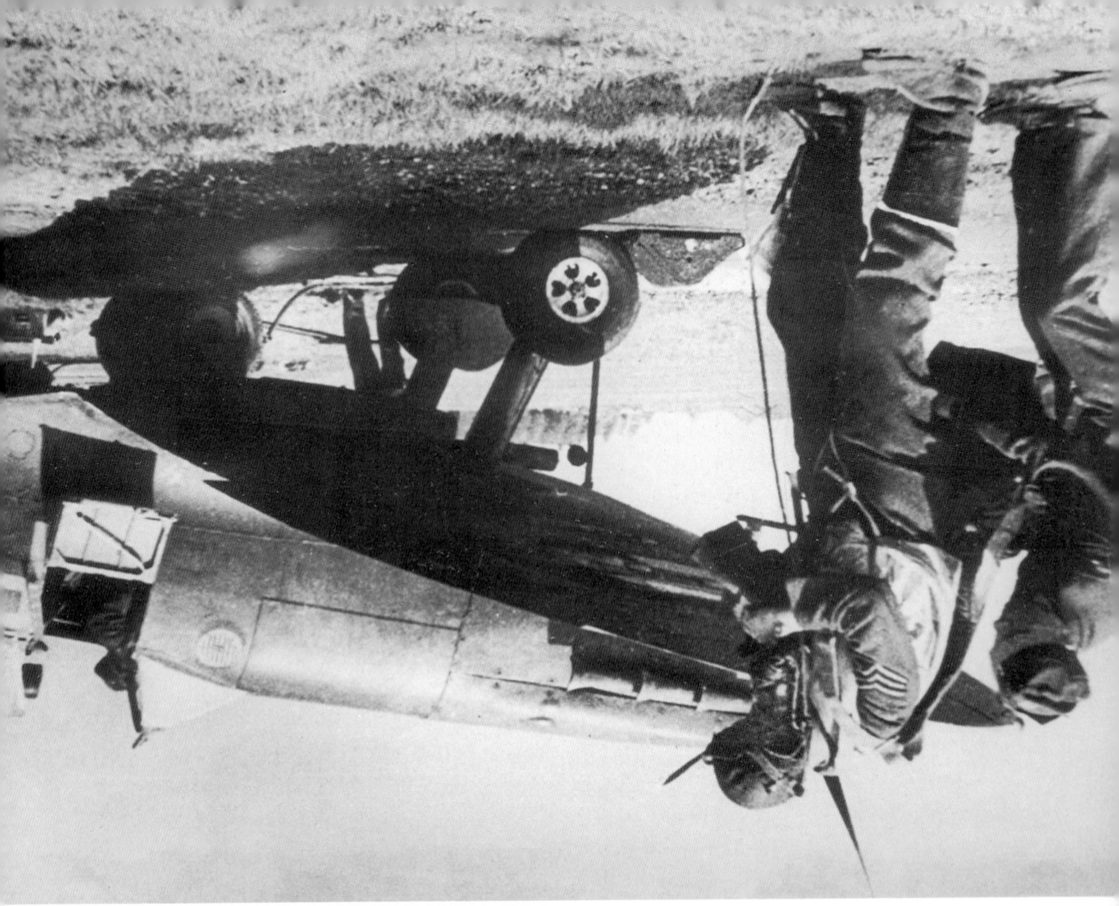

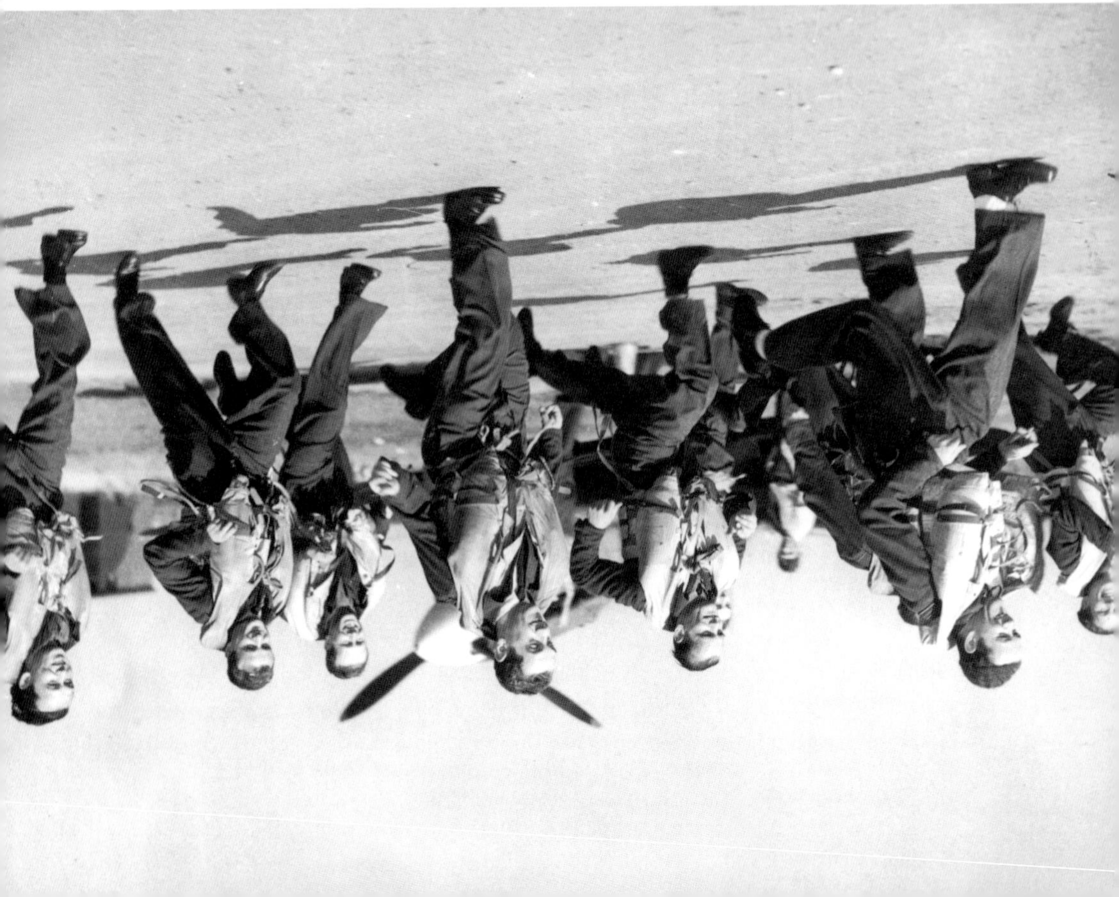

Opposite page:

Polish fighter pilots of 303 Squadron scramble

Polish fighter pilot of 303 Squadron

1940, Polish fighter pilot during the Battle of Britain

Polish fighter pilots of 303 Squadron

Opposite page:

1942, fighter pilots of 303 Squadron show off
fragment of downed German *JU.88* aircraft

Pilots from 303 Squadron

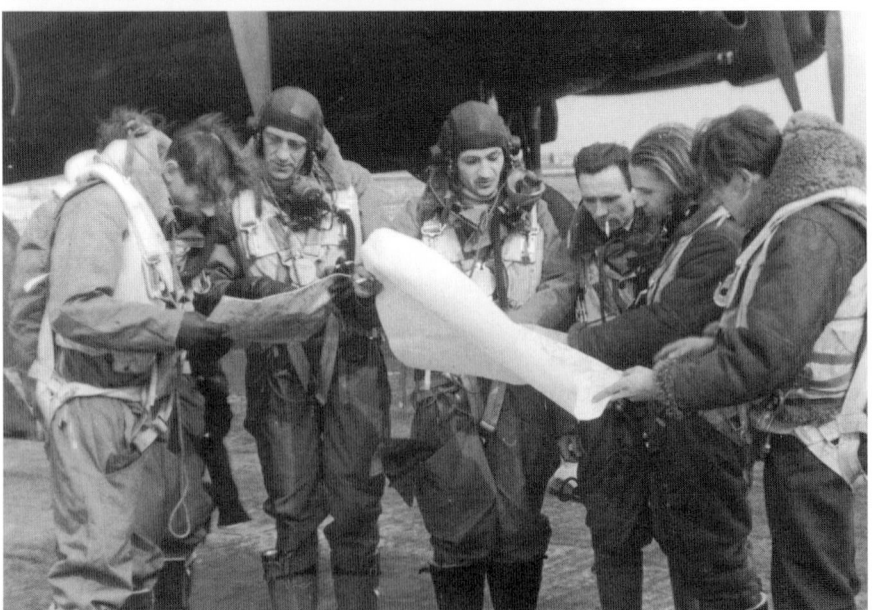

A *Wellington* of 300 Squadron in flight over
the Bay of Biscay

Polish bomber aircrew of 300 Squadron

THE 178TH GERMAN
AIRCRAFT DESTROYED
BY 303 POLISH (F) SQDN.
3.1.42

JU.88.

result of enemy action, but mainly through postings to other branches of the Armed Forces. This despite the fact that 290 airmen had arrived in Great Britain from Palestine, having reached the Middle East by a variety of routes.

Various attempts were made to solve this problem, the least effective being transferring people from the Army. A few pre-war airmen were serving with the Carpathian Brigade, which was prepared to relinquish only flight personnel, while the newly forming armoured division was trying to get its hands on every suitable man. Younger men volunteered willingly for the Air Force, but these were the very men that other commanders did not want to lose, hence many applications went astray and barely 120 men were added to the Air Force's rolls. Several hundred volunteers arrived from the United States, and a further several hundred from South America, who, for the most part, were more suited for support duties. Only towards the end of 1941 and in 1942 did the situation change when, as a result of the military agreement with the Soviet Union, almost 2,000 airmen and former Air Force Training Corps personnel arrived in Great Britain.

Despite these difficulties, plans to expand the Air Force went ahead, for the Poles saw these squadrons as an essential element in any eventual general rising in Poland. The British were helpful, making an exception to their own iron rules by looking the other way when Polish squadrons had only 80% of their required ground crews. However, this shortfall meant that the Poles were more dependent on the British than the original air force agreement had envisaged. There were no Polish operational commands, while communications and most support services had British personnel.

After the formation of the Polish fighter and bomber squadrons which were operational in 1940, three further fighter squadrons were formed: 315 Dęblin Squadron, 316 Warsaw Squadron and 317 Wilno Squadron; and two bomber squadrons: 304 Land of Silesia Squadron and 305 Land of Wielkopolska Squadron. Starting on the 15th of April 1941, 303, 306 and 308 Squadrons formed No. 1 Polish Fighter Wing, and from the 18th of August, 302, 316 and 317 Squadrons formed No. 2 Polish Fighter Wing. Altogether, at the start of 1942, the Polish Air Force in Great Britain consisted of 8 fighter squadrons, 1 fighter reconnaissance squadron and 4 bomber squadrons, with 144 fighter aircraft, 72 bombers and 12 reconnaissance aircraft. These were supported by flying schools and repair shops.

After its defeat in the Battle of Britain, the *Luftwaffe* ceased attacks on the British Isles and restricted itself to the occasional sortie, and so operational roles began to change. The British now began offensive sorties as the prelude to the battle for air supremacy over Europe. Initially, these sorties were harassing in nature, but they grew in strength. Bombing raids began against military and industrial targets in Northern France, Belgium and then Germany.

Polish fighter and bomber squadrons played their part in these operations with some success. The fighters either escorted bombers, or took part in large sweeps of fighters over enemy-held territory to take on any enemy aircraft they encountered. 315 Squadron shone at these sorties and on the 14th of August 1941 shot down 8 *Messerschmitts* over France for no loss. Two days later, 306 Squadron took down 6 similar aircraft and 308 Squadron in one day twice downed 5 German aircraft. The Polish squadrons were especially good at escorting bombers. The Germans were still carrying out offensive sorties and Polish squadrons were involved in dogfights with them. All the squadrons underwent night-flying training and 307 Squadron became a specialist night fighter squadron. It began patrolling British airspace in the spring of 1941 using *Defiants* and in August received radar-equipped *Beaufighters*. The squadron chalked up its fair share of *Heinkels*, *Junkers* and *Dorniers*. In 1941, the Polish fighter squadrons were officially credited with 198 'kills', either in aerial combat or on the ground, as well as 52 'probables' and 57 damaged. This figure represented 27% of all British-based fighter successes.

After the initial phase, all four Polish bomber squadrons were equipped with Mark I *Wellington* aircraft, 16 per squadron. Interestingly enough, there was a difference in operational procedures between the British, where the aircraft captain was always the pilot, and pre-war Polish practice, where the navigator was captain. The British insisted that all foreign air forces operating under RAF command follow British practice, however, they were prepared to make an exception for the Poles.

In 1940, when there was still a threat of a German invasion of the British Isles, 300 and 301 Squadrons took part in bombing German barges in Boulogne, Calais and Ostend, followed in 1941 by raids on targets in Northern France, Belgium and Germany. Railway junctions at Cologne, Mannheim, Düsseldorf and Frankfurt, manufacturing plants in Duisburg and airfields in Essen were attacked. It was an emotional moment for the Polish airmen, especially when they eventually flew over Berlin. These were exceptionally difficult operations, requiring great physical and mental stamina and they took place exclusively at night. Over the period covering the end of 1940 and the whole of 1941, the four Polish bomber squadrons carried out 1,454 sorties and dropped 1,855 tons of bombs.

On the 16th of July 1941, a special drumhead service was held at RAF Swinderby, 301 Squadron's home station, when General Sikorski, in the presence of the British Chief of the Air Staff Air Chief Marshal Sir Charles Portal, presented to the Inspector General of the Polish Air Force colours embroidered in Wilno by Polish women and smuggled out to Great Britain. 300 Squadron received the colours first and every three months they were handed over to the next squadron in numerical sequence.

However, very strong German anti-aircraft defences and night fighters were taking a heavy toll of the Polish bomber squadrons, for the *Wellington* was slow,

ZA WARSZAWĘ

Opposite page:

Loading mines onto a *Wellington*
of 300 Squadron

A bomb marked '*For Warsaw*' loaded up

A de Havilland *Mosquito* fighter-bomber
of Polish 305 Squadron

1941, General Sikorski and Air Chief
Marshal Portal present Air Force colours
made in occupied Poland

reaching about 290 kph (175 mph) and fully laden could reach an altitude of only 6,000 m (18,000 ft). By the end of 1941, 145 Polish airmen had lost their lives, 5 were unaccounted for and 67 had been taken prisoner. The Poles also lost a further 38 airmen and 49 aircraft during training.

The Polish Air Force was suffering from a manpower shortage and since it was continuously engaged in operations, it was also losing men. Whereas, at the beginning of 1942 it had consisted of 8 fighter squadrons, 1 fighter-reconnaissance squadron and 4 bomber squadrons, it grew by only one army co-operation squadron, 318 City of Gdańsk Squadron, which was formed in March 1943 in Britain to work with Eighth Army artillery in Italy. At the beginning of 1943, 301 Bomber Squadron was re-organised, owing to a shortage of crews. There now arose the need to form quickly a special duties flight for supply flights to occupied Europe, mainly Poland, consisting of 7 crews, and so 301 Squadron was disbanded and its remaining crews posted to 300 Squadron. The new flight was numbered 1586 and was attached to 138 Squadron RAF. In fact, the Poles had difficulty manning their current roster and were coping only thanks to the arrival of 1,500 men from the USSR and 500 volunteers from the USA, as well as to the fact that the British authorities, who badly needed the squadrons, turned a blind eye to under-manned ground crews.

After the intensive operations of 1940 and a rather more peaceful 1941, things continued relatively quietly in 1942, during which the Poles shot down only 90 aircraft. The Polish Wing, consisting of 302, 306 and 308 Squadrons, together with 303 and 317 Squadrons, took part in the Dieppe Raid on the 19th of August 1942. However, 1943 was far more intensive, for the great strategic bombing raids over Germany were going apace. The bombers were accompanied by a fighter screen, in which the Polish squadrons distinguished themselves by using a new tactic of covering the bombers both from below and above. A special group of Polish fighter aircraft, 'Skalski's Circus', under Colonel Stanisław Skalski—Poland's most successful fighter pilot—also took part in operations in North Africa as part of a British squadron. Altogether, in 1943 Polish fighter aircraft shot down 113 enemy aircraft, with 66 damaged and 42 'probables'.

It turned out that 1942 was the Polish bomber squadrons' high point, as well as the year of their highest losses. The British were by now prepared for the great raids, their war industries were in high gear and on the 30th of May they sent 1,000 aircraft over Cologne. Two days later another 1,000-bomber raid took place. Polish bombers took part in both raids, 104 aircraft in each. This was an enormous effort for the Poles and men had to be brought in from the training schools to make up the numbers of aircrew. Throughout 1942, Polish bomber squadrons carried out 2,450 sorties and dropped 2,764 tons of bombs and 528 tons of mines. They lost 291 airmen, 16 were missing and 91 were taken prisoner. A further 39 were killed during training and in accidents, and 89 aircraft were lost.

During 1943, there was a great emphasis on the Battle of the Atlantic and thus Polish bomber squadrons for the most part found themselves attacking German ports, mainly Hamburg. They also mined French ports used by the Germans, such as Brest, Lorient and St. Nazaire, as well as the Dutch coast. The lack of aircrew reduced the squadrons' overall effectiveness and only 1,306 sorties were carried out and 784 tons of bombs and an equal amount of mines dropped. Losses totalled 112 airmen lost, 1 missing and 19 taken prisoner, as well as 28 aircraft lost.

In the first half of 1943, in anticipation of a landing in France, the British formed Tactical Air Force for close co-operation with ground forces. The Polish fighter squadrons were organised into two Wings, Nos. 1 and 2, and the plan was to move them to Northern France after a successful invasion. This had a deep effect on the Poles, since such a move would bring them closer to Poland. In the autumn of 1943, 302, 308 and 317 Squadrons of No. 1 Wing were equipped with Mark IX *Spitfires*, while in March of 1944, No. 2 Wing's 306 and 315 Squadrons received Mark III *Mustangs*. Out of the bomber squadrons only 305 Squadron was transferred to Tactical Air Force, 300 Squadron remaining in Bomber Command and 304 Squadron in Coastal Command. As we have already seen, 301 Squadron had been disbanded when 1586 Special Duties Squadron was formed.

Polish aircrews were also assigned to Transport Command. The largest Polish transport unit was formed in the Middle East and initially operated from the Gold Coast; it was later transferred to Cairo where it operated on Middle Eastern routes and, starting in 1943, on longer flights as far afield as India, Sri Lanka, Algeria and South Africa. There was also a Polish unit in 45 Group, Transport Command which worked the Canada-GB-Middle East route, as well as a further unit in 229 Group, Transport Command operating in India and Burma. An additional 26 Polish airmen served in 4 RAF squadrons. Within Transport Command the Poles carried out 23,202 flights, ferried 12,635 aircraft and carried 25,187 people and 1,769 tons of assorted supplies.

The Polish Air Force also set up a number of training establishments, which in the second half of the war even included higher education. Some Polish aircrews were trained in Canada, and over the course of the war, 4,434 Poles were trained in Great Britain and in Canada. In April 1944, a new Air Agreement granting the Polish Air Force complete autonomy was signed with the British and General Iżycki became AOC.-in-C. Polish Air Force.

There was also a Polish balloon squadron, consisting of 5 officers and about 150 men, which manned barrage balloons over Glasgow, then over other sites in Scotland and lastly, starting at the end of June 1944, over London as part of the defences against the V-1 flying bomb.

Polish fighter squadrons also took part in the invasion of Europe and subsequent fighting. The two Polish Fighter Wings (131 and 133) and an RAF wing formed No. 18 Fighter Sector, 2nd Tactical Air Force, which was command-ed by a Pole, Lieutenant Colonel (later General) Aleksander Gabszewicz. The Sector was tasked with covering the landings and its squadrons flew several sorties daily. Between the 6th and the 8th of June, the Sector shot down 30 enemy aircraft. The 11th was an emotional day for Polish 302, 308 and 317 Squadrons when they landed on French soil in Normandy.

In mid-July, the ground-support fighter formations were disbanded to form part of a larger fighter group. Colonel Gabszewicz assumed command of 131 Wing, which flew cover in Normandy, with the squadrons making as many as 50 sorties a day. The Wing then moved to the area of the Belgian-Dutch border.

A week after D-Day, starting on the 13th of June, London became the target of V-1 flying bombs and Fighter Command, equipped mainly with *Mustangs*, had its hands full. The V-1s could in fact be caught and shot down by a diving aircraft. Those Polish squadrons which had remained on British soil took part in these operations, as well as two from 133 Wing, which was withdrawn from France on the 9th of July and committed to the defence of British airspace. Over the period from the 13th of June 1944 to the 29th of March 1945, when the last flying bombs were launched, the squadrons fared as follows: 306 Squadron—60 V-1s, 315 Squadron—53 V-1s, 316 Squadron—74 V-1s. This represented around 10% of the 2,000 V-1s shot down. The squadrons also continued to fly ground-support sorties over Northern Europe, with 307 Night Fighter Squadron carrying out similar duties, which included covering the airborne landings at Arnhem.

Overall, during 1944, Polish fighter aircraft in the West had 100 definite 'kills', 8 'probables' and damaged a further 24. The most successful was 315 Squadron, with 45 'kills'. Two Polish bomber squadrons, 300 and 305, carried out sorties over Germany attacking railway junctions, fuel depots and airfields. 305 Squadron, whose OC was always a Pole, included Britons, Canadians, Estonians and Norwegians, many of them quite senior and older officers.

During the final months of the war, the Polish armed forces in Western and Southern Europe saw the arrival of 663 Army Co-operation Squadron, which had been formed in September 1943 in Italy as part of Second Corps, but which had become operational only at the start of the following year. Its role was combined operations with British Eighth Army artillery. By now the fighter squadrons were flying fewer sorties, for the Germans were running low on fuel and had reduced flight operations to a minimum. Between the 16th of December 1944 and the 5th of January 1945, the last unexpected German counter-offensive was launched in the Ardennes. Polish 131 Fighter Wing took part in air opera-tions against Field Marshal Gerd von Rundstedt's supply lines, which led to the Germans attacking Allied airfields in France and Belgium on the 1st of January, during which 18 Polish fighters, mainly from 302 Squadron, were destroyed at an airfield at Ghent and 2 pilots were killed. Returning from their sorties, the two other Polish squadrons, 308 and 317, attacked the Germans, shooting down

18 aircraft. This was one of the last major encounters with the *Luftwaffe* in the West. In 1945, Polish fighters shot down 36 enemy aircraft, with 308 Squadron claiming a third of them.

The two Polish bomber squadrons, 300 and 305, were kept busy, since the Allies wanted to end the war in Europe as speedily as possible by carrying out major raids on the Third Reich. 300 Squadron's Lancasters' final mission was as part of an attack on Hitler's Alpine residence at Berchtesgaden on the 25th of April. 305 Squadron, flying *Mosquitoes*, flew its final mission during a night attack on the 25th/26th of April on German supply routes in Northern Germany.

At the end of the war there were almost 14,000 members of the Polish Air Force in Great Britain and over the course of the war 186 Polish airmen had been awarded the DFC, 8 the DSO and 1 the DSO and bar; 1,903 had lost their lives. The Polish squadrons were disbanded starting in 1946 and some of the Polish aircrew were offered permanent commissions in the Royal Air Force. One of these men, Aleksander Maisner, was eventually to attain the rank of Air Vice-Marshal, retiring from the RAF in 1977 and dying in December 2008.

The Polish 1st Armoured Division

In 1939 and 1940, Poland had only a single armoured formation, the 10th Armoured Cavalry Brigade. Thus, from the very beginning of his time in Great Britain General Sikorski dreamed of raising an armoured corps, but he was stymied by the lack of manpower. The Poles initially raised two mechanised rifle brigades with their own armour and more or less at full strength, but a further five brigades could be raised only in cadre form with a full complement of

Polish 1st Armoured Division

2nd Motorised Artillery Regiment breast badge

officers, but lacking other ranks. In 1942, the 2nd Rifle Brigade was re-named the 10th Armoured Division and put under Poland's foremost tank commander, General Stanisław Maczek, who had commanded the 10th Armoured Cavalry Brigade in Poland in 1939 and its re-creation under the same name in France in 1940, but it was still far from a fully-blown armoured division. In the absence of major operations, this was acceptable, but once preparations for the Cross-Channel invasion began, things had to change.

Every available man was brought in from the Middle East, more han 1,000 were squeezed out from other countries, but this barely sufficed for a division, as well as a parachute brigade. While the British were calling for the Poles to take part in the invasion, they hesitated over equipping under-strength units. However, Churchill had the final word and a modern

A Polish Sherman tank in Northern Europe

A German *Tiger* tank destroyed by the Polish
1st Armoured Division

Following page:

Polish troops in Northern Europe   Crew of Polish *Sherman* tank 'Warsaw'

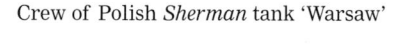

1944, Polish tanks waiting to cross the Seine

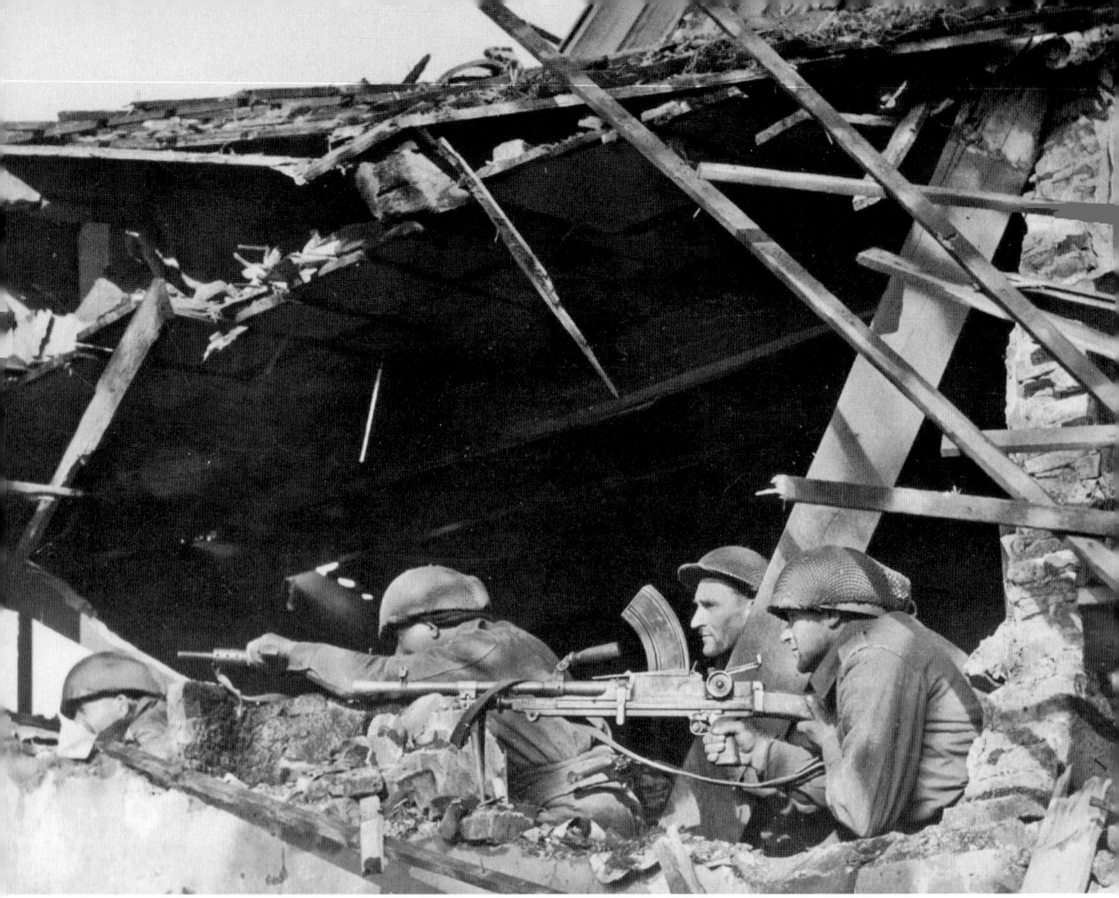

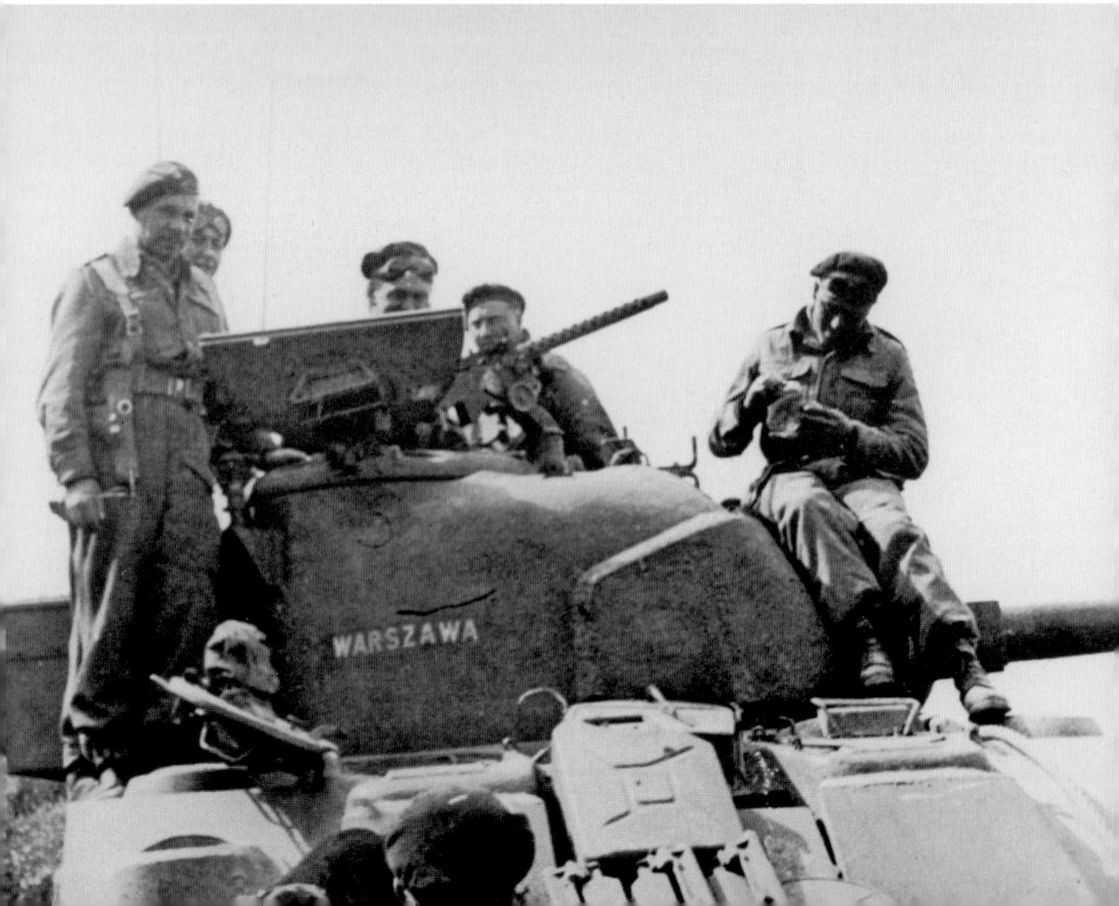
WARSZAWA

Polish anti-aircraft battery on watch for
German fighter-bombers

Polish casualties are evacuated from
the battlefield

Polish forces are in the thick of the fighting
to liberate Europe

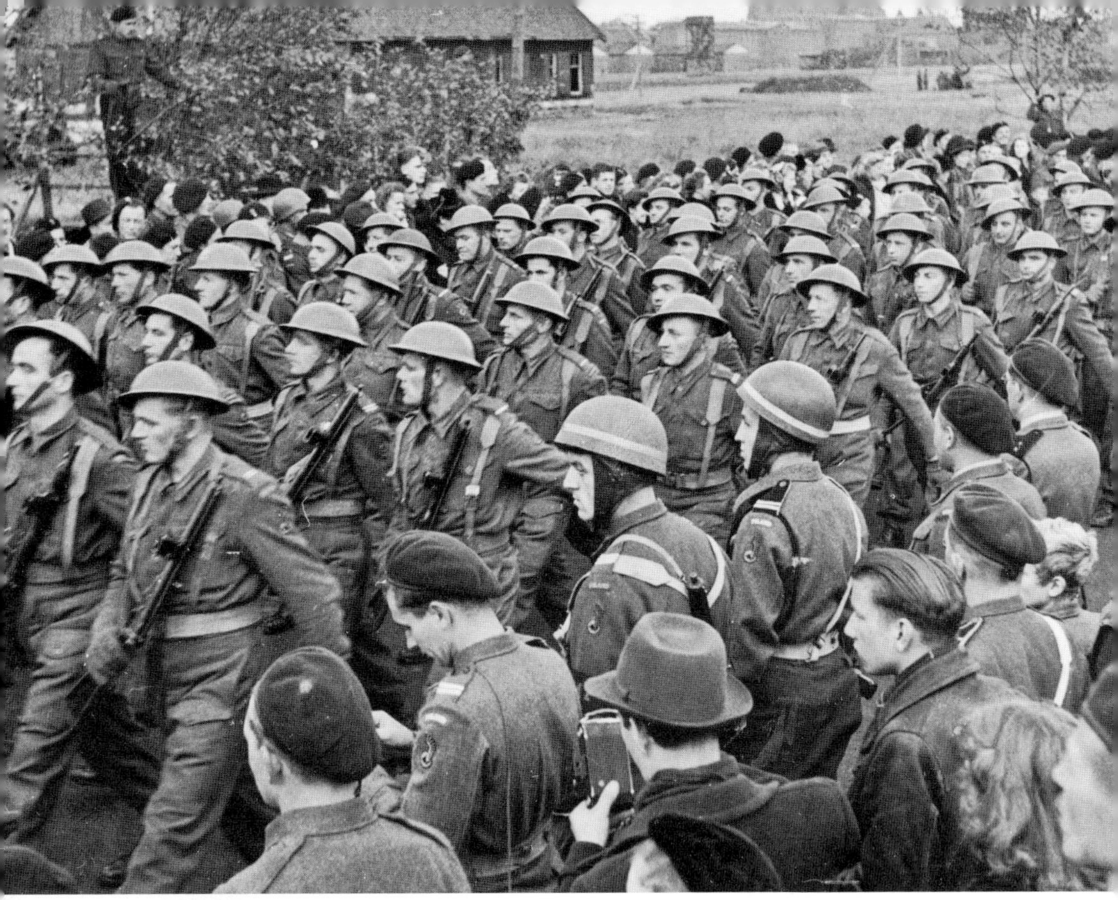

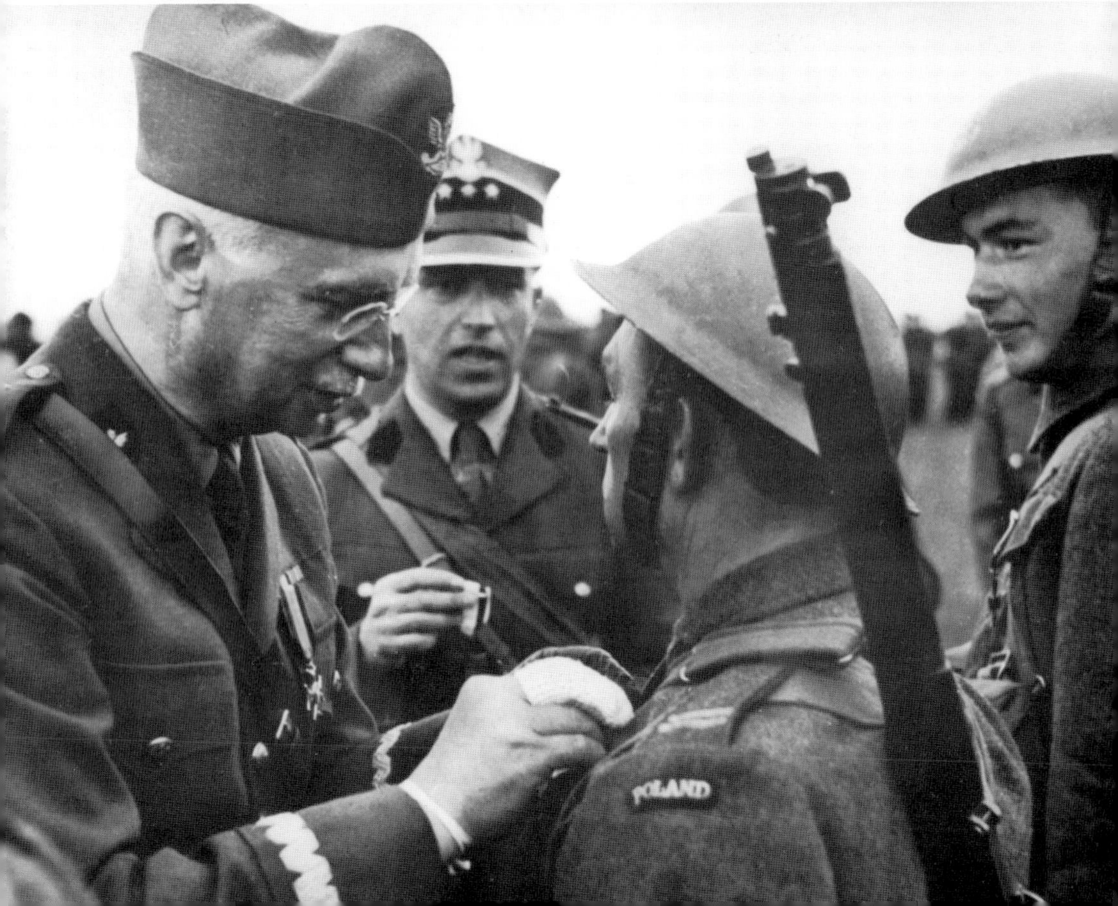
POLAND

Previous page:

1944, Polish forces receiving the freedom
of the city of Breda in Holland

General Sosnkowski decorating a soldier
from the Polish 1st Armoured Division

1944, Polish tanks from the Polish
1st Armoured Division in Holland

May 1945, Polish forces under General
Stanisław Maczek capture Wilhelmshaven

1944, General Juin decorating General Maczek of the Polish 1st Armoured
Division in France

armoured division was readied for the invasion. The work went slowly, men were continually being brought in and there was a struggle for equipment, but finally, in spring 1944 the 1st Armoured Division, General Maczek commanding, was by and large ready.

Including reserves, it had 885 officers and 15,210 other ranks and was composed of the following units: the 10th Mechanised Brigade, the 3rd Rifle Brigade, a reconnaissance regiment, divisional artillery, engineer units, a signals battalion, a provost company, supply and medical detachments, a reserve armoured squadron and other supporting arms. Its equipment consisted of 381 *Sherman* and *Cromwell* tanks (the latter for the reconnaissance regiment), 473 guns and 4,050 vehicles.

On paper, all was in place, however the Division was never at full strength, never mind reserves, and there was a question mark over the physical fitness of the rifle battalions, given the age of many of the men. However, once the decision to form the Division had been taken, the British turned a blind eye and supplied the necessary brand new equipment and provided training, while inspection teams did not enquire too closely. The Division was to form part of the invasion's second echelon and was moved from Scarborough to Aldershot only in July, where it impatiently awaited its final movement orders.

The long-awaited Allied invasion of France began on the 6th of June 1944. The Poles were not in the first wave and only at the end of July was the Division loaded onto ships at Tilbury Docks. On the 1st of August, after an uneventful crossing of the English Channel, Polish soldiers stood on French soil again for the first time in four years. They were returning in strength, with a fine well-equipped force.

The Division was assigned to Canadian II Corps, part of Field Marshal Sir Bernard Montgomery's 21st Army Group and almost immediately came under fire. The Germans were continuing to counter-attack and the Canadian Corps was ordered to hit the Germans from the north in the direction of Falaise. The going was hard, for the Germans defended stubbornly, supported by their superior *Panther* and *Tiger* tanks. The Polish Division came through its baptism of fire well, gaining in confidence and experience. However, the initial losses were 656 men killed or wounded and 66 tanks put out of action.

An opportunity now arose to encircle the retreating Germans in the so-called Falaise Pocket. The Canadians and the Poles set about their task and on the 15th of August (co-incidentally the anniversary of the Poles' famous victory over the Bolsheviks before Warsaw in 1920), things went well for the Division: it succeeded in capturing the bridge over the River Dives and the nearby fords, which tanks could cross. On the afternoon of the 17th, the 10th Regiment of Mounted Rifles reached the town of Trun, but that evening it received orders to continue its advance as far as Chambois, about 4 miles south-east of Trun. Interestingly enough, captured German prisoners revealed that to the east lay the 2nd German

Panzer Division, the same unit which the then Colonel Maczek's armoured brigade had engaged in September 1939.

Between the 19th and the 21st, the Division was involved in heavy fighting, since the Germans were strenuously attempting to break through the closing encirclement. The worst day was the 20th with the German 21st Panzer attacking from the east, but the 4th Canadian Armoured Division arrived in support from the north on the following day. The strings of the closing pocket were held and the German attacks began to peter out.

Overall, the Division lost 325 men killed, including 21 officers, 1,002 were wounded, including 35 officers and 114 were missing, presumed killed. This number of 1,441 represented about 10% of the Division's total strength, and in some units it was as high as 20% or even 30%. In percentage terms, these losses were higher than those of Second Corps at Monte Cassino, but the propaganda effect was smaller, since the Division was fighting as part of the Canadian Corps, which was credited with the overall success. The Division also took 5,115 prisoners, including one general and 136 officers, 55 tanks, 44 guns, 38 armoured vehicles and 207 other vehicles, not to mention light weaponry and horse-drawn vehicles.

After Falaise, the 1st Armoured Division, after a few days' rest, headed off in pursuit of the retreating Germans towards Abbeville and Ypres. The Poles were enthusiastically welcomed by the French along the way. They took Abbeville, and Saint-Omer, as well as the historic Belgian towns of Ypres and Ghent. Over the course of about a fortnight, the Division covered almost 500 km (300 miles) taking 4,000 prisoners and a great deal of equipment. After joining the British to take Antwerp, by the middle of September, the Division was on Dutch soil and before it stood Breda, the capital of the Catholic part of Holland.

General Maczek, wanting to avoid destroying this historic town, planned a successful attack from the east, which began on the 27th of October. Within a few days, the town fell. After some further mopping-up operations, the Division settled down for the winter in Breda. This was essential, since after losing 367 killed and 1,325 wounded, numbers, especially in some of the rifle companies, had fallen to 60% of strength.

The time spent in Breda was one long round of receptions and enthusiasm. The hospitality and gratitude of the Dutch took the Poles by surprise. The whole Division was fêted and given the freedom of the city and the men felt as if they had liberated their own country. To this day, the Dutch of Breda fondly remember their Polish liberators.

News of the decisions taken at Yalta sent a shock wave through the 1st Armoured Division, offensive operations in Holland more or less coinciding with the Crimean Conference. However, unlike the Second Corps, most of the Division's men were not from the lost Eastern lands and were thus less personally affected. The Division was again part of Canadian II Corps and had been reinforced by a Belgian paratroop battalion and a Canadian field artillery regiment. Its task was to advance north along the Dutch-German border, with the eventual goal of taking the German port of Emden. Its objective was then changed to Wilhelmshaven.

It was April when the Division's final push began. There was some heavy fighting between the 19th and the 29th, and the same month the Division liberated a female other ranks POW camp at Oberlangen (Stalag VI-C) in Germany, containing women from the Home Army who had been taken prisoner after the Warsaw Rising. The Division reached Wilhelsmhaven during the first days of May and two days after the cease-fire on the 4th, Colonel Antoni Grudziński, 2 i/c of the 10th Armoured Brigade, took a symbolic surrender.

Over the course of its operations from August 1944 to May 1945, the 1st Armoured Division had taken prisoner 2,200 officers and over 50,000 other ranks, destroyed 260 tanks and self-propelled guns, 310 anti-tank guns, 30 armoured cars, not to mention shooting down 13 aircraft and 9 V-1 flying bombs. The Division's losses were: 304 officers and about 5,000 other ranks, 240 *Cromwell* and *Sherman* tanks, 22 guns, 96 tank transporters and 71 trucks.

The Division was now involved in the symbolic task of occupying Germany. The British authorities, aware that the Third Reich contained many thousands of Poles from POW, concentration and forced labour camps, assigned the city of Haren on the River Ems to the Division. All the town's inhabitants were moved out, its name was changed to Maczków and for the next two years it would have a Polish administration, with schools, a theatre, newspapers and magazines, thus becoming a small Polish enclave on German soil under the protection of the Division. General Klemens Rudnicki took over the Division in May, General Maczek moving to Great Britain to take over I Corps. The Division was finally demobilised in 1947.

The Polish 1st Independent Parachute Brigade

Badge of the Polish 1st Independent Parachute Brigade

On the 9th of October 1941, after a visit to the 4th Rifle Brigade training in Scotland under its commander Colonel (later General) Stanisław Sosabowski, General Sikorski issued an order renaming it the 1st Independent Parachute Brigade.

The British, who hitherto had simply been keeping an eye on Polish efforts in this area, began to take a real interest and at the start of 1942 they allowed Polish troops to use their central parachute school at RAF Ringway near Manchester. British parachute operations were in their infancy and so German operations in Holland and Crete were studied, great attention was paid to the actual jump and the Polish instructors' experience came in very handy. Indeed, their value was so appreciated that they were assigned men from other allied nations: Belgians, Czechs, Dutchmen and Norwegians.

The nucleus of the Brigade was formed quite quickly, but then the same manpower problem that bedevilled all the Polish armed forces in the West slowed things down. Seeing this, the British reduced the supply of equipment. The Brigade needed 2,500 men, but it still had fewer than 2,000. However, General Sikorski believed that the recruitment target would be met and on the 7th of September 1942 he established the Brigade's order of battle: HQ, four rifle battalions, an engineer company, a signals platoon and a medical company. In fact, it now required 3,000 men, a number which was never achieved, and in May 1944 the fourth skeleton battalion was disbanded. On the 15th of June, the Brigade was presented with colours by the Polish President, Władysław Raczkiewicz, at Cupar in Scotland. The colours had been embroidered by the women of Warsaw and brought over to England on one of the three 'Bridge' missions.

From the very beginning, General Sikorski had planned for the Brigade to be used in Poland as soon as the decisive moment for a general rising approached, thus it remained under his personal command and was not part of First Corps. However, things turned out differently: the allied advance in Italy was halted in its tracks and the invasion of Northern France postponed until mid-1944, so it was the Red Army which entered Polish territory first. It was clear by now that the decisive events in Poland would take place while the Western armies were too distant to be able to help, even if political decisions were to turn in Poland's favour. Moreover, flying the 1,500 men of the Brigade to Poland with enough arms and ammunition for just 1 day would have required 265 specially modified *Liberators* with reduced crews. This number of suitable aircraft simply did not exist and in fact SOE used no more than 24 *Liberators* for all its national groups. In other words, it was technically impossible to send the Polish Parachute Brigade to Poland. Hence, a decision had to be taken whether it should be released to the British for use in Northern Europe.

By 1944, the general Polish consensus was that the Brigade should be released to the British with no caveats as to its use. In May 1944, the Polish Cabinet took the decision in order to be seen as a good ally, and at the beginning of June, General Sikorski's successor as Polish Supreme Commander, General Kazimierz Sosnkowski, formally informed the British authorities of this in writing. Final equipping now began. However, it is unclear whether General Sosnkowski made it crystal clear to the Home Army in Poland that this important decision had been taken.

The outbreak of the Warsaw Rising hit the men of the Brigade especially hard, since they were unable to go to their capital's defence. The Polish paratroops had not been part of the first 'D' Day echelon, for they were still being equipped, thus they formed part of the second echelon. In mid-September, Field Marshal Montgomery, whose forces had already crossed the Somme and taken Brussels and Antwerp, produced a detailed plan for an operation aimed at shortening the war. The main route to the Ruhr was protected by the Siegfried Line stretching from the Swiss border to Belgium. Therefore, Montgomery proposed that, instead of a frontal assault due east, the Siegfried Line be outflanked from the north through Holland. There were two elements to his plan: British and Polish paratroops were to secure the bridge over the Rhine at Arnhem, while ground forces were to attack from the south. Their task was to reach Eindhoven and Nijmegen, where they would link up with American paratroops and then advance as far as Arnhem, where they would join the British and Polish units. General Eisenhower accepted the plan and allocated two American airborne divisions, the 82nd and the 101st.

There was an additional dimension to this plan. The first V-2 rocket had landed on London on the 8th of September causing considerable consternation, since, unlike the V-1 flying bomb, there was no known defence against it. The Germans were launching the V-2 rockets, with a maximum range of 320 km (190 miles), from Holland and their sites lay in Montgomery's path.

Polish paratroopers boarding an aircraft
for Operation 'Market Garden'

Polish paratroopers on parade

General Sosabowski prior to Operation
'Market Garden'

1944, General Sosabowski at Arnhem during
Operation 'Market Garden'

Polish paratroopers in action

Polish paratroopers on the march
at Arnhem

The hastily prepared Operation 'Market Garden' began on the 17th of September. Both American airborne divisions took their objectives and, four days later, British XXX Corps broke through to make contact, but its further advance was halted by a stubborn German defence. This had dire consequences, given that further north, at Arnhem, things were going badly. The British 1st Airborne Division had been dropped several miles from its objective, the bridge at Arnhem, thus losing the element of surprise. A day later, German pressure was beginning to tell and the following day, elements of the Polish Parachute Brigade arrived in gliders, followed by further elements 24 hours later. The bulk of the Brigade took off on the 21st in 114 aircraft, but British commanders called off the drop in mid-flight. However, only 61 aircraft received the order and turned back, the remainder continued, dropping 1,067 paratroopers, including the Brigade Commander, General Sosabowski.

The now under-strength Brigade landed south of the Rhine under German fire. The tactical situation was bad: Arnhem was in German hands and the British were on the other side of the Rhine in the town of Oosterbeek and completely surrounded. The Poles needed to set up a defensive perimeter and also to cross the river to come to the aid of the British. About 60 of them made it across, Sosabowski having already made contact with the British divisional commander, and the following night the Poles managed to get about a battalion with some anti-tank weapons across the Rhine. On the 23rd, the rest of the Brigade was dropped some distance from Driel, which it reached on foot and then set about trying to cross the river, but in vain, for German fire was too intense. On the 25th, the order was given for all units still north of the Rhine to cross over the river, link up with the Poles and then withdraw to the south. Only 2,163 men from the British 1st Airborne made it across the river, together with 140 Poles, most of whom swam across. The operation was a failure and the bridge at Arnhem remained in German hands for another 6 months or so. The Polish Brigade lost 49 dead, (4 officers), 159 wounded (12 officers) and 173 missing (16 officers). Sadly, not only had this élite Polish formation failed to find success, but it did so knowing that Warsaw was suffering at the same time.

The 1st Independent Parachute Brigade also took part in the Occupation of Germany. After the Battle of Arnhem, it had returned to Great Britain and had been re-organised with reinforcements of Poles from the German Army, who had been taken prisoner. Its commander changed, for General Sosabowski left to be replaced towards the end of December by Lieutenant Colonel Stanisław Jachnik who in turn handed over command in April 1945 to Colonel Antoni Szczerbo-Rawicz. The Brigade was now put on stand-by, for the plan was to use it against an isolated German position, which was holding out in Dunkirk. However, by the time it was landed at Ostend on the 8th of May, hostilities had ended and the Brigade was sent to the Bersenbrück area, near Meppen, where the Polish 1st Armoured Division was stationed. The Brigade now came under the Division's operational command and the two then occupied a considerable stretch of Germany. In addition, the Brigade assumed humanitarian responsibilities for many thousands of Poles left stranded by the war on a hostile shore. The settlement of Emmerich, which contained a Polish civilian camp, was called *Spadochronowo*, which loosely translated as 'Parachuteville'.

The Brigade was demobilised in 1947.

The Polish Section of SOE
and Poland's 'Silent and Unseen'

Breast badge of the cichociemni special forces of the Polish Underground: 'The Silent and Unseen'

Winston Churchill was nothing if not creative. In the early days of the war he conceived of an irregular organisation which would help to undermine Nazi rule in Occupied Europe. In July 1940, the War Cabinet accepted his concept and out of an amalgamation of several existing intelligence departments was born SOE (Special Operations Executive) to come under the Ministry of Economic Warfare, with Sir Frank Nelson, a man with an unusual background, appointed to head it. Nelson's appointment had something of the symbolic about it, since he represented the new organisation's most characteristic features: its independence from the regular armed forces, its unorthodox nature, anathema to many regular officers, and its imaginative personnel selection and operational methods. SOE had a number of sections in Europe and the Far East and at its high point employed almost 10,000 men and 3,200 women, a great many of them commissioned officers or agents of comparable rank.

France, being the closest occupied country, became the initial object of SOE's attentions and the French Section was the first to be formed, followed, interestingly enough, in the summer of 1940, by the section for distant Poland. Almost from the start, the Head of the Polish Section was Captain (later Colonel) Harold Perkins, who stayed in post until the end of the war. Perkins had owned a small textile plant in Bielsk in Poland before the war, he spoke Polish and he knew the people. His section worked closely with Special Department VI (Homeland Liaison) of the Polish General Staff, which became SOE's only real window into Polish affairs and Poland herself. Contrary to the practice of other SOE sections, which sent their own people to occupied countries and reported to their superiors in London, the Poles were granted the exceptional privilege of

Cichociemni parachute training

Successful landing!

cichociemni undergo advanced weapons training in Scotland

Field-radio communications are an important part of *cichociemni* training

cichociemni are taught to live off the land

Many *cichociemni* are parachuted into Poland to take command of Polish Home Army units and give instruction in sabotage techniques and guerrilla warfare tactics

autonomy. They recruited their own emissaries, couriers and covert operations experts to send to Poland, each of whom took the oath of the underground Home Army of which they became soldiers immediately upon landing on Polish soil. SOE's task was to help Department VI in this work, to provide supplies and to ensure good communication between the Poles and the appropriate British authorities. However, it was agreed that all intelligence gathered by the Poles was to be handed over to British Intelligence, except that dealing with Poland's internal affairs.

Immediately after the formation of SOE's Polish Section, Department VI began discreetly to recruit volunteers to parachute into Poland for special duties. The object was to inject into the Polish underground military a number of specialists trained in areas such as staff work, covert operations, intelligence, document forging, demolitions, signals and general sabotage skills. This was very much in line with SOE's primary mission.

There was a gratifying surge of volunteers for the dangerous assignment to return to Poland, which included:

> 1 general officer
>
> 112 staff officers
>
> 894 junior officers
>
> 592 NCOs
>
> 771 privates
>
> 15 women
>
> 28 civilian political couriers.

Of these 2,413 volunteers, 606 completed the training and 579 qualified to jump. Hence the selection was exceptionally rigorous, with exactly one in four candidates completing training. Once accepted and trained, a volunteer became a *cichociemny* and a member of what later came to be known collectively as the *cichociemni* (the 'Silent and Unseen').

First of all, however, the candidates had to take a number of tests, after which they were sent for special training, since each of them would become a specialist in several skills. A great emphasis was laid on physical fitness, marksmanship and map-reading and this was followed by courses in covert operations and explosives. In September 1940, SOE set up the first covert operations course for Poles at Inverlochy Castle near Fort William in Western Scotland.

This initial training was followed by an array of specialist courses (some of them optional) in sabotage, communications, unarmed combat, intelligence, codes, ciphers, invisible inks, document forging, German armour, partisan warfare and propaganda. There were also courses on psychological warfare, called black propaganda. The Poles ran an assault course in Scotland and the British a street-fighting course in Battersea , South London, as well as a commando course designed to produce experts trained in sabotage of industrial facilities, railway lines, telegraph lines, power stations, power lines and similar installations.

At the beginning of January 1941, the first course in partisan warfare began at the SOE training camp at Briggens near London. The *cichociemni* also took practical courses in personal survival, hence the so-called 'roots' course run by the 1st Polish Independent Parachute Brigade in the Scottish mountains, which trained parachutists for lengthy periods of concealment and living off the land. There were also British courses on urban survival run in Birmingham, Liverpool and Glasgow. Parachute training took place either at the British parachute school at RAF Ringway, or at the Polish training centre for the Parachute Brigade at Largo House near Leven, popularly known as the 'monkey grove'.

The final part of the course was pre-flight preparation which was designed to change a regular soldier into a resistance fighter. The first such courses were not strictly speaking courses: in addition to a few lectures, they really consisted of final group preparation. Real pre-flight preparation courses began in July 1942 at the SOE station at Audley End House in Essex run by the Poles. After qualifying to jump into Poland the parachutist took the AK oath of allegiance, chose one and more frequently two noms de guerre, which were essential for conspiratorial work where real names were never used, and left for a holding station.

The pre-flight preparation course lasted from 2 to 6 weeks. A *cichociemny* prepared a 'legend', in other words a cover story tailored to his new persona. He received false identity papers, and completed his civilian wardrobe. He was familiarised in detail with conditions of life in Occupied Poland, as well as with the structure of the Polish Underground, the German Army and Administration. The underground press, as well as German publications and the occupation 'collaboration' press were put at his disposal. It was important that these courses be taught by people who had recently arrived from Poland. Later the parachutist did exercises covering the organisation of the drop zone team, what to do after the jump, how to find a contact point and a safe house, given that all jumps took place at night. In his spare moments a parachutist would spend as much time as possible on the firing range.

An individual parachutist's equipment consisted of civilian clothes, none of which could be English in style or cut, since that would immediately give him away. In addition, the jumper had his military equipment: a jump suit and parachute, a folding spade to bury the parachute and a poison capsule, if he wanted to take one, concealed in a button. Ten of the parachutists would later have to use their poison capsules. There was also a wide webbing belt with pouches, which held money (usually dollars) for AK High Command as well as six-months' pay.

Towards the end of 1943, training courses for volunteers from Second Corps were started in Southern Italy and the Polish directing staff were sent out from England. The training, although simplified, was similar to that carried out in Great Britain. The last pre-flight preparation course in Italy ended in July 1944 and in Great Britain in September of the same year.

The first drop of parachutists into Poland took place during the night of the 15th/16th of February 1941. The aircrew on this initial mission was British and the aircraft barely made it back on its last drops of fuel. Sadly, the very next day the whole aircrew was to perish when their aircraft was shot down. Nevertheless, they were to receive posthumous Polish awards for gallantry, with the pilot receiving Poland's highest gallantry award, the *Virtuti Militari*.

Virtuti Militari

*Poland's highest
gallantry award*

This initial trial operation was followed by a long break lasting until November, which was used to fine tune what were extremely difficult operations, given the range of aircraft in 1941. For the Poles it was very important that Polish airmen be allowed to take part in the flights to Poland, and since all SOE work was carried out by 138 Squadron RAF stationed at RAF Newmarket and later at RAF Tempsford, in the autumn of 1941, three Polish bomber crews reported for duty there, followed by a further two. These were volunteer crews, who had already completed their regular tours of duty and who had received additional training in low-level night flying and astral, as well as visual, navigation, given that Poland was not covered by radar navigational aids.

The first flight to Poland was carried out by heavy and slow *Whitley* bombers, and subsequent ones by four-engine *Halifaxes*. The *Halifax* was also slow, achieving a maximum speed of 300 kph (180 mph), and its range was no greater than 2,500 km (1,500 miles) with a load of 1,900 kg (4,000 lbs) and a crew of 7. Since the distance from London to Warsaw flying over Denmark was around 1,600 km (950 miles), the aircraft required modifications and additional fuel tanks were fitted, increasing its range to 3,500 km (2,100 miles), but with a reduction in load to 1,200 kg (2,400 lbs). Flights had to take place at night, and since the return trip lasted over a dozen hours, they could be done only during the autumn, the winter and early spring. The need for visual navigation to find the drop zone required a full moon, which meant that realistically there could be only about 40 night flights during a single year.

General Sikorski, who attached a great deal of importance to these operations, began trying to obtain a number of *Liberators* from the Americans. These aircraft could fly almost 5,000 km (3,000 miles) at a speed of just under 480 kph

(300 mph) and their carrying capacity was substantially greater than that of the British bombers. He also discussed with the British forming a separate Polish squadron.

During the first mission, the *Whitley* flew the shortest route 'cross-country' over Germany. In the autumn a new circuitous route crossing Denmark was planned and was called Route No. 1. It crossed the North Sea to the north of the Island of Sylt, cut across Denmark, then around Bornholm the route took a turn to the south and the aircraft headed for the area of the Jamno and the Bukowo Lakes. From there it led over the Charzykowskie Lake towards Toruń and then on into the Płock region. The aircraft now headed for their designated drop zones. The Polish crews, who had an excellent knowledge of the area, did not always stick to the route and often chose their own alternatives when they were over the Baltic.

Since German night fighters were appearing more frequently over Denmark, the route began gradually to shift north on the most dangerous sector. Thus Route No. 2, which was flown in the autumn of 1943, eventually became established. It skirted Denmark to the north and crossed Sweden where it turned south.

In April 1943, Polish C Flight (informally called 301 Flight, thus preserving the number of 301 (Polish) Squadron which had been disbanded to provide the flight's manpower) was formed within 138 Squadron. In November 1943, it was re-constituted as 1586 Special Duties Flight and transferred to 334 Special Duties Wing operating in the Mediterranean Basin mainly over Yugoslavia and Northern Italy, the first American *Liberators* having finally arrived in September. In mid-December, the flight carried out several missions to Poland from Tunisia, after which before Christmas it finally settled in Southern Italy whence it carried out flights to Poland until the end of 1944, supported by 148 Squadron RAF from 334 Wing and, during the Warsaw Rising, by an additional two Liberator squadrons: 178 Squadron RAF and 31 Squadron SAAF. However, given the exigencies of SOE work, the Poles never had their own flight dedicated exclusively to flights to Poland.. In November 1944, the Flight became fully fledged 301 Special Duties Squadron and was eventually the only Polish squadron to receive a unit decoration of the *Virtuti Militari*.

When the base for air operations to Poland was shifted to Brindisi in Apulia in Italy in late 1943 three routes were used. Route No. 3 crossed the Adriatic, Dalmatia and Croatia, and then the recognisable feature of Lake Balaton in Hungary and from there it led over the Tatra Mountains. Route No. 4, after crossing the Dalmatian coastal towns of Bar and Kotor, crossed Montenegro towards Hungary to the east of Budapest and entered Polish airspace east of the Tatra Mountains. Route No. 5 led over Durras in Albania, then over Serbia and from Bazias on the Romanian/Yugoslav border it headed for Lwów.

The next critical issue was to obtain suitable military equipment for the underground army in Occupied Poland. The Polish Armed Forces, as had been agreed, were to be equipped by the British and all would have been simple had Great Britain itself possessed adequate supplies. While British industry was slowly beginning to get into top gear, the needs were enormous and although the Polish Section of SOE did what it could to fill Department VI's requests, it was never enough.

The final issue was how to organise an appropriate reception for parachute drops in Occupied Poland, set up efficient and accurate associated radio links and provide adequate protection for such operations. This was no easy matter, for drop zones had to be set up on fields almost a third of a mile long and about half as wide, as far from main roads as possible and near a bend in a river or a lake in order to be able to locate them at night. Suitably trained underground troops had to put out lamps forming a lighted arrow indicating the wind direction and then, after a drop, meet the parachutist and pick up the containers. There also had to be 'safe houses' prepared for arriving *cichociemni* and couriers.

At the same time another partisan group, located on nearby high ground, had to pick up radio signals sent by the BBC from London. There, at the Polish Section, only one person knew the dozen or so 'reserved' tunes whose titles had been sent to Poland in the greatest secrecy. If at the end of a programme the radio announcer said that such and such a tune was to be played, then the partisans waiting at a drop zone knew that the planned flight would in fact take place. They knew too which of the waiting drop zones would be targeted, how many parachutists and how many containers there would be, for earlier radio signals had carried the relevant information. It is also worth adding that sometimes, for reasons of security, a drop zone had to be protected by partisan detachments with not infrequently several hundred men.

Aircraft left for Poland in four successive operational seasons, which were tied closely to the arrival of longer nights. It was possible to fly from Great Britain from the end of August to the first half of April, while from Italy, which was a shorter route, from July to the end of May, thus almost continuously.

The period of trial flights began in February 1941 and ended in April 1942. The subsequent seasons were given code-names: 'Intonacja' —September 1942 to April 1943, 'Riposta'—September 1943 to July 1944 and 'Odwet'—August to December 1944. Flights took place on moonlit nights with a full moon, or in the so-called third phase between the beginning of the second and the end of the third quarters of the moon. At the beginning of 1943, trials were made flying on moonless nights, initially only with supplies, but from the spring of 1944 with parachutists too.

During 'Intonacja' 42 drops were made, 28 with *cichociemni* and the rest just with supplies; 106 *cichociemni* were dropped, as well as 9 couriers and a Hungarian radio-telegraphist who was later slipped into Hungary. One of the *cichociemni* was killed jumping, and a further 3 perished together with their Polish aircrew.

'Riposta' began with flights from England, followed by a short period from Tunisia and then from Brindisi in Italy. Two hundred and five missions were carried out, of which 36 carried parachutists. They also included 3 'Wildhorn' missions (called 'Bridges' by the Poles) when *Dakota* aircraft actually landed on Polish soil. One hundred and forty-six parachutists were carried—135 *cichociemni*, 10 couriers and 1 woman. One of the *cichociemni* was killed jumping and three of them perished with their British aircrew.

'Odwet's' main effort focused on helping the Home Army during the Warsaw Uprising. There were 229 successful missions out of 410 attempted, not counting those which ended in 'blind' drops, all carried out by American, British, Polish and South African aircrews. *Cichociemni* were dropped in only 7 missions. Thirty-one *cichociemni*, 2 couriers, as well as the 4 British members and 1 Pole of the British Military Mission were dropped. One of the *cichociemni* was killed jumping.

Seventy aircraft, of which 30 were piloted by Poles, were lost flying to Poland; out of these 112 Polish airmen, 6 were rescued by the AK, 28 became POWs in German camps and the rest perished

The final flight with *cichociemni* took place on the night of the 26th/27th of December 1944, and the final flight carrying only supplies two nights later.

Altogether, 317 *cichociemni* were sent to Poland (in reality 316, since one of them jumped twice) including 1 woman and 29 political couriers (in reality 28, since one of them also jumped twice), 1 Hungarian who had taken the partisan warfare course and 4 Britons and 1 Pole in the 'Freston' British Military Mission of December 1944.

Therefore, 307 *cichociemni* landed on Polish soil. Each one was promoted a rank upon landing. They did not serve as a cohesive military unit; they were not a combat formation. From their individual application to service in Poland through their training in small groups and then while awaiting a drop the *cichociemni* were at the disposal of Department VI of the General Staff. After their jump, they each received an individual posting depending on the current needs of the Home Army High Command and their specialist skills and they were then to be found in all areas of underground military operations.

Scattered by their postings throughout the whole of Poland and even abroad—to the east in Ukraine as far as the front and to the west in the depths of the Reich wherever AK intelligence operated—they served in the most dangerous sectors. The worked at many levels of underground warfare: in covert operations, intelligence, operational communications, on staffs, as weapons instructors, as partisans; some of them worked as couriers between Poland and the West. During their years of service their assignments often changed as required by current conditions.

The *cichociemni* provided a number of senior military leaders for the Underground. The last AK Commander-in-Chief, General Leopold Okulicki, as well as

8 military district commanders and deputy commanders, 1 sub-district commander, 8 chiefs of staff, as well as a dozen or so department heads at AK High Command and at regional, district and sub-district level were *cichociemni*.

Cichociemni specialising in intelligence work were employed by the Department of Offensive Intelligence in Department II on the Staff of AK High Command. The Head of Department II was a cichociemny. They were initially all assigned to stations and to the intelligence network of the two most important departments: 'East' which was conducting intelligence work behind the eastern front and 'West' which extended into Germany, Austria, Czechoslovakia and Moravia. They brought professionalism to intelligence work and the large percentage of losses incurred by this small group of 37 *cichociemni*, 15 of whom were killed or arrested by the Gestapo and the *Abwehr*, is proof of the ferocity with which they were pursued by German counter-intelligence.

As the war continued and Poland was elbowed aside to make way for the Soviets, the Polish Section of SOE found itself in a ticklish position. While the British were perhaps understandably rather more reluctant to provide the Poles with military equipment if the Poles were going to use it against the Red Army, a supposed ally, SOE felt a debt of obligation towards the Poles. It was, perhaps, this sense of obligation which prevented SOE from ever really making it plain to the Poles how their political situation had changed by 1944, which certainly contributed to the disaster of the Warsaw Uprising.

Commemorative badge of AK Battalion 'Parasol'

Almost 100 *cichociemni* were in Warsaw or in the area of the Kampinos Forest nearby when the Warsaw Uprising broke out. Their contribution to operations during the Uprising was considerable. They were to be found everywhere: on the front line they commanded well-known detachments such as 'Parasol', 'Baszta', 'Czata 49' and 'Rum'. They worked on staffs, in communications and in weapons manufacture. Eighteen of them, 20%, were either killed or were missing in action. One of them was in on the final act, the capitulation, which was signed in Ożarów by Colonel Kazimierz Iranek-Osmecki, a *cichociemny*, on behalf of the AK Commander-in-Chief. After Warsaw's capitulation, some of the *cichociemni* went into captivity. Others left the city with the civilian population in order to keep working underground until the end of the war.

It is unclear when and where the name *cichociemni* (*The Silent and Unseen*) was first used. The earliest document in which the term appears is a Department VI directive of September 1941. However, during the war the term was unknown in Poland; at the time people referred to parachutists as 'birds from the sky' or 'drops'. It was only after the war that Polish historians adopted the term *cichociemni*, usually written without quotation marks and all in lower case. Many of them who settled in Great Britain were later awarded British decorations, either the King's Medal for Courage in the Cause of Freedom, or a King's Commendation for Brave Conduct.

Polish Women in World War II

Poland's brutal introduction to total war in 1939 meant that women and even children found themselves on the front line from the very start. In Poland, both the Germans and their new allies, the Soviets, showed little restraint in their treatment of unarmed civilians. Hence the front ran through everyone's lives and women stood shoulder to shoulder with men in every area of underground life and activity.

Many women had had an introduction to military life before the war by serving as girl guides in the Polish Scouting Movement, which had a patriotic and military ethos to it. Others had belonged to the Women's Auxiliary Corps under the auspices of the Ministry of Defence.

In February 1940, the Polish Ministry of Military Affairs, still in Paris, laid out guidelines for forming a women's military service. At this stage a number of women joined the Red Cross and served with the Polish forces' medical services in the Norwegian campaign.

A Women's Auxiliary Service (to be called the Women's Military Service in 1942) was formed in Poland as early as October 1939 as part of Department I in the High Command of 'Serving Poland's Victory'—a precursor to the Home Army. It was an auxiliary service, based on the law of April 1938 on universal military service, which stated that women could be called up, but only on a voluntary basis. It was commanded by Major Maria Wittek, who had commanded the pre-war Women's Auxiliary Corps and who after the war would become the first woman to be reach general officer rank in the Polish Army, having attained the rank of colonel during the Warsaw Rising.

Members of the Women's Military Service served as couriers, messengers, nurses, tailors, cooks and bakers, signallers, teachers, ammunition carriers, cipher clerks, distributors of the underground press, guides through the sewers during the Warsaw Rising and in a multitude of other permanent or ad hoc positions, sometimes also taking part in covert operations and combat. There was in fact a women's sabotage formation called 'Dysk', led by Major Wanda Gertz. Women worked in the Home Army both in Intelligence and Counter-Intelligence, often in very dangerous circumstances.

The women were supported by the girls' section of the 'Grey Ranks' scouting movement, which, like the boys', was strongest in central Poland, especially in Warsaw, and which trained girls to carry out auxiliary roles, such as nurses,

Stefania Wojtulanis aboard a *Spitfire*

Anna Leska, an ATA ferry-pilot

Women played an important role during the Warsaw Uprising 1944

Krystyna Skarbek, Polish-born SOE agent also known as Christine Granville, was celebrated for her daring secret missions to Nazi-occupied Poland and France

Woman soldiers of a Polish Army Transport
Company during training in Palestine

A female soldier of the Home Army undergoing
weapons training in a forest encampment

messengers or cooks. The girls were also very active in combating the occupying Germans and, together with the boys, formed the backbone of 'minor sabotage'. The 'Grey Ranks' girls' section later became part of the Women's Military Service.

In 1941, the Women's Auxiliary Service was formed in the USSR from women who had been deported to the Soviet Union and left with the Polish forces in 1942, many of its members later serving with the Polish Second Corps in Italy in support formations. Among the Poles in the USSR there were over 1,000 female volunteers and nurses, as well as 1,000 boys and girls of the Young Volunteers Association. General Sikorski's daughter, Zofia Leśniowska, who perished with him at Gibraltar in July 1943, became the Service's first Commandant. She was replaced by a formidable woman, Col Maria Lesniak, who served in post until the end of the war. The Service, whose members were known as 'pips' (*pestki*), provided women for a number of support functions such as clerks, drivers, nurses, cooks, librarians, teachers, air traffic controllers, cipher clerks and mechanics.

Three women, one of whom was Jadwiga Piłsudska (Marshal Piłsudski's daughter), also served as ferry-pilots in the Air Transport Auxiliary and indeed women were perhaps able to help plug the manpower shortage in the Air Force better than in the other arms, serving also in various ground capacities. At the end of the war, the Service, which by now also had its Air Force and Naval sections (the women in the Naval Section were rather charmingly called 'little gulls' [*mewki*]), had about 7,000 women in its ranks. The Service was disbanded in 1946.

Many women who had been unable to leave for Iran with the Polish Army in 1942 joined or were conscripted into what became known as the Polish First Army serving alongside the Red Army. The most famous women's unit was the 1st Emilia Plater Independent Women's Battalion, which was formed in August 1943 and initially attached to the 1st Kościuszko Infantry Division. It was named after Emilia Plater who was a 19th century Polish revolutionary and patriot who fought during the 1831 uprising, ironically against the Russians. The battalion was a fully-fledged infantry battalion, but was always commanded by a man. Only one its units, a fusilier company, actually saw action, in 1943 at the Battle of Lenino alongside the 1st Division. The battalion eventually arrived in Warsaw in October 1944 where it remained until the end of the war carrying out security duties. The battalion was disbanded in October and November 1945.

From 1939 until the collapse of the Warsaw Rising the Head of all underground communications and couriers in Poland was Major Janina Karaś. A number of the international couriers were women, with a couple of them attaining real eminence. The first was the legendary and glamorous Christine Granville, whose real name was Krystyna Giżycka née Skarbek. She served as an

SOE agent both in Poland and later in the Middle East and France, for which she was awarded the George Medal by the British.

The second was Elżbieta Zawacka, who died in early 2009 aged 99, often known by her war-time *nom de guerre* 'Zo'. She crossed the German frontier over 100 times carrying secret despatches and intelligence. After being sent to Britain as a personal emissary of General Rowecki to General Sikorski (a rare distinction), she returned to Poland in 1943 as the only woman to be dropped by parachute as one of the 'Silent and Unseen' SOE operatives. During the Warsaw Rising she served in the Women's Military Service and after the war she would be the second woman to achieve general officer rank in the Polish Army.

It has been calculated that about 50,000 women served in the Home Army and over 5,000 with the regular armed forces. During the Warsaw Uprising, over 17% of the underground fighters were women, of whom 3,000 lost their lives.

The Polish Army on the Eastern Front

Polish 1st Tadeusz Kościuszko Infantry Division badge

When General Anders and his army departed from the Soviet Union for Iran in 1942 many thousands of Poles were left behind. The evidence suggests that the Soviet leadership had been planning for such an eventuality. As early as 1940, a group of Polish officer POWs, including a regular Polish army officer, Lieutenant Colonel (later General) Zygmunt Berling, had been pulled out of a camp and in September they had been brought to Malakhovka near Moscow where they were accommodated in a comfortable house, which was later given the telling name 'The Villa of Happiness'. Conditions there were good, the food excellent and they received a daily dose of lectures and political seminars, together with discussions of military matters, and it appears that the idea of raising a Polish army under Soviet command was considered, although no final decision was taken at the time.

Stalin's agreement to allow General Anders and his army to leave the USSR was a logical consequence of the change in Polish-Soviet relations, which had gone through a number of phases. The first phase began after the Fourth Partition of Poland in 1939 when Stalin had even opposed the formation of a 'rump' Polish state. This doctrine led to the great deportations from Poland's eastern lands in 1939 and 1940, to the liquidation of the Polish intelligentsia and to the decision on the fate of thousands of POWs. It even affected Stalin's attitude to the Polish Communists in those areas controlled by the USSR. Since the Comintern had dissolved the Communist Party of Poland in 1938 under the pretext that it had been penetrated by the Polish police, the Polish Communists were treated warily by the Soviets and a great many had been sent to labour camps and prison. Only those who showed no signs of nationalist tendencies and who uncritically accepted Soviet policies were tolerated. One of these was Wanda Wasilewska, a pre-war member of the Polish Socialist Party, who now revealed herself to be a fervent supporter of Soviet ideology. She was elected to the Supreme Soviet and attracted the attention of Stalin himself, who summoned her from Lwów for a talk in March 1940.

Immediately after the German attack in June 1941, some of the men at 'The Villa of Happiness' began calling for Polish Communist forces to be formed in the Soviet Union. Stalin was not yet prepared to go that far. However, after General Anders's army had finally left, it made both political and military sense for the Soviets to raise such forces, although Stalin did not begin this process while he maintained diplomatic relations with the Polish Government-in-Exile in London. Even after he had broken off relations over Easter 1943, he waited to see what would be his western partners' reaction. Only when he was convinced that Churchill and Roosevelt would not take any firm action in support of the Poles, did he move.

At the end of April, after diplomatic relations with the Polish Government-in-Exile had been broken off, Wasilewska raised the issue of a new Polish Army with Stalin. Soon thereafter, a meeting was held in Moscow, at which it was decided to form the Tadeusz Kościuszko Infantry Division and that its commander would be Colonel Berling. On the 8th of May 1943, a communiqué appeared in the Soviet press as well as in a new weekly Polish paper in the USSR, *Free Poland (Wolna Polska)*, in which the Soviet Government expressed its agreement to raising the Division.

Yet before there was an overt change in Soviet policy towards Poland, secret talks were held in the USSR on the creation of new Polish political leadership, composed of Communists and completely dependent on the Soviet Union. On the 1st of March 1943, an Executive Committee of the Union of Polish Patriots was formed in the Soviet capital, under the chairmanship of Wanda Wasilewska. On the 8th of March, this committee produced the first number of *Free Poland* which became the Union of Polish Patriots' mouthpiece. There could no doubt of the new organisation's aims and whose interests it would serve, for as early as the 16th of April an article entitled 'Poland's Place in Europe' appeared in *Free Poland*. It stated openly that Poland's eastern lands must be relinquished to the Soviet Union, since the Ukrainian, Belorussian and Lithuanian populations living there must be given the right to join Soviet republics. It also showed a willingness to move Poland west, for the editorial raised the issue of Poland's access to the Baltic and of her right to German land.

Unlike the situation in the West, there was an extensive Polish manpower

The Polish Communist Army on the Eastern Front using a
Willys MB US Army 'Jeep'—one of thousands supplied to
the Soviet Union under the US Lend-Lease programme

pool available in the Soviet Union. First of all there were those willing volunteers who had been unable to reach Anders's army and who simply saw this as a chance to get back to Poland, without necessarily subscribing to Communist ideology. Then there were about 100,000 Poles who had been called up by the Red Army but, labelled as 'unreliable' after the German attack, had been transferred to labour battalions. There were also those who had been called up by the Red Army, but had not been transferred to labour battalions and who had received permission to join the Polish division. A certain number of recruits were found too amongst those Soviet citizens who were of Polish descent, often the descendants of exiles from Czarist times, and who were serving in the Red Army either as professional soldiers, or who had recently been called up.

There was no difficulty recruiting private soldiers from this mass of volunteers, for nothing more than a medical examination was required. However, a problem arose finding officers. Trainloads of volunteers would arrive at the recruiting centres with almost no officers, with the exception of a few reservists who had concealed their rank when deported. The reason for this was that those who had been able to had left with General Anders, those murdered at Katyń and elsewhere in 1940 were unable to rise from the grave and the 'Villa of Happiness' had had only a dozen or so residents.

Therefore, the Soviet authorities had to bring in a great many native Russian officers, who had no connexion with Poland and who spoke no Polish. They were later to be called POPs (*Pełniący Obowiązki Polaka*— 'carrying out the duties of a Pole', also a play on the colloquial Russian word for an Orthodox parish priest, 'pop'). The Division's officer corps was thus composed of three groups: the largest were men of Polish descent living in the USSR, the POPs followed, with the smallest Polish one composed of friends of Colonel Berling, reserve officers, newly-promoted good NCOs, and graduates of the recently-opened military schools. There was also a serious lack of NCOs and the problem was tackled by training selected soldiers in the divisional training battalion and on regimental junior leaders' courses.

Following Soviet practice, such a diverse group of soldiery had to undergo thorough political training and indoctrination, which was left to the Division's political training wing. Only the Union of Polish Patriots was to provide instructors, who had to be Communists and native speakers of Polish to ensure that no part of the course was lost in translation.

The Division was structured along Soviet lines with three infantry regiments, a light artillery regiment and a number of independent units, such as a training battalion, an engineer battalion, a signals company and so on. Since the eventual idea was to expand the Polish forces in the USSR, the division also included an armoured regiment, an anti-aircraft detachment, a mortar detachment, a flight of fighter aircraft and a women's battalion. Following this model, the Division's strength was to be: 1,095 officers, 3,258 NCOs and 7,093 other ranks—11,446 in all. However, the high number of recruits meant that already by July the Division's strength was at 14,380.

As planned, Colonel Berling became the divisional commander. When the Division exceeded its planned size, a reserve regiment was formed, but the flow of volunteers was so great that the possibility arose of raising a full Polish corps. Stalin agreed to this and so, on the 10th of August 1943, a decree was issued by the Committee of National Defence of the USSR permitting the formation of a corps. Its commander was to be the now General Berling, who also remained GOC Polish 1st Division. General Karol Świerczewski, a Red Army officer but a Pole, became military 2i/c. In addition, the following units were raised: the 2nd Henryk Dąbrowski Infantry Division, the Józef Bem Artillery Brigade, the 'Heroes of Westerplatte' Armoured Brigade, the 'Warsaw' Air Regiment, a parachute battalion, a reserve infantry regiment and a number of independent smaller units. Later, at the beginning of 1944, the 3rd Romuald Traugutt Infantry Division began to form comprising above all Poles from Silesia, Pomerania and Wielkopolska, whom the Germans had forcibly recruited into the Wehrmacht and who had been captured by the Soviets. By the early spring of 1944, the strength of the Corps was 43,508, of whom 4,564 were officers.

After its decisive victory at the Battle of Kursk in the summer of 1943, the Red Army moved steadily west. The Polish Division was assigned to the Thirty-Third Army and passed through recently liberated Smolensk reaching the Lenino area, to the east of Orsha. There it was to force a crossing of the marshy Miereja River. On the 9th of October, just before launching the attack, the divisional commander issued an order appointing all education officers political officers. This proof of the formation's political character was underscored by General Berling's eve-of-battle order: '… Since we are fighting, since we are shedding blood and we are marking our road home with graves, then our voice will be heard in Poland, it cannot and will not be ignored… We shall set up a provisional government and we shall allow it to do its job. We shall be vigilant to ensure that fascism not return to Poland in any form. We shall guard our alliance with the Soviet Union with whom and with whose sincere friendship we shall keep faith.' A single division was now talking of seizing political power!

On the 12th and 13th of October, the Division carried out the planned assault together with its neighbouring Soviet divisions. They crossed the Miereja and its marshes, the infantry regiments penetrating the German lines to a depth of a mile or two, but German resistance, supported by artillery and air power, was too stubborn. The Poles were unable to break through and the adjacent Soviet divisions never got off their start lines; then German counter-attacks developed leading to a serious threat of encirclement. A quick withdrawal from the most advanced positions partially saved the day, but many men from the 1st Infantry Regiment were taken prisoner. For a time the situation was chaotic, senior officers lost their heads and young inexperienced soldiers, under fire for the first time in their lives, died in a hopeless struggle. During the night of the 13th/14th, the Division was pulled out of the line. Losses were considerable: 502 killed, 1,776 wounded and 662 missing in action.

The participation of this Polish formation fighting alongside the Russians was certainly necessary for political reasons. Hence the Battle of Lenino was widely trumpeted by Communist propaganda, even though it had been dreadfully conducted and there had been far too many casualties.

After the battle, the whole of Polish I Corps was moved to the Smolensk Region, where it remained until March 1944 re-organising, rebuilding its manpower and undergoing further training. Meanwhile the Red Army had moved far to the west, had re-taken the Ukraine to the west of the Dnieper and was already in the south-east of Poland in Volhynia and Podolia. Despite the great deportations in 1939-1940, many Poles still lived there thus providing the Corps with a fine recruiting opportunity. Therefore, the Union of Polish Patriots approached the Soviet authorities with the idea of expanding the Polish forces to a whole army. On the 16th of March, the appropriate decree was issued by the Praesidium of the Supreme Soviet of the USSR. Sumy in the Ukraine, over 180 miles to the east of Kiev, was designated as the site for the formation of these new forces.

First Polish Army had three major components; the Field Army, the Principal Training Staff and the Polish Partisan Staff. The Training Staff was initially located at Sumy, but in July it was moved to Zhitomir and it was commanded by General Świerczewski. The following units were raised: 4th Jan Kiliński Infantry Division, 1st Cavalry Brigade, 2 and 3 Howitzer Batteries, 14th Anti-aircraft Regiment, 2nd Regiment of Night Fighters and a number of other units. Later, I Armoured Corps and 5th and 6th Infantry Divisions were raised and an officers' school established.

The task of the Polish Partisan Staff, under General Aleksander Zawadzki, was to support partisan detachments in German-occupied Poland. It trained radio operators and taught ciphers, signals, enemy identification and other skills needed for guerrilla warfare. It controlled the larger Communist partisan detachments: the Grunwald Brigade (following Soviet practice, partisan formations were called brigades), the Wanda Wasilewska Brigade, the 'Poland Still Lives' Formation, the Tadeusz Kościuszko Brigade and several smaller formations. Partisan groups were parachuted into Poland for reconnaissance and covert operations and these Polish formations worked with Soviet partisan forces, some of them of significant strength, which were supplied by air.

The major element of First Army was the Field Army, consisting of the 1st, 2nd and 3rd Infantry Divisions with supporting arms. Towards the end of April,

Artillery unit of the Polish Communist Army

Artillery unit of the Polish Communist Army

The Polish Communist Army arrives
in Warsaw January 1945

it was moved to Volhynia, where it became the second echelon of Marshal Rokossovsky's Belorussian Front. The Army was tasked to conduct the defence of the eastern bank of the Styr near Luck. When the Front's left wing began an offensive on the 18th of July, units of First Army took part, crossing the Bug on the 20th. The Soviets claimed that this event marked the arrival of First Army units on the most easterly point of Polish territory, whereas in reality they were already in the central part of pre-war Poland.

At the time of the start of the final Soviet offensive, the First Army had over 93,000 men in five infantry divisions, a cavalry brigade, four artillery brigades and other arms. It also had 172 tanks, 1,213 vehicles and 118 aircraft. On the 4th of October 1944, General Berling was replaced as Head of the Army by General Władysław Korczyc, to be replaced in turn on the 18th of December by General Stanisław Popławski, both men having served in the Red Army.

After taking Warsaw, the Army moved into the second echelon covering the junction between 1st and 2nd Belorussian Fronts, but during the course of the new offensive it found itself once again in the front line on the northern wing of 1st Belorussian Front. Its armoured brigade was detached in March and placed under command of Soviet First Guards Tank Army, where it took part in taking Gdynia and Danzig (Gdańsk). During the first part of March, its advance elements fought for Kołobrzeg and a little later, its 1st and 2nd Infantry Divisions, after fighting for Kamień Pomorski, reached the Stettin (Szczecin) Lagoon.

The First Army, while operationally under Soviet command, came under the control of the Ministry of National Defence of the newly-established Communist Polish Committee of National Liberation. The Ministry's Head, General (later Marshal) Michał Żymierski, issued an order on the 20th of August 1944 to begin raising Second Army. Unlike the Polish armed forces in the West which were always short of reinforcements, the Communists had access to far greater manpower resources, given that they were operating on Polish soil and could conscript men. They also took AK men, whom they absorbed into the ranks either by force or under threat of deportation to Siberia. In addition to the Communists' desire to raise as many forces as possible, thus improving their standing both with the Polish population as well as with the Soviets, their aim was also to sweep up all those younger folk who were not favourably disposed to a Soviet occupation and who could well turn to active resistance.

At the beginning of July 1945, the hastily-raised Second Army had 4,968 officers and 51,343 other ranks and consisted of five infantry divisions: the 5th Saxon, the 7th Sorbian/Lusatian, the 8th Dresden, the 9th Dresden and the 10th Sudeten. It also had two anti-tank brigades, the 9th Dresden and the 14th Sudeten, as well as an anti-aircraft division and an engineer brigade. At the beginning of February, the Army was reinforced by Soviet 16th Armoured Brigade. The Army was initially commanded by General Świerczewski, with a short interlude between the end of September and mid-December under General Popławski. While it was being formed, the Army was exclusively under Polish command and after the start of the January offensive, it was transferred to the Warsaw, Kutno, Łódź and Piotrków Trybunalski area, while the 10th Infantry Division, as the reserve, was transferred to Kraków and Katowice. On the 20th of February, the whole Army, as well as First Army, came under the 1st Belorussian Front and was transferred to the Piła, Krzyż Wielkopolski and Czarnków area and later to Gorzów Wielkopolski, where it entered the second echelon. An essential change was made on the 20th of March, when the Army was moved to the 1st Ukrainian Front and was reinforced by Soviet I Armoured Corps with 268 tanks. By now, the Army had almost 90,000 men and it moved to an area north of Breslau (Wrocław). At the beginning of April 1945, it was in the first echelon and was to take part in the assault on Berlin.

On the 11th of April, the Second Army, commanded by General Świerczewski, held a position on the eastern bank of the Western Neisse River along an 30 km- (18 mile-) front, where it formed the core of a formation covering the left wing of 1st Ukrainian Front, whose main forces were to go for Berlin. Second Army's task was to break through German defences and advance towards Dresden. The attack was launched on the 16th of April meeting with initial success. However, a gap opened up between the divisions heading for Bautzen and Dresden and others further to the north into which German armour was able to penetrate, breaking the Army in two, which led to very heavy fighting, with considerable losses on both sides. General Świerczewski withdrew his main forces from Dresden directing them to the area of the German breakthrough. The enemy was held in the Bautzen area and by the end of April, a new front had been stabilised along the line Kamenz-Doberschütz-Dauban and Second Army was able to prepare for an advance towards Prague. Losses had been considerable, but over 20,000 Germans had been killed, with 550 prisoners taken, and 314 tanks and 135 guns and other armoured vehicles destroyed.

In the first half of April, First Army, under General Popławski, operating along the Baltic, made a quick turn to the south and headed for Berlin. Its mission was to encircle the German capital and on the 30th, it broke the German defences on the Havel Canal and its 1st Infantry Division was moved to Berlin, where it took part in street-fighting there. First Army's remaining divisions moved further west, and on the 3rd of May they made contact with the US Ninth Army on the Elbe. Its losses had been considerable: 2,958 officers and other ranks had been killed and 9,247 wounded.

These forces, serving alongside the Soviet Red Army, were later to form the nucleus of the armed forces of the new Communist Polish People's Republic.

Unfinished Business—An Epilogue

Once the Soviet Union and the United States entered the fray in 1941, it was really only a matter of time before Hitler's Germany was ground down and defeated and the war would have been won without the Poles. Yet their consistent efforts to 'punch above their weight' were inspirational. Breaking the German Enigma codes in the 1930s and then unconditionally handing over the fruits of their labours to the French and the British in 1939 was arguably a critical contribution to the common cause. Furthermore, once the war had begun, Polish Intelligence, with an extensive network of agents throughout Europe and elsewhere, contributed enormously to the Allied war effort.

Polish engineers were responsible for a number of excellent technical innovations during the war, such as Rudolf Gundlach's swivelling tank periscope, which was installed in the British *Crusader* 2, *Churchill*, *Valentine* and *Cromwell* tanks. Then there was Tadeusz Heftman's successful *Peepstock* radio transmitter/receiver designed for use by intelligence agents and resistance movements in occupied countries. Józef Kosacki's Mine Detector (Polish) Mark 1 was used for the first time in North Africa in 1942 and played a significant part in the Battle of El Alamein and the subsequent North African campaign, as well as in Europe in 1944. Lastly, there was Jerzy Podsękowski's 22 mm light anti-aircraft gun, the *Polsten*, which the British proceeded to mass-produce.

In General Sikorski the Poles had a genuine statesman of world-class stature, in General Anders they had a first-rate battlefield commander and in General Rowecki an outstanding leader of the underground Home Army. All three of these men were to have a profound effect on Poland's fortunes over the course of the war, but only one of them was fated to survive it.

The Poles suffered two genocidal tragedies during the war. First was the fact that the Nazi Holocaust was carried out mainly on Polish soil. Then there were the 1940 Katyń massacres by the Soviet NKVD of unarmed Polish prisoners-of-war in 1940. While the Germans have apologised to the Jews and the Poles for their conduct during the war, with the then German Chancellor Willy Brandt kneeling at the site of the Jewish Ghetto in Warsaw in December 1970, the Russians have never shown much contrition for their behaviour in Poland. Indeed, there are those Russian nationalists who still to this day maintain that Katyń was a Nazi crime and that the documents proving NKVD involvement produced by Presidents Gorbachev and Yeltsin were fakes designed to curry favour with the West.

'V' for Victory

Polish patriotic badge

Tragically, when the war ended in 1945, Poland's ordeal did not come to an end and a new foreign occupation began, the baleful results of which are apparent to this day. Unlike British or American servicemen who returned to their homes, a great many Poles no longer had homes to return to. Much of the country, especially the cities, had been badly damaged and, despite many protestations to the contrary, the Western Allies had to all intents and purposes abandoned Poland to a hostile power: the Soviet Union. Nor was it likely that Poland, an overwhelming Catholic country, would take kindly to coming under the influence of her atheist Communist neighbour.

The Western desire to please, or at least not to antagonise the Soviet Union at the end of the war was never so plainly visible as in the British Labour Government's decision to refuse to invite representatives of the Polish armed forces which had served with the British to take part in the Victory Parade in London in June 1946. Significantly, the Polish Communist Army had taken part a year earlier in the June 1945 Victory Parade in Moscow.

The Poles had hoped that their contribution to the common cause would encourage the Western Allies, the United States and Great Britain, to ensure that Poland did not emerge from the war, undiminished. However, losing the eastern part of Poland with the cities of Lwów and Wilno to the Soviet Union was for the Poles emotionally comparable to the United Kingdom losing Scotland, or the United States, Texas, to an unfriendly neighbour. This was all the more distressing, given that the Poles had been fighting the Germans from the very first day of the war and had, unlike many of the occupied countries, produced no quislings nor military units to fight alongside the Germans.

The inexorable process whereby Poland was physically moved west at the end of the war was rationalised and accepted at the two major conferences that the 'Big Three', Winston Churchill, Franklin Roosevelt and Josef Stalin, held at Tehran in 1943 and at Yalta in 1945, and that Stalin, Churchill, Clement Attlee and Harry Truman held at Potsdam later that same year. To put it simply, the Soviet Union was determined to retain the territory lost to Poland in the 1920 war and regained in 1939 and neither the Americans nor the British were prepared to stand in Stalin's way. An additional and unfortunate consequence of shifting Poland westward was to the forcible and often brutal expulsion of the German inhabitants from the country's new western provinces: an issue which continues to create ill-will to this day.

Over the last twenty years Poland has made great strides. Now a thriving, independent country, Poland belongs both to the EU and NATO and is proud of that fact. Yet the Poles cannot easily forget those dark days, which began on the 1st of September 1939 and whose 70th anniversary we commemorate this year.

JAREK GARLIŃSKI

June 2009

First to Fight: Threads of History

Memories which are still alive

Colonel Stanisław Berkieta

It came to me recently that seventy years have elapsed since the start of World War II and that perhaps it would be wise to put down on paper those memories which are still alive and to share them with others.

For us as young men it was, of course, a great and at the same time terrible adventure which changed our lives forever. The difficult experiences that each of us went through during the entire duration of the war were, of course very different, depending on the places and circumstances in which we found ourselves, and so, in order to prevent this turning into a large volume, I will describe the most important and the most memorable events that befell me.

Although I was involved in the underground army in Warsaw, I felt quite desperate because of the German occupation and so I came to the decision that, regardless of any dangers I might encounter on the way, I would endeavour to reach the Polish Army which, at the time, was interned in Hungary. And so, in April 1940, I began my journey. However, fate was against me and, in May of that year, after crossing the artificial Soviet/German border in Przemyśl, on the river San, Poland, I found myself in a Russian prison on the false charge of being a spy.

I spent nine months in two of the prisons, namely Przemyśl, and then in Starobielsk, in the Ukraine. I was sentenced to five years of hard labour in Kotlas. The conditions in the hard labour camp were utterly inhuman and the daily food rations were determined by work quotas set by the camp authorities and impossible to achieve. The starvation rations led to malnutrition, giving prisoners the haunting appearance of walking cadavers. Thanks to the Sikorski-Maisky agreement, I only served nine months.

After the release of the Polish prisoners of war from the prisons and labour camps, General Anders began to assemble the first detachments in August 1941, which was when he gave his first order to the newly formed Polish Army. In

March 1942, having overcome endless obstacles, I, too, finally succeeded in joining the Polish Army, a section of which was being organised at that time in Lugovaya, Kazakhstan.

The conditions in which the Polish Army in Russia underwent its training were exceptionally difficult: the lack of regular rations allocated by the Russians, problems with accommodation—particularly during the long winter months when the temperature dropped to below −43°C, the absence of uniforms, the constant interference of the Russian authorities, but most significantly the lack of fighting equipment. All this made normal training impossible. Even we, as parachutists/commandos of Battalion 'S', did not possess anything related to our function, apart from the parachute practice tower which, however, was somewhat useless without the necessary parachutes, which we never received prior to our departure from Russia.

After difficult negotiations with Stalin, General Anders secured the evacuation of the Polish Army, and as many of the surviving Polish families as possible, out of Russia to Persia. This took place between March and September 1942. It must be said that, by this time, some of the detachments were close to resembling an army—but not quite.

Intensive training, at long last, took place in Iraq with fighting equipment such as tanks, armoured cars, means of communication etc., suitable for military operations. Our enemy called us 'the tourist army' since, after leaving the Soviet 'hell', we spent several weeks recuperating in Persia, after which we were transferred to Iraq, then Palestine and finally to Egypt where, after a short sojourn, we left to fight the Germans in Italy.

The war, for me, began with the Italian campaign after we arrived in Taranto on an English passenger ship which had been adapted for the transportation of troops. In Italy, we fought as part of the British 8th Army. I was in charge of the 3rd Platoon of the 4th Squadron, 15th Poznański Lancers' Regiment, which was assigned to the 5th Kresowa Infantry Division as the reconnaissance regiment.

I participated in the entire action of the 2nd Polish Corps, beginning with the Battle for Monte Cassino (11th-18th May, 1944), the bloody but victorious battle, after which we were in pursuit of the retreating German Army along the whole length of the 'boot' of Italy, including Loretto, Ancona etc, all the way to Bologna. From there, in December 1944, I was sent to Egypt as an interpreter in the British Army Training centre situated in Abbasia, near Cairo.

In the meantime, my regiment, the 15th Poznański Lancers, was transferred from Italy to Egypt. Therefore, when my term as interpreter on Abbasia came to an end, I was returned to my regiment, which subsequently was sent back to Italy in 1945.

Once back in Italy, I commenced my engineering studies at the Institute of Technology in Fermo, studies which I took up again after my arrival in England.

In September 1946, at the invitation of the British Government, the entire Polish Army left Italy and arrived in England, as political exiles. The invitation from the Government was one thing; the reception by the British public was another. The dire economic situation in Britain after the war, with high unemployment and the rationing of practically everything, was not conducive to creating a welcoming atmosphere. Notices with the words 'Poles go home', together with the negative attitude of the press, did nothing to ease those early post-war years for us exiles in a foreign land, who had lost everything we had fought for, while those around us celebrated their victory. As for the Victory Parade, at the insistence of Marshal Stalin, the Polish Army was excluded from participating.

After several years of being fed with propaganda films (promoted by the British Government) heaping praise upon the communist ally, namely, Stalin and his regime in the Soviet Union, English people were unable to understand why we could not go back to Poland. What we told them about the suffering we had endured in the Soviet Union was often greeted with disbelief and treated as anti-Soviet propaganda. It was difficult to explain that Poles, particularly Polish officers, could not go back to their own country for fear of being arrested upon arrival as being an enemy of the state, that is, the communist state imposed upon Poland by the Stalin regime. The punishment could be deportation, once again, to a prison in Russia.

One of the major problems we encountered in England was the attitude of the trade unions, which were so very pro-communist and anti-Polish; this usually meant that only the worst kind of jobs were available to us.

The majority of Polish soldiers and their families remained in England as political exiles. Everyone had to go through the transition into 'Civvy Street' and become independent and self-reliant, regardless of the post-war conditions. An organisation was set up specifically for this purpose, known to the Poles as the PKPR (Polski Korpus Przysposobienia i Rozmieszczenia or the Polish Resettlement Corps).

I returned to my studies, financed in part by an army grant and partly by means of earnings from menial jobs, which helped me to support my family and to ensure that my children received a good education. Once my studies were completed, I was fortunate enough to find my successful career as an engineer which enabled me once more to see the world, as not only the war, but also my work, took me to many interesting places I might not have otherwise seen.

Whilst constrains of space and time have prevented me from going into greater detail about my war experiences and the many adventures they contain, I trust that others might like to share their memories in a similar vein.

Telling Times

Lieutenant Colonel Stanisław Dmowski, by his children

Adam Mickiewicz, the famous Polish-Lithuanian poet, wrote a verse where he said that Poles were famous all over the world because they loved their country so much that they were ready to leave it, to travel to the end of the world, to wander in poverty for many years and to fight and give their lives, if they had the slightest glimmer of hope that this might contribute to Poland's freedom and independence. The children of Lieutenant Colonel Stanisław Dmowski wrote in his obituary in 2002 that Adam Mickiewicz's verse sums up perfectly their father's life.

He was a trained army man graduating from the Officer Cadets Schools at Różan? and Ostrów Mazowiecki in 1934 and already 30 years old when the Germans invaded Poland. In the Polish September Campaign of 1939 he was commanding the 3rd Machine Gun Company of the 10th Infantry Regiment, part of the 26th Infantry Division.. On 6th September 1939, the Division was in the area of Inowrocław, where it was used in the Battle of the Bzura, covering the eastern wing of 'Pomorze' Army. After the initial success of the Polish offensive, the Division recaptured several locations, the Germans organised a counterattack in which the 26th I.D. was subsequently destroyed.

On September 17th, wounded in both legs, Dmowski was taken prisoner and sent to a German hospital, from which he later escaped, as he had heard that Polish Army units were being re-formed in France. Crossing the Carpathian Mountains on foot and travelling further south through Hungary to Yugoslavia, he obtained passage to France with the assistance of the Polish Consulate.

On his arrival in France he joined the 2nd Polish Infantry Division, as a company commander taking part in the French Campaign. After Dunkirk, when France was about to capitulate, he was ordered by the Polish Army High Command to lead his company, along with other Polish troops, across the border into Switzerland where they were to be interned.

However, he and others did not like the idea of spending the rest of war in internment so after a five week 'holiday' in Switzerland, they crept back across the very same border and travelled south through Vichy France, planning to escape to Britain. He failed in his first attempt and after a taste of a French colonial prison in Oran, he was returned to Marseille.

His second attempt to escape from France was by crossing the Pyrenees and he managed it this time. Travelling through Spain into Portugal and arriving in Lisbon, he was again arrested, this time as an illegal immigrant! Fortunately, the Polish and British diplomatic services were able to help him and after a few weeks in a Portuguese jail he was released and via Gibraltar reached Scotland in October 1941, where he joined the Polish Forces there.

After several postings in Scotland, Dmowski volunteered for, and took part in the Commando and Diversion Course. Graduating from the Polish Staff College, he was posted to the Polish Motorised Division, which was going to take part in the Normandy landings in June 1944. He was due to travel on a reconnaissance mission to France, but at the last moment he was ordered to go to London instead. There he was briefed and sent to Italy, and from where he was flown to Poland and dropped at night by parachute into the country as a *cichociemny* (Silent and Unseen) operative (Polish Forces equivalent to SOE).

In Poland he made contact with the underground Polish Home Army (AK), using the pseudonym 'Podlasiak' he fought in Battalion 'Andrzej' operating in the area of Silesia, disrupting German communications and harassing their retreating forces.

After the arrival of Russian forces, Poland came under an interim government controlled by them, and Dmowski remained at the disposal of the Area Commander of Kraków where he was Chief of Action 2 and Military Intelligence, Home Army Headquarters. However, on January 19th 1945 the last commander of AK—General Leopold Okulicki made a decision to dissolve the military organisation.

Eight months later, in September 1945, Captain Stanisław Dmowski decided to reveal his identity to the Polish Home Army Liquidation Commission. Subsequently, he joined the Polish Forces of the Provisional Warsaw Government. After completing a Brigade Commanders' and Armoured Brigade Chiefs of Staff Course, he became Chief of Staff of the 4th Armoured Brigade, but because of his background, he was not trusted and the Security Police kept a watchful eye on him. Several months later, in March 1946, he was released from the Polish Forces of the Provisional Warsaw Government and was immediately arrested by the Security Police on suspicion of being a spy. During his interrogation it was only his knowledge of agriculture work, acquired in his youth, that saved him from being imprisoned. One of the interrogators, who was of peasant stock, remarked that no bourgeois spy could have known so much about farming!

Released by the security police he decided not take any more chances and left Poland again using his Carpathian route south. This time he headed for the American zone in Austria, where again he was arrested and accused of being a Russian spy this time. After military superiors in Britain confirmed his identity, he was released and returned to Britain in July 1946 where his life changed completely. In the Polish Resettlement Corps, he was trained as a watchmaker and repairer, later he obtained qualifications as a draughtsman and worked for many years for GEC but his life in civvies was never as exciting and full of adventure as a *cichociemny*.

 **MINISTRY OF DEFENCE** CS(RM)2c
Bourne Avenue Hayes Middlesex UB3 1RF

Mr Stanislaw Dmowski

Former Service and History: Joined an Officer Cadets School Course at Rozan and an Infantry Officer Cadets School Course at Ostrow-Mazowiecki from 15.10.1931 to 15.8.1934. Posted to the 10 Infantry Regiment 15.8.19.34 to 29.3.1939. Company Commander of the 26 Infantry Division 29.3.1939 to 16.9.1939. Commander of the 3 Machine Gun Company, 10 Infantry Regiment 23.3.1939 to 29.3.1939. Attached to the Independent Machine Gun Company, 26 Infantry Division 29.3.1939 to 31.8.1939. Took part with the 10 Infantry Regiment in the campaign in Poland from 1.9.1939 to 17.9.1939 (Czerlin, Galancz, Znin, Barcin, Lubien, Rybno, Sochaczew, Defence on the River Bzura. Attack from Kompina Village east of Lowicz towards Skierniewice, defenc of Kompina Village, attack from Gagolin-North Village towards Sochaczew, retreat to Osiek III north of Lowicz, defence of Osiek III, night march in the direction of the southern woods Wyszogrod, attack from the southern woods Wyszogrod). Wounded in action in the leg on 17.9.1939 and admitted to German Field Hospital in Blonie 19.9.1939 to 28.9.1939. Escaped from hospital to his parents 28-29.9.1939. Crossed the frontier to Slovakia at Jasliski, 17 klm south of Rymanow 14-15.11.1939. Via the Balkans made his way to France and crossed the French frontier on 22.11.1939. Enlisted with the Polish Forces under French command at Bessieres Camp Paris on 24.11.1939. Posted to the 8 Company, 5 Infantry Regiment, 2 Polish Infantry Division on 5.2.1940. Took part in the campaign in France May 1940 - 23.6.1940. On crossing the frontier to Switzerland interned 23.6.1940 - 27.7.1940. Escaped from internment, stayed in France and after an unsuccessful attempt to make his way through Africa, via Spain and Portugal arrived in Gibraltar (3 weeks arrest in Oran, Algeria and 5 weeks imprisonment in Lisbon, Portugal) 27.7.1940 to 11.9.1941. Arrived in the United Kingdom and came under British command as above. Served in the United Kingdom 1941-1944 and 1946-1949 until finally relinquished his Commission. Assigned to the 7 Rifle Brigade Cadre 12.11.1941 to 22.2.1942. Completed a Rifle and Heavy Armaments Company Commanders Course at the Infantry Training Centre 22.2.1942 to 9.5.1942. Attached to the 2 Officers Training Battalion 10.5.1942 to 1.6.1942. Transferred to the 1 Independent Rifle Brigade 1.6.1942 to 24.10.1942. Assigned to the Infantry Officer Cadets School 24.10.1942 to 6.11.1942. Completed a special course 6.11.1942 to 5.4.1943 and then a Military Academy Preparation Course 5.4.1943 to 10.7.1943. Joined the 3 Military Academy Course 12.7.1943 to 18.12.1943. Completed a special course 18.12.1943 to 20.2.1944. Attached to the 1 Polish Armoured Division 20.2.1944 to 6.7.1944. At the disposal of the Personnel Unit, General Staff 7.7.1944 to 26.12.1944. Transferred to the Polish Home Army and parachuted into Poland on 26.12.1944. Served with the Polish Home Army from 26.12.1944 to 10.9.1945 (Home Army Battalion "Andrzej" in January 1945, at the disposal of the Area Commander Krakow 15.2.1945 to 25.2.1945, Chief of Action "2" and Military Intelligence, Home Army HQ, Slask-Dabrowski Region 25.2.1945 to 10.9.1945. Revealed his identity to the Polish Home Army Liquidation Commission on 15.9.1945. Registered with the Regional Commission Minsk-Mazowiecki on 19.9.1945. Joined the Polish Forces of the Interim Warsaw Government on 22.9.1945. Completed a Brigade Commanders and Armoured Brigade Chiefs of Staff Course at Modlin 23.9.1945 to 4.1.1946. Chief of Staff of the 4 Armoured Brigade 6.1.1946 to 3.3.1946. Released from the Polish Forces of the Interim Warsaw Government on 28.3.1946. Imprisoned by the Polish Communist Security Police (U.B) in Warsaw 27.5.1946 to 23.6.1946. Escaped from Communist Poland dominated by the Soviet Union and reported to the 1 Polish Armoured Division at Meppen, Germany on 1.8.1946. Arrived in the United Kingdom and rejoined the Polish Forces under British command on 25.8.1946 (Special Liquidation Commission, General Staff). Completed a two year contract with the Polish Resettlement Corps. Commissioned 2nd Lieutenant on 15.8.1934. Promoted to Lieutenant on 19.3.1937 and Captain on 1.3.1944.

From Soldier to Sailor

Feliks Keidrowski by Andrzej Formaniak

Feliks Keidrowski, 88 years old, has always been known as an ex-navy serviceman, however, as his whole WW II experience unfolds, we find a man with two different military career paths: a serviceman in the infantry but also one in the navy. At the beginning of 1939, when political tensions between Poland and Germany were mounting with every passing day in the expectation of a war that finally blew up in the summer 1939, when he was just eighteen and he says, "I had done my military course and was convinced that when the day of confrontation arrived Poland would be ready to fight Germans".

"On September 1, 1939, whilst cycling in the neighbourhood, I met my youngest brother, who told me I had been called up to the Army. I tried to find out where I had to report, but the Army centre sent me away. It was finally on September 5th, 1939 that I reported to an 800-strong unit, The Battalion of Youth. The following day the Nazis gave the unit a taste of what to expect. We were marching towards Warsaw when a German plane flew over us, returned, and opened fire resulting in 30% of the unit being killed or wounded".

When Poland was defeated by Hitler's three-week blitzkrieg, many soldiers and officers wanted to carry on fighting against the Germans. Those not captured as POWs or discovered by Nazis as soldiers, tried to sneak out of Poland to join the Polish Army in France. Romania had proclaimed itself as neutral, granting refuge to members of Poland's fleeing Government and the Polish Army. Although this neutrality could not be maintained for long, as shortly after conquering Poland the Nazis invaded Denmark, Norway, Luxemburg, Holland, Belgium, and in May 1940, France.

Feliks Keidrowski and his comrades crossed the Romanian border on September 18, 1939, where the authorities placed them with Romanian families allowing them complete freedom but more and more soldiers were disappearing from Romania every day, making their way to France.

'About six of us formed a group in January 1940 and as we were well supplied with American dollars, we thought we would be able to bribe Romanian soldiers. We were not lucky and were caught by a soldier who was resistant to our bribe. We were detained in a high-security prison.' A couple of months later his misery was ended by the intervention of the Red Cross. 'They came to check the prison and said that at the age of 19 I was too young to be in a maximum-security jail', he recalled. Freed in March 1940, he moved to a Boy Scout camp where he could enjoy the luxury of shelter, a bed, sanitation and food—but for him, it was not enough. He and his colleagues still wished to join the Polish Army in France, so as escapees, they decided to take a train to Bucharest. By this time, Romania was already 'hosting' Germans on its territory and identification was needed to travel. Feliks Keidrowski spoke German but had no documents. He bribed the train conductor to smuggle them on board the train but couldn't believe it when they were placed in a compartment full of German soldiers! It turned out to be a very clever move as the Germans were never checked for security and consequently they managed to get through all the borders.

So, via Constantia, Romania and Turkey, they reached the Palestinian port of Haifa on 11th November 1940, joining the Polish Independent Carpathian Rifle Brigade the very next day. This Polish military unit, part of the Polish Army in France, was formed in 1940 in French Syria, from Polish soldiers exiled after the invasion of Poland in 1939. It was commanded by General Stanisław Kopański. Based in Latrun, the Brigade was equipped with British weapons and reinforced and trained by the French.

In October 1940, Feliks and his comrades left Palestine for Egypt when the Brigade moved to Egypt to undertake garrison duties and other tasks such as guarding POW camps and preparing the fortifications of Alexandria, a port on the west bank of the Nile Delta. However, as Poland was still formally at peace with Italy, the unit could not be sent to the German/Italian front in North Africa. From Alexandria they transferred to Tobruk, in Libya in July 1941. Transported in seven convoys, between 21 August and 28 August 1941, the Brigade took over the westernmost perimeter of the Allied defences and took part in what became known as the 'Siege of Tobruk'.

However, sometime before, on 23 July 1941, Feliks Keidrowski had been severely burned on his back when a small petrol dump he was guarding had exploded. He lost consciousness but survived. He was under sedation for a long time and only regained consciousness after he had been brought back to Alexandria, where he made a full recovery, eventually rejoining the Brigade.

On 9th December 1941, in the final night attack on Tobruk, during Eighth Army's Operation 'Crusader', the Polish brigade seized the strategically-important 'Madauar Hill' town of Acroma, breaking through to the British Eighth Army and ending the siege. Because of their impact on this battle, the Polish soldiers were allowed the prestigious title of The Rats of Tobruk by their Australian 'comrades in arms'.

On 15 December, the Brigade, attached to the XIII Corps of the Eighth Army, took part in the attack on the Axis of Gazala's defensive line, held by Italians. The following morning the Italians tried to take their position back. 'We were short of ammunition so all 6,000 soldiers had four rounds each. As I was a machine-gun carrier I had 40. The order was not to fire randomly. We stayed in position without shooting facing thousands of advancing Italian soldiers. They were 50-100 yards away from us and still no single shot, our nerves wrecked by the fear of not being able to hold back the Italians, now 50 yards from us still no flare signalling to us "open fire". Instead the order went out: "fix bayonets!" We charged towards them with a roar and all 16,000 Italians got out anything they could wave and surrendered—just like that. We didn't even fire a shot we took them all as prisoners.'

On 17 March 1942, the Brigade was withdrawn from the front to the El Amiriya camp and returned to Palestine, where it was reformed into the 3rd Carpathian Rifle Division, once the Polish forces of General Władysław Anders joined them, after their evacuation from the USSR. The Brigade officially ceased to exist on 3 May 1942. This is when Feliks Keidrowski changed his military career and joined the Polish Navy. He travelled to various places across the world, including Cape Town in South Africa, Rio de Janeiro, Canada and New York.

In August 1942, he took part in the North Atlantic Convoys, carrying cargo outbound from the British Isles to North America during the Battle of Atlantic. His crew escorted aircraft convoys to Malta. But on November 12, 1942, an event happened which would destroy Feliks Keidrowski's naval career forever. He was on the Polish destroyer, ORP *Błyskawica* when on November 11, the *Błyskawica*, while escorting a big ship with soldiers to Bougie, North Africa, was attacked by the German air force and a German submarine at the entrance to the port. The destroyer with her anti-aircraft guns battled against 40 planes for several hours. One of planes dropped a bomb that almost hit the ship and an anti-personnel bomb exploded 10 yards behind the ship's stern but she also survived the attack. The ship was holed in 200 places, fortunately all of them above water level. A few navy men were killed but many more were injured. Feliks Keidrowski was amongst the badly wounded. A piece of shrapnel became lodged in the bone of his left arm. Another piece went through his nose, half an inch from his eyes. He had to have skin grafts and plastic surgery but he survived again. After 17 months in hospital he was no longer fit to resume naval duties and was invalided out of the service.

Many years have passed since the War, during which Feliks Keidrowski married and settled in England, coincidently in Alrewas next to the National Memorial Arboretum. More importantly he has finally lived to see the Poles' contribution to the Allied victory in WW II commemorated by the Polish Forces War Memorial—just where he lives!

"It is never late to say 'thank you' to those who sacrificed their lives for our freedom. One of my friends, Stanley Puc, died on November 12, 1942, half a yard away from where I was standing."

"I always wanted to visit the Armed Forces Memorial, so I could lay a wreath in his memory and I finally got to do that."

Feliks Keidrowski

The Sewers of Warsaw

Marzenna Maria Schejbal by Andrzej Formaniak

There is an old Polish saying, 'where the devil doesn't dare to go, there he sends a woman', an interesting motto to highlight a short account of Mrs Marzenna Maria Schejbal's WW II experiences that made her a living legend in London.

She was born as Maria Karczewska before the war and was only 15 when the Germans invaded Poland in 1939. During the German Occupation she got involved in making up cigarettes for Polish soldiers lying wounded in hospitals. She and her sister Ewa would make parcels for them, or take them soup cooked in special field kitchens, she says. Polish resistance forces against the German Occupation consolidated in the Polish Home Army or Armia Krajowa – (AK), and by 1944 the AK numbered 300,000 men and women and maintained a campaign of harrying the German garrison forces, keeping open routes for escaped prisoners and setting up a very successful intelligence service. The AK spy network supplied the Western Allies with invaluable early warnings of the German V-weapon programme.

However, Marzenna's parents had forbidden both their daughters to join the resistance. Her father was already helping to smuggle Jews and partisans to safe houses, and feared the girls might compromise these efforts. Despite this, her sister Ewa, slightly younger, somehow had already got involved in the AK through her boyfriend and so it became inevitable that Marzenna would soon follow in her footsteps.

By the summer of 1944, the whole of Warsaw was in a state of conspiring, and the momentum of untamed hatred against the Germans was growing with the speed of light. Almost five years after the German invasion of Poland, the bubbling lava of the Polish Underground was ready to erupt. Almost by accident, both girls stumbled upon 'W' hour, the 5pm start of the Warsaw Uprising on

August 1st 1944. They were out in the city centre when the shooting and shelling started which trapped both sisters. It took four days to cover the two miles to get back home to say they were safe. Shortly after this episode, they reported for duty to the nearest AK unit. Ewa was already sworn in as an AK soldier, now it was 'Marzenna' (her pseudonym), who recited the oath to Poland's Black Madonna and so became an AK soldier too.

Marzenna was not trained to fight but she was ready to do anything and was soon acting as a messenger, stretcher-bearer, and forager for medical supplies. Female soldiers represented at least 10% of AK personnel. There were about 5,000 women who fought in the Uprising, which was meant to last less than a week!

After the first week, the AK seized the central districts—happy days when they all celebrated these first victories. Slowly, however, the whole military situation changed as the Germans amassed additional forces and as August progressed, the Germans relentlessly wore down the Poles using flamethrowers, rockets, explosive charges and remote-controlled tracked vehicles fitted with explosives—'*Goliaths*', to supplement their tanks, artillery and bombers. As the Poles fought their way through the streets of Warsaw, the Germans behaved in a particularly brutal fashion, executing civilians and prisoners alike, setting fire to hospitals full of patients, and driving civilians in front of their troops when attacking AK positions.

On the nights of the 1st and 2nd of September, Warsaw's Old Town was about to fall, the Poles, cut off from each other, kept communications going through their city's intricate sewer system. Marzenna was in the group fighting in the Old Town and once cut off from other AK troops, the group decided to escape from the area using the sewers. Her sister who had been wounded on August 13th was in a hospital and Marzenna didn't want to leave her to face the Germans. During the evacuation of her sister from hospital, a '*Goliath*' exploded killing three hundred people. Luckily, she survived and managed to find her sister and piggybacked her to safety. Ewa was then transferred with other wounded personnel through the sewers to the town centre.

Marzenna stayed on with her group of 39 soldiers; they were almost the last people to leave the old town through the sewer. She had no idea what it would be like to crawl through an 80 cm diameter pipe; it was a terrifying experience. They were told that the whole journey would take two and a half hours—it lasted seventeen hours! Somebody had died in the tunnel in front of them and the swollen body blocked the whole tunnel. They couldn't move—so they had to push the body to another manhole with a bigger opening. Everything was done in darkness as the Germans were becoming vigilant and could throw gas, petrol or grenades into the sewers. People panicked and started shouting, especially the men who became claustrophobic; some were ready to give themselves up to the Germans, and others who wanted to survive silenced them by covering their mouths. There was some fighting as they were calmed down to allow the group to get moving. People were so exhausted that the first person who reached the last open manhole couldn't get out and collapsed from the sudden onslaught of fresh air after so many hours in the sewer. After this, the others were pulled out with ropes. Marzenna developed a fever and later collapsed when they were washing themselves in the public bath. Fortunately, she was found by her colleagues and the group doctor, who was in the sewers with them, tended her scratches and infections. A few days she recovered and returned to her duties—this time finding food for starving wounded soldiers. The Uprising was nearing its end with only one month's fighting left. On 2nd October 1944, the Warsaw Uprising was finally over. After 63 days of long struggle, General Tadeusz Bor-Komorowski, the Home Army Commander-in-Chief surrendered to the German Commander, SS General Erich von dem Bach-Zelewski.

AK soldiers were recognised by the Germans in the armistice as army personnel under the Geneva Conventions. The Polish troop leaders gave their soldiers two days to decide if they wanted to stay in the town or go as prisoners to a POW camp with the Germans. The capitulation agreement guaranteed that women fighters would be treated as soldiers, with the same rights as the men.

By this time, Marzenna knew that her mother hadn't made it through the sewers and that her father's fate was unknown, so together with her sister they decided to go as POWs not wanting to be liberated by the Russians. Marzenna and Eva, and 1,728 other Warsaw women were designated as the first women POWs in WW II. After a few transit camps, they ended up, in the freezing, rat-infested barracks of Oberlangen in Germany, near the Dutch border. This camp, previously closed by the Red Cross as completely unsuitable for POWs, was then re-opened for the Polish women soldiers.

Over six months later at 18.00 hrs on 12th April 1945, the Oberlangen camp was liberated by soldiers of General Maczek's 1st Armoured Division. The immense joy of being liberated by a Polish force lasted for weeks, but since the war was still on, and they had to wait another month before the women soldiers of the Polish Home Army and former POWs in the Third Reich could start the next chapter in their lives.

She found out that mother had been sent to Bergen-Belsen and had survived but that her father had been taken to a labour camp and perished. He was never seen again.

After Oberlangen both sisters ended up in Murnau. Oflag VII-A Murnau was a POW camp for Polish Army officers and generals in the Bavarian town of Murnau am Staffelsee. After the end of WW II, it became one of the camps for displaced persons. The girls did not want to go back to Poland as they knew what it would be like under Russian rule. Instead they chose Italy and after a few months there, the two sisters and their mother, who had by then joined them, left and arrived at a refugee camp near Pulborough in West Sussex.

Another chapter opened up in Marzenna's life who was by now married to Witold Schejbal whom she had met in Murnau. This however is another story to be told on a different occasion. Marzenna's struggle with the vagaries of life did not stop there but throughout her life as a civilian she remained as decisive, bold and efficient as she was in the AK. A woman who had resisted her fate by her persistence and untameability, perhaps that old Polish proverb should read, 'Where the devil doesn't dare to go, there he sends Marzenna'.

Marzena and her sister as ex-Home Army combatants

Cavalry Charge !

Lieutenant Andrzej Żyliński by Jan Żyliński

There is an historical myth that in 1939 Polish Cavalry units charged German tanks with mediaeval lances and sabres. Over the years many historians have disproved this propaganda spread by the Germans and the Polish Socialist regime. Let's look at one of them which took place between 11th and 12th September 1939, in fields outside the town of Kałuszyn near Mińsk Mazowiecki, and known as the Battle of Kałuszyn,

Major General Wincenty Kowalski, commander of both the prestigious Polish 1st Legions Infantry Division and the Wyszków Operational Group formed around it, was one of the most successful officers in the Polish Army at that time. When the German forces seized the town of Kałuszyn, cutting off Kowalski's men from safe passage towards the Romanian Bridgehead, a decision was taken to go straight through the German cordon.

The Polish aim was to re-take the town and break through the German encirclement before German panzer reinforcements arrived and enemy resistance stiffened. After short preparations, the battle started overnight with a Polish assault on the villages surrounding the town. Polish forces managed to break through the positions of the enemy's 44th Infantry Regiment, which was disorganised and had underestimated the Polish forces still present in the area. At one point the commander of the Polish 6th Legion's Infantry Regiment ordered the 4th Squadron of the Polish 11th Uhlan Regiment to advance towards the town itself. This order was mistakenly understood as an order for a cavalry charge and the Squadron, numbering 85 men at arms and commanded by Lieutenant Andrzej Żyliński, rushed towards the enemy positions with their sabres and rifles. The effect of this accidental charge was that the Poles broke through to the town, despite suffering significant casualties (33 dead out of the

85 Uhlans who took part in the charge). The Polish infantry followed into the breach in the German defences and by the early morning the town had been liberated and the German division in retreat.

Losses on both sides were significant, but the German 44th Regiment had almost ceased to exist. Its commanding officer, Major Krawutschke, committed suicide. In the course of the heavy fighting, the town was almost completely destroyed. After the end of World War II, the battle of Kałuszyn was one of 24 battles of the 1939 Campaign to be featured on the Tomb of Unknown Soldier in Warsaw.

Jan Żyliński, one of Lieutenant Andrzej Żyliński's sons recalls this story in his father's own words:

'It was a dark, moonless night. I felt the cold and the pain of my broken arm which had not yet healed. We had been waiting at least two hours during the night of 12th September on the Jakubow-Kałuszyn road. At about 2pm I went up to Colonel Engel and asked what was happening. He replied that we were on the outskirts of Kałuszyn which was probably full of Germans. He was awaiting the return of his recce patrols. I went back to the squadron. A few minutes later a fire fight began at the head of the column which quickly ceased. In the ensuing silence I heard Colonel Engel's voice: "Cavalry Forward !". I took it as an order repeated by his HQ staff. The order: To take Kałuszyn.

Of course I was angry, because it was against regulations for cavalry to charge at night. Yet I knew that with cavalry charges seconds can make all the difference. I yelled' Squadron gallop and charge." The soldiers issued a blood-curdling roar and charged. We passed our HQ Group, the infantry positions and the forward scouts. The sand track was getting narrower, hemmed in by ditches on both sides. We reached a river ford and then galloped across the bridge. On the other side we met our first Germans, 6 or 7 of them. We couldn't tackle them because the roadside ditch was too wide to jump. So we rode on. Very quickly we reached the first gardens and vegetable plots on the outskirts of Kałuszyn. Masses of Germans were running away like rabbits, through the fences and gardens of the town. We drove on yelling our battle cries at the top of our voices. We reached a fork in the road with many abandoned German trucks and continued towards the town centre. Suddenly it was as bright as day. The Germans had set off illuminating flares. In front of us, dozens of Germans were fleeing as fast as their legs could carry them. An officer was trying to stop the rout. A few soldiers turned around and started firing back. I looked behind me and realised I was alone apart from one or two horsemen and Sergeant Rudziński. The rest of my squadron were busy giving furious chase to the fleeing Germans. That was the moment I reined in my horse and shouted "Regroup"!'

So as Jan Żyliński says 'Led by my father, the Polish cavalry had taken the town. Hitler boasted that the German Army went through Poland like a knife through butter. There were many occasions when the Poles were able to pay back in kind.'

The cavalry charge of 4th Squadron, 11th Cavalry Regiment on 12th September 1939 was certainly one such instance of many charges of similar intensity by other units.

It is important to state that cavalry charges were not considered to be a way of conducting the fight against the enemy. In normal circumstances, horses were taken away and uhlans were supposed to fight on foot. However, as Poles say, 'blood is not made of water', so there were occasions where this 'normal' way of conducting battles was overruled.

There were many charges during the German Invasion of September 1939. Indeed lances and swords were often used in addition to rifles, automatic weapons and the devastating power of surprise, shock and speed which gave brilliant results.

Some of them are being better known than others. Italian war correspondent, Mario Appelius, who witnessed a Polish cavalry charge in Wólka Węglowa on September 19th, 1939, wrote:

'There was a heroic advance of several hundreds of Polish Uhlans who all of a sudden appeared from the bushes. They advanced with their banner. All German machine guns stopped shooting, only artillery was covering the field with shells over a distance of 300 metres in front of the German defence. Poles were attacking like it was in mediaeval pictures with their commander with his sabre raised. The distance between the attacking cavalry and the wall of German shelling was diminishing with every second. It was unthinkable to continue this charge against certain death. But the Poles went through....'

General Juliusz Rómmel gave up his own Virtuti Militari Cross to Corporal Mieczysław Czech who picked up the Squadron banner from Captain Maziarski when his horse had fallen.

Polish soldiers who survived the battle of Wólka Węglowa were taken as POWs. The Germans asked them to admit who had taken part in the cavalry charge promising their release home in recognition of their heroism. This promise however was not kept, and all those who admitted their involvement were subsequently executed.

The undefeated spirit of Polish fighting men had been developed over centuries of defending the country against its foes. In fact 108 years earlier in 1831, the previously-mentioned Kałuszyn had also been a battlefield. That time it was Russian regiments that had been defeated!

Lieutenant Andrzej Żyliński

Troubled skies

Wacek Włodarczyk by Danuta C Wlodarczyk

Wacek Włodarczyk was born in 1917 in the small town of Łask in the heart of present-day Poland. At the time, however, Poland did not exist as a country but shortly afterwards, at the end of the first World War, Poland was to become an independent country again after 123 years of territorial divisions of Poland by Russia, Prussia, and Austria.

One day, when Wacek was about twelve years old, youngsters in the town almost burst with excitement when they heard that a plane been forced to land nearby. He and a crowd of other boys ran to the river and saw the pilot emerge unscathed from his fragile single-seater. Aviation was still in its infancy at the time. Blériot's first cross-Channel flight had taken place only about twenty years before, but the new Polish government encouraged amateur flying and aero clubs had sprung up around the country. Polish pilots excelled in the annual flying races known as the European Challenge.

From the moment that Wacek first set eyes on the little plane and its leather-helmeted pilot, his ambition was to learn to fly. He attended the local grammar school but sometimes had to take a year out working in a bakery to earn money to finance his education as his family could not otherwise afford the fees. After passing his leaving exam in 1938, he applied to Dęblin, the Polish Air Force Officer Training Academy, and was thrilled to be accepted.

He began his training in 1938 at the age of 21, starting with a gliding course in the Tatra mountains. His year group were under the supervision of Wing Commander Bajan, a national hero who had twice won the European Challenge.

Unfortunately war broke out before Wacek finished his training. On 1st September 1939, Germany invaded Poland and airfields were one of the main targets for their bombers. At five o'clock in the morning Dęblin came under attack and 48 cadets lost their lives. The airfield and most of the planes were destroyed. After further attacks, the remaining cadets were ordered to leave on foot for south-eastern Poland, marching by night and sleeping in the forest by day to avoid bombardment by the Germans.

On September 17th, they were shocked to hear that Russia had invaded Poland from the east. Unable to defend their country without planes against the combined might of Germany and Russia, the surviving Air Force personnel were then taken by bus into Hungary and Romania. It was planned that they would continue to fight for Poland under the command of General Sikorski along with Poland's allies, France and Britain.

Wacek spent three weeks in Nagycata, Hungary. Then he and his comrades were ordered to make their way to France individually or in small groups. They were issued with civilian clothes and false passports. Now a 'student', Wacek and three friends were given train tickets from Budapest to Athens. Here they were taken to Marseilles, crammed on a ferry with hundreds of other Polish troops. On arrival they were despatched to Bron airfield near Lyon where the Polish Air force was gradually re-grouping in France.

From Bron, small groups of fully-trained personnel left every few days for England where some were able to play a significant and heroic part in the Battle of Britain. For the cadets who remained, it was a frustrating time. Their training had been interrupted and they could take no part in the action. They had to kill time, first in Bron and then in Paris until May, 1940, when the Germans invaded France. The remaining military personnel were then evacuated by train to St. Jean de Luz in south-west France. Wacek caught the last boat to leave the port, a converted liner called the Arandora Star.

They crossed the Bay of Biscay and disembarked in Liverpool. Wacek and thousands like him were taken to Blackpool where they were billeted in the many hotels and guest-houses. English courses were arranged for the foreign troops and at last the Polish officer cadets could resume their training. It took them a year to master subjects such as navigation, meteorology and mechanics with all the lessons in English, a completely new language for most of them. Among the first words Wacek learnt were: "A pennyworth of chips, please".

Then as now, Blackpool was a fun place to be. It seemed to be full of pretty girls and the best dance bands of the day regularly played at venues such as the famous Winter Gardens, a favourite haunt of the Poles. Romances with local girls blossomed, and one evening in the spring of 1941, Wacek met his future wife, Sheila, whom he married in 1943.

By June 1941 the cadets were considered ready to take to the air again and were dispersed to complete flying courses at airfields all over the country. After completing one of these courses, the young pilots were assigned to train either as fighters or bombers. Wacek was sent first to South Cerney for training on *Oxford* bombers, then to Bramcote in Warwickshire where he learnt to fly *Wellingtons*. By this time, Polish squadrons were being formed under RAF command. Wacek joined 300 Squadron, the first Polish bomber squadron, which was now operating from airfields in Lincolnshire such as Hemswell, Ingham, Faldingworth and Syreston.

From May 1942 until January 1943, Wacek took part in 30 bombing raids over Germany, targeting cities such as Duisburg, Düsseldorf, Essen, Bremen and Hamburg. Losses were severe. Many comrades did not return from their missions. During the course of the war, 300 Squadron lost 85 aircraft and hundreds of crew. Wacek was one of the lucky survivors, although tragedy struck just before his final mission. He returned from a week's leave expecting to fly his last raid with his regular crew. Instead, he was shocked to hear that they had not returned from a raid on Kiel undertaken with another pilot during his absence.

After finishing his tour of 'ops', Wacek took a course in instructing and spent about nine months training younger pilots at the Operational Training Unit at Bramcote. Then, at the end of 1943, he was posted to Cairo to join RAF Transport Command. Here he spent the remainder of the war in a unit ferrying new American bombers, mainly *Liberators,* across North Africa and to the Middle East. Pilots were required to pick up these new planes in the Western Mediterranean or West Africa. Then they ferried them to the places they were needed such as Cairo, Baghdad or Karachi.

The thrill of flying in cloudless blue skies and of landing in numerous exotic locations are still among Wacek's most vivid memories and helped to blot out some of the more tragic aspects of the war. Off duty, he was able to visit the Pyramids, Alexandria and the Holy Land. Wherever he went, life was punctuated by chance meetings with fellow Polish airmen in favourite haunts such as Shepheard's hotel or Groppi's bar in Cairo.

Wacek flew to England from Algiers on May 8th, 1945. Flying over France, he heard on the radio that the war in Europe was over. On landing at Lyneham, he was in time to join the celebrations in the officers' mess before heading home to join his wife and the baby daughter he had never seen. These celebrations were muted for the Poles, however, as the independence of their country for which they had fought so hard had not been achieved. Wacek continued flying with RAF Transport Command until January 1946. He piloted Warwick aircraft carrying passengers and cargo, including newly minted currency, to the liberated countries of Western Europe.

After many years not knowing how his family had fared in Poland, Wacek eventually received news from his sister. Sadly, his mother had been killed by German bombing on 1st September, 1939. His youngest brother had been deported to Germany and was never heard of again. Conditions in Poland were grim. A few of Wacek's former comrades returned home, but ominously, nothing was heard from them. Very few Poles were able to stay on in the RAF after the war. The Polish Resettlement Corps assisted the others in re-training for new professions. On leaving the RAF in 1948, Wacek had to 'come down to earth' quite literally. It was time to face the next challenge of forging a new life for himself and his family in post-war Britain.

300 Squadron, Polish Air Force
breast badge

Wacek Włodarczyk, August 2009

Polish Women Pilots with the
Air Transport Auxiliary Service (ATA)

Based on an interview, Jadwiga Piłsudska-Jaraczewska
with dr. Marek Stella-Sawicki, Warsaw, April 2009

The role of Polish pilots during Battle of Britain is widely known today: one is reminded of it by the Polish War Memorial highlighted on the A40 at Northolt as one drives into London from the north-west. Less glamourous yet essential war work was done by pilots of the Air Transport Auxiliary Service (ATA) who delivered all sorts of aircraft across the length and breath of the UK: brand new machines from factories to RAF airfields, and exhausted machines in need of major refitting from airfields to repair shops (so-called maintenance units)—and back. Among these ATA pilots were a number of Polish women, including Jadwiga Piłsudska, the second daughter of Poland's Marshal Józef Piłsudski (1867-1935).

Jadwiga's love of flying began in pre-war Poland where, as a teenager, she took up gliding as a hobby in 1937. Flying was becoming very popular in the country, and was inspired by Polish successes in international air competitions, notably by Żwirko's and Wigura's victory in the Challenge 1932. By the time of the outbreak of the Second World War the 19-year-old Jadwiga had spent over a hundred hours in the air and had received the highest international gliding qualification.

Shortly after the outbreak of war, Jadwiga with her mother Aleksandra and her sister Wanda had to leave Warsaw; on 17th September they crossed the border into Lithuanian territory. Their mother was never to see Poland again; the two girls would not see their country for over half a century. They managed to reach England via Sweden. In 1942, Jadwiga volunteered for the ATA in which she was to serve for two years, attaining the rank of Second Pilot Officer. Jadwiga piloted the entire range of single-engined planes used by the RAF and also many light two-engined ones. Her favourite aircraft were *Spitfires* of all marks. She found the *Spitfire*, especially of the Supermarine class, beautifully responsive and exceptionally easy to handle; in the sky she felt that she and the machine had merged into a single living entity. Some of the aircraft were ready for action and were fully armed. She often flew Hurricanes and Fireflies from Heathrow.

When it came to flying a new type of aircraft, preparation consisted of studying a thoroughly produced comprehensive technical manual, listening to a few tips from ground personnel, and spending 15-30 minutes on board familiarising oneself with all the controls. Not only was there no radar, but it was forbidden to use the radio to avoid interference with radio communication used by combat aircraft in action. There was also no radio contact with the place of destination; the pilots only had a compass and maps. The airfields she was heading for, always simply left markers authorising landing. Incidentally, Jadwiga in her interview mentioned that Polish pilots were quite incorrigible in talking to each other in Polish over the air, which was against RAF rules, and that Polish women pilots would probably have done the same! Having made her delivery, usually in southern England and frequently in Scotland, Jadwiga and other ATA pilots would be collected en route by so-called 'taxis', usually Avro Ansons, and flown to other airfields for their next mission. Indeed, much of her time in the air was spent being ferried around the country in this way. The ATA pilots were granted short periods of leave, but, weather permitting, they normally flew on a daily basis and spent little time at airfields. Jadwiga estimates that she must have delivered well over two hundred aircraft during her two-year service.

The proverbial British fog frequently delayed missions or forced pilots to break the journey; on one occasion Jadwiga had to wait ten days for the fog to lift before she could take off. It was in circumstances such as these, when she was alone in the air, alone to evaluate air conditions and alone to make appropriate decisions, that Jadwiga found her pre-war gliding experience absolutely invaluable. Needless to say, her work was dangerous, and flying machines that were not fully airworthy carried particular risks, but these Jadwiga simply accepted 'like changes in the weather'. Her mother and sister regarded her chosen field of military service as a patriotic duty that the family had performed in every generation; if they did worry, they never spoke of it to Jadwiga.

Jadwiga left the ATA after two years and embarked on the study of architecture in Liverpool where a Polish School of Architecture had been established (there was an analogous Polish School of Medicine in Edinburgh, and a Polish Law Faculty at Oxford); Jadwiga graduated in 1946. Her older sister Wanda studied medicine and qualified as a psychiatrist; much of Wanda's professional life was spent in a Polish hospital near London where she often had to deal with victims of the war.

During her residence in wartime London Jadwiga was in touch with the exiled Polish community there and with other Polish pilots passing through the British capital, including aces such as Urbanowicz. She still vividly remembers the horrors and the destruction wreaked during the Blitz.

Jadwiga Piłsudska trained on her favoured *Spitfires*

Jadwiga Piłsudska in her brand new ATA uniform

Jadwiga Piłsudska (third from left) with American pilots including last in line Mary Ford

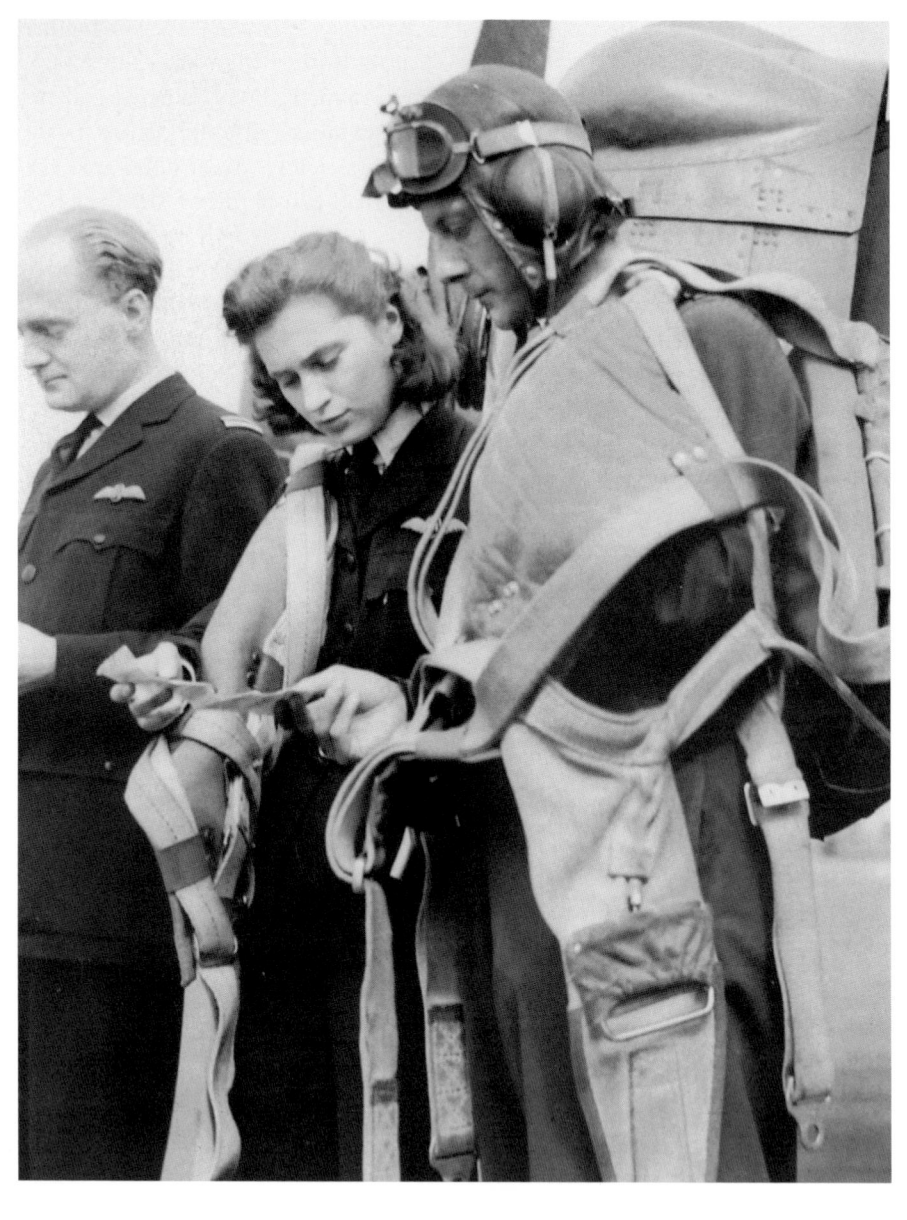

Jadwiga Piłsudska with members of White Waltham flying team

Jadwiga's British colleagues in the ATA were mostly women who like her had developed a passion for flying before the war; later they were joined by a large number of lively and enterprising American women pilots. Jadwiga had two close Polish friends and fellow ATA pilots: Stefania (although called Basia) Wojtulanis and Anna (Anka) Leska. Both were many years older and had considerable experience of flying engined aircraft before the war: in 1939 they had evacuated a variety of Polish transport and reconnaissance planes to Romania, before making their way to France. In England, Basia Wojtulanis was stationed with Jadwiga at White Waltham (the ATA administrative HQ) near Heathrow, while Anka Leska was further away at Hamble. Because of their greater experience, Basia and Anka also delivered bomber aircraft. Basia served in the ATA for five years and probably clocked about a thousand flights. Jadwiga kept in touch with her friends after the war, although their paths eventually separated. Jadwiga (and her family) chose exile rather than return to a Soviet-dominated Poland, and remained in England where she pursued a career as an architect and town planner; in 1944 she married Andrzej Jaraczewski, an officer in the Polish Navy. Basia Wojtulanis moved to the USA with her husband General Karpiński, also a Polish pilot; they lived near Los Angeles. Anka Leska worked for a time in London before returning to Poland with her husband who had been a prisoner-of-war. Jadwiga and her sister Wanda were only able to return to Poland in 1990 after the fall of communism in her country. Jadwiga now had the possibility of seeing Anka very often, until Anka's death. Jadwiga also kept up for a long time with some of her wartime British friends and with the association of former members of the ATA. Obviously, with the passage of time, this proved increasingly difficult to maintain.

Jadwiga Piłsudska-Jaraczewska,
Warsaw, 2009

A Debt of Honour Repaid

"The valiant Poles who were first to stand up to Hitler should march in the van of the Victory Parade"

Five years after this statement to the House of Commons, victory had been won and on 8th June 1946, thousands upon thousands of soldiers, sailors and airmen of 134 Allied nations marched through London in the Victory Parade to celebrate the defeat of the Axis powers.

Victory Celebrations, London, 8th June 1946—not a single Pole is among them!

"The parade is notable for the exclusion of all Polish servicemen. 303 Squadron was the only Polish unit invited; it declined because the invitation was not extended to any other Polish units, despite Poland being the fourth largest European ally during World War II. This is considered one of the causes of the feeling of 'Western Betrayal' in Poland."

Fifty-seven years after the Parade at a lecture on The Katyn Massacre at the Imperial War Museum, Michael Moszyński, son of one of those Polish servicemen witnessed an impassioned speech by a Polish veteran, who said that after everything that Poland had suffered in the War, from Katyn to Yalta, it was distressing for Polish fighters who had helped win the war but had lost their homeland, to be excluded from the Victory Parade. The veteran finished by saying:

> *"I had to watch the soldiers from the other nations march past from a street corner with tears streaming down my eyes. For me and all my comrades this was the final betrayal".*

This was a bolt from the blue. How could this be? As an avid reader of military history, particularly of anything to do with the Polish contribution in the Second World War, Michael Moszyński had never heard of this disgraceful episode. At that very moment, he decided to find out about it, why it had happened and, most importantly, to do something about it.

Michael's father, Stefan Moszyński had been a Captain in the 10th Mounted Rifles, the reconnaissance regiment of the 1st Polish Armoured Division. Unable to return to Poland after the war (the Russians had sent his family to Siberia) he settled in England like thousands of other Polish servicemen. Michael's father died when he was very young and so he had not learnt Polish but his English mother ensured that he at heart remained close to his Polish roots. When he asked his mother about the Parade she told him: 'Oh yes. Stefan had to watch the Parade from the streets and was very upset about it for the rest of his life".

> ## *"Without the Poles in their Hurricanes and without the Polish cryptographers cracking the Enigma code, the 1946 Victory Parade could well have been in front of Hitler".*
>
> The Spectator, 3rd December 2003

A quick search on the internet soon provided the background to why the Poles were not invited to the Parade. This was how the review in the Spectator of *"For Your Freedom and Ours"* by Lynne Olson and Stanley Cloud summarised the issue:

> *"Britain's dilemma, having entered the war as guarantor of Poland, and with so many Poles fighting under her command, yet utterly bound to an America which cared little about this and had anyway outgrown British advice, grew steadily worse. Churchill's sufferings as his sense of honour was put to the sword are painfully portrayed. Exhausted, nearly 70, ill after such titanic efforts, what irony to find himself, in his own estimation, comparable to Neville Chamberlain at Munich, whom he had so castigated for selling out an ally to appease a dictator!*
>
> *From underhand agreements at Teheran in November 1943 to*

outright betrayal at Yalta in 1945 the slope to infamy got steeper, the
promises thinner, the Poles' despair deeper. Finally General Anders
asked for his Polish II Corps to be withdrawn from the Eighth Army
and pilots questioned the point of taking off. They had seen the
Warsaw Uprising left to be destroyed, with derisory help from the
Allies, while Stalin stopped his advance to look on, content that the
SS was saving him some bullets. The Polish Parachute Brigade,
formed specifically to drop into Poland, clamoured to go, were
refused, then dropped into Arnhem and massacred, all because the
Russians would not allow Western aircraft to land and refuel (until
far too late). Churchill wanted to send aircraft regardless and call
Stalin's bluff, but the Americans would not hear of it.

Nevertheless, Anders and the pilots fought on for the sake of their honour, this being all they had left. Even this was derided at the end of the war when the Attlee Government would not allow them to march in the Victory Parade for fear of annoying the Soviets. They were treated as a nuisance, an extra expense to a bankrupt country, to be got rid of, with no thought that without the Poles in their Hurricanes and without the Polish cryptographers cracking the Enigma code, the Parade could well have been in front of Hitler. So the facts surrounding the issue and the why it had happened were now understood. The key question was what to do about it?

Clearly the answer had to be to secure an apology from the British Government. And the way to achieve that was to try a personal approach by writing a letter to the Prime Minister, Tony Blair. As with everything in life, timing is all. As Blair was about to embark on a trip to Warsaw to secure support for a joint initiative within the EU with the Polish Government, now was the time to strike.

On 22 May 2003, Fiona Millar who was then the partner of Alastair Campbell, Communications Director at Downing Street, puts a letter from Michael Moszyński on Tony Blair's desk. This was one week ahead of the British Premier's visit to Warsaw where he was to deliver a speech encouraging Poles to vote 'Yes' in the European Referendum. Poland was at that time being extensively covered in newspapers all over Europe. President Bush was in Cracow, Günter Verheugen, EU Commissioner for Enlargement of the European Union, was visiting Warsaw and in Iraq, a Polish Sector was being created.

Among thousands of Blair's concerns, this issue did not seem to be the most important. Blair reads however;

"I am writing to you today in the hope that you may be able to correct
one of the more shameful deeds of the British Government in 1945,
which left a permanent scar on the reputation of Great Britain in the
mind of her most loyal ally."

"After all that happened to my Father's country in those terrible years, the final insult took place during the Victory Parade in London."

"To our great dishonour, the British Labour Party acquiesced in the Soviet Government demand that no Polish servicemen serving under British command should participate in the Parade. After almost 60 years this feeling of treachery has not vanished."

In the following paragraphs it is proposed that in 2005 on the 60th anniversary of VE Day, that not only should the Polish veterans be invited but also that they should lead the Parade. "I think that this is the least Britain should do" writes Moszyński.

"Now is the time that our generation should consider what to do for those magnificent Poles who helped us to preserve our freedom, now, when at last they have regained theirs."

The letter ends referencing the motto:*"For your freedom and ours".*

Just a few days later a reply arrived from the Prime Minister's Office.

This letter was duly circulated to the British and Polish media which covered the story. This is how it was reported in *The Polish Daily*:

"The British Government apologises for V-Day parade without the Poles.

A Debt to Parents Finally Repaid"

The Polish Daily, 11th September 2003

It had finally happened: the British Government had officially expressed regret for not inviting Polish Combatants to take part in the famous Allied Victory parade in 1946.

However, the scale of the wrong meant that just an apology was not enough and a reply was sent to the Prime Minister stating that actions spoke louder than words, and reiterated that allowing the Polish veterans to lead the 60th Anniversary Parade would be appropriate recompense.

The next months saw fruitless discussions with the 'spin doctors' of the Ministry of Defence who gave evasive answers as to why this request was not possible.

Applying that great Polish trait of tenacity, over the next two years a letter-writing campaign was launched that generated support from many people

1O DOWNING STREET
LONDON SW1A 2AA

From the Private Secretary   18 June 2003

Dear Mr Moszynski,

Thank you for your letter which you passed to Fiona Millar concerning Polish representation in commemoration of the 60th anniversary of VE Day.

The Polish units serving in the British Armed Forces played a distinguished and gallant part in the Second World War and it is fitting that their contribution should be remembered and honoured. We very much regret that Polish contingents did not take part in the victory parade.

Because of the age of the veterans of the War, we do not intend to hold a marching parade in 2005. There will be a suitable commemoration of the anniversary of the end of the war for veterans to take part in, but we have still to consider the precise details. We will ensure that veterans from Polish forces that fought with the Allies will be represented in these events.

Yours sincerely,

Matthew Rycroft

MATTHEW RYCROFT

Mr Michael Moszynski

including Norman Davies, Lord Lichfield, Frederick Forsyth, General Sir Mike Jackson and the Duke of Edinburgh.

Also after the article in *The Polish Daily*, a call was received from Wojtek Fudakowski, son of Jan Fudakowski, an officer who had also served with in the 10th Mounted Rifles. Wojtek had been a scout in a partisan group and was involved with the Home Army Veterans Association. It transpired that whilst the other Polish veterans' associations had received invitations to the 60th Anniversary events, the Home Army Association had not, as it was deemed not to be under British Command during the war. This was factually incorrect: in order to grant POW status and thereby protect the survivors of the Warsaw Uprising after the surrender in October 1944,the Home Army or AK was recognised as an integral part of the Polish Armed Forces which served under British command.

A letter was then written to the Leader of Her Majesty's Opposition, Michael Howard who in turn contacted Geoff Hoon, the Defence Secretary, to put the record straight. Needless to say, the appropriate invitations arrived and the Home Army Association in turn invited Michael as their only non-veteran guest.

"Polish veterans to take pride of place in victory parade"

By Kwan Yuk Pan, Financial Times: 5 July 2005

Leading up to the Parade, the letter-writing campaign began to pay off. Frederick Forsyth wrote a powerful piece in the Daily Express about the Poles deserving recognition in the Anniversary Parade. At the same time, he contacted the Chief of the General Staff, General Sir Mike Jackson, whilst one of Lord Lichfield's relatives, the Duke of Edinburgh, applied pressure in the right places.

Amazingly just before the 60th Anniversary Parade, a letter arrived from Commodore Edwardes, officer in charge of the parade, stating that *"the Poles would be in the van"* of the Parade of Colours at Horse Guards.

The news was greeted with great enthusiasm by the Polish veterans and again was covered in both the Polish and British media. This is how the *Financial Times* of London reported the story four days before the Parade:

> *Among the veterans who will march along The Mall on Sunday in a parade marking the 60th anniversary of the end of the second world war, few will participate with the same pride as a contingent of elderly Poles.*

For the Poles and their military colours will be present for the first time in a British victory parade. Even though Poland made one of the largest contributions to the Allied war effort and there were thousands of Polish troops stationed in the UK at the time, the country was excluded from the original London celebration in 1946.

Stalin, who had established communist rule in Eastern Europe, indicated that he did not wish Poland to be represented and the British authorities agreed for fear of offending their former ally.

Now Britain is making amends by putting the Poles at the head of Sunday's parade.

"It's very good that it's happening. But it's a bit late in the day," says 95-year-old Witold Leitgeber, a former Polish army captain who, like many others, settled in Britain after the war.

Jan Zielonka, lecturer in European politics at Oxford University, says: "Historically, the Polish contribution to the war has never been sufficiently acknowledged. Poland provided the fourth largest Allied army in the war yet the Poles were excluded from marching in the celebration because Stalin wanted it so."

The invitation to the Polish veterans is the latest in a series of British gestures to respond to historical Polish grievances.

Tony Blair, the Prime Minister, has addressed these complaints as part of efforts to build relations with the European Union's new members, especially Poland.

The parade coincides with the start of the UK's presidency of the EU, but British and Polish officials insist that the invitation has nothing to do with the UK's current political challenges in Europe. "It's not about politics. It's about acknowledging the Poles' valuable contributions to the Allies' victory," said the Foreign Office.

Officials said the invitation was issued in April, after months of planning. The ground was laid two years ago when Mr Blair formally expressed regret to Poland for the 1946 parade snub.

However, putting right the historical record has improved bilateral ties in a broader sense.

Adam Rotfeld, Poland's Foreign Minister, told the Financial Times yesterday: "These issues are important in Poland because Poles have been deceived so often about their history (notably, under communism). This matters to our national identity."

As you can imagine on Sunday 9th July when the Red and White Colours of the Poles led the march in Horse Guards Parade in front of the Queen, many were moved to tears. But this time they were tears of pride.

As a final footnote, Michael Moszyński, on leaving Horse Guards at the end of the ceremony with two Home Army veterans bumped into Tony Blair. Michael introduced the two veterans and explained that it was he who had written to him about the Poles attending the Parade. He shook their hands and said "Wonderful people, the Poles. We owe them a great deal".

"Not so far from central London, is RAF Northolt, where during the Battle of Britain Poles used to take off to defend British skies. It was there, that long after the war, Polish airmen themselves, not grateful Great Britain, erected the monument for those who never returned. It carries an epitaph:

We gave our souls to God,

Our hearts to Poland,

Our bodies to the British soil.

That about tells the whole story, why those who remained after the war, and those who are still alive, were never invited to the Victory Parade. Time gradually heals all scars, but memories stay forever".

RUDOLF FALKOWSKI

A Debt Repaid—Polish Colours at Horse Guards Parade, 9th July 2005

© *Marek Kepa*

A Debt Paid at Last

From the author Frederick Forsyth, CBE

My childhood was spent in a small market town in the heart of Kent and my years from two to seven were occupied by the Second World War. Thus Ashford was at the centre of the Battle of Britain in which the Poles played a glorious part (although I was too young to know it then) and constant enormous troop movements between the coast and the hinterland of our country for the whole period.

Opposite our house was a patch of waste ground, home to an AA battery firing at the German bombers that almost nightly droned overhead towards London. The gunners were Poles.

My parents took me across the road to meet them and I recall—I was about five in 1943— they made a huge fuss of me. All had a wallet full of pictures of their own families, so far away and some never to be seen again. As a child I knew none of this. I just marvelled at the amazing language of which I understood not a word.

And they came across when invited for tea, sitting bolt upright in the drawing room, jumping to their feet whenever my mother entered or left the room. I was much impressed. Then they were gone. The Luftwaffe came no more so the guns fell silent that had kept us awake for three years. Both my parents had developed a great tenderness for those boys.

Of the Attlee government's shameful decision to exclude the Poles from the great Victory Parade I also knew nothing. I do not think my father did either; it was pretty hushed up. Years later I tried to analyse why Attlee had capitulated to Stalin's insolent demand. I think there were probably four reasons.

Back then we were the heart of the Honeymoon Period with the USSR. The massive casualties of the Soviet armies were common knowledge, and the Soviets were thought to be our helpful and friendly allies.

Stalin personally still seen as the jovial Uncle Joe, forever beaming and smiling on our newsreels. The true horrors of the Gulag and Katyn came much,

much later. This was the spirit in which we also shamefully sent back by force Cossacks and Ukranians to Stalin's execution machine.

Secondly, the Soviets had tens of thousands of Allied prisoners of war liberated from German camps by the Red Army. We know now that Stalin made brutally plain that their speedy return would depend on our compliance with his wishes.

The third reason that might lurk behind the Labour Government's decision was that at least half that party was very far left indeed, hero-worshipping Moscow and everything Russian. When the cold War really started during the Berlin Blockade and lasted until the 1990's there would remain a huge question mark over the loyalty of the Labour left.

And finally, Attlee was advised by the Foreign Office, a department neither pre-war, or then nor now alien to the concept of appeasement of powerful foreign tyrants. I think it likely that a combination of all four of the above swayed Attlee, who was not personally a dishonourable man. But the decision to acquiesce was truly appalling.

Being fascinated by history I learned all this later; about September 1939, Katyn, Monte Cassino, the Warsaw Uprising, Arnhem, Stalin's crushing of post-war Poland, the betrayal of all the pledges of Yalta which Roosevelt had so naively believed.

Sixty years passed and my friend Patrick Lichfield passed on to me a letter from Michael Moszynski about the memorial parade and his move to entreat the authorities to include the Poles in 2005 and at the forefront of the marchers. Could I think of anyone to write to?

It was obvious what had to be done. It was a debt of honour to the men in the Spitfires and Hurricanes that had wheeled in the sky above my head when I was two, and the lads from the gun battery across the road.

It occurred to me that if there was one man whose voice in the background would carry irresistible force, had been in the war himself, who carried the clout and the rank to over-rule all the other organisers born after 1945 it was the Duke of Edinburgh. So although we had met only twice at charity receptions and aware that he would not recall me from a knot-hole in the wall, I just wrote a letter.

There was a polite reply from an equerry to acknowledge receipt. Then suddenly it happened. The parade went ahead and there were the Poles, the remaining ones, right up front with their banners flying at last. It made Patrick and me immensely happy.

Frederick Forsyth

Frederick Forsyth

'SQUADRON 303'

by Arkady Fiedler

First published in 1942, *Squadron 303* was the only Polish book
written abroad and then published in Underground Poland, 1943.

SELECTED EXTRACTS

*For very real security reasons at the time of publication
all the names in this edition of the book were fictitious.
The true names were given in subsequent post-war editions.*

Chapter 1

"I Am Delighted"

It is the last day of August 1940, six o'clock in the evening. The Polish Fighter Squadron 303 is up, patrolling the outskirts of London. It is their last training flight. Tomorrow the Squadron will appear on the Fighter Command operational map and take part in the Battle of Britain which has now been raging for weeks. For three weeks the Polish fighter pilots have been counting the days, eager to be in the thick of the fight.

The sky is blue and the reddish evening sun casts a golden glow on the countryside. England, twenty thousand feet below, looks like a dreamland of peace and quiet, basking happily in the mild sunshine of late summer. The beautiful England of August! The Polish airmen yield to England's charm—and dream of coming battles.

Squadron Leader K., an Englishman, is a short and rather plump man with an apparently jovial expression. He is a splendid fighter pilot and has shot down seven German planes in France, but to-day there is something on his mind. He has been in charge of the Polish Squadron for only a few weeks and he has some doubts about the men, though he shares his command with a Polish Squadron Leader. He feels a little uneasy and he sometimes wishes he had a plain, straightforward squadron of British boys to lead into battle. How, he wonders, will the Poles stand up to their task? Apparently they have fought in Poland and in France. They are not all bad fellows, but the Squadron Leader cannot help wondering why these strange and unknown pilots from Central Europe have been entrusted with one of the most vital sectors—in fact the most important of all—the defence of the Metropolis itself. Probably a case of inter-allied courtesy. But wasn't this rather overdoing it?

London is there on the left, a huge patch of grey. Even on the sunniest day a haze of smoke and mist hangs over the city. Above the haze emerge the swollen bodies of the barrage balloons, rosy in the setting sun. But the Squadron Leader does not enjoy the beauty of his England.He looks down on London and thinks of the morrow and the days to come. If only he could know how the Poles would work...

Twelve minutes past six. A voice croaks in the earphones. It is an order from the ground.

"Squadron 303, Flight A, course 90 degrees!"

Now what's up? A new manoeuvre? Six machines break away from the formation and fly east, in the appointed direction, under Squadron Leader K..

Soon there is a new order: "Course 100 degrees!"

It sounds rather well, like the promise of real business. The five pilots following the Squadron Leader are thrilled. Perhaps it's beginning?... Then comes a sharp order: "Course 140 degrees!" No doubt about it, they are leading them on. Probably towards the enemy.

Indeed after a few minutes they see, far away, slightly to the left, a formation of German bombers. The bombers are flying towards France. Obviously returning from a raid, for one or two are trailing a little smoke. Behind and above, as usual, flies the escort of a score of *Messerschmitts*.

Without hesitation the flight goes into attack. It is in a good position, flying out of the sun. It has to cut across the path of the bombers before they leave England. The pilots are filled with enthusiasm. At last they will have a whack at the Germans!...

They had their whack, but not in the way they had hoped for. They did not reach the bombers. They were still about two miles away when three *Messerschmitt* 109s appeared out of the blue a few hundred yards in front of them. The German fighters lagging behind their main formation. By a strange coincidence they failed to notice the Polish flight: coming up in a broad curve, the Germans had the *Hurricanes* below them, and hidden by their own wings. Moreover the flight was dead in line with the blinding sun.

The Squadron Leader and Sergeants Szaposzka and Kar leap at them like a flash. The three get on the three Germans' tails, each choosing his man. The Germans are still unaware of their existence. At a distance of a hundred yards the Squadron Leader opens fire and in a moment the middle *Messerschmitt* catches fire, giving the flight a grand spectacle. The German machine explodes and drops like an enormous torch; a comet with a red tail.

The other two Germans save themselves by a sudden turn, and dive. But the sergeants are as swift in the attack. They cling to the enemy like leeches. Szaposzka in a fantastic, almost vertical dive, calculates exactly the angle, and calmly aims below his opponent's fuselage so that he has to pass through a stream of bullets. The heavy fire acts as though tearing the entrails out of a living body.

Meantime Kar in his dive keeps right on top of the third *Messerschmitt*. Not firing. He waits. And watches. When the last German begins to pull out of the dive, the Sergeant is right on his back, like a vulture. At close range he fires three

Jan Zumbach with Jan Kazimierz
Daszewski (Long Joe) sharing a cigarette

Pilot Jan Zumbach with a member
of the ground crew

Jan Zumbach's *Hurricane*. The firepower of the *Hurricane*, with its 8 guns,
was a revelation to the Poles

A destroyed *Hurricane*

Witold Urbanowicz returning the salute of a member of the PAF

Jarosław Giejsztowt, Juliusz Frey and Wojciech Kołaczkowski

short bursts into the engine and the top of the cockpit, and the enemy, a streak of dense smoke, crashes to the ground.

The encounter and the destruction of the three *Messerschmitts* lasted only a few seconds, less time than it takes to describe. But during those few seconds another drama was enacted behind the backs of the victorious section, and Squadron Leader K. had no idea that his life had hung by a thread.

While he and his two Poles were attacking the German marauders, three more *Messerschmitts* came suddenly to the rescue of their comrades. They opened fire at a distance to drive off the attackers. Their fire was without effect. Besides they had come too late, for the first three machines were already doomed.

In their blind frenzy the rescuers made a capital error: they neglected the two Polish fighters guarding the rear of the flight. As if the *Hurricanes* were not there, the Germans flashed past them, a blurred vision of black crosses rushing into battle. The rearguard, Pilot Officer Ox and Sergeant Zych, went instantly full boost after them.In this furious pursuit the machines drew a complicated pattern: in front were three Germans in flames, behind them Squadron Leader K.'s section, then three more Germans, and finally a couple of Poles.

The second section of German machines was just coming within effective range of the Squadron Leader and Szaposzka, when the two rearguard pilots caught up with them. Ox went for the right-hand, Zych for the left-hand machine. They fired almost simultaneously and with identical results: mortally wounded, the two *Messerschmitts* plunged downward, one emitting billows of smoke, the other a great mass of flame. The third seized the opportunity to slip off.

A nice scrum! Five German machines sent down, an evil omen for the enemy. Two Jerries bailed out, the other perished in the flames of the wreckage of his plane. A victory all the more remarkable because it had been achieved so easily, with so little effort, It was the best type of team-work, a clean game well played.

And overwhelming, too. The Polish pilots were amazed. These *Hurricanes*! what a thrill to be wielding this incomparable instrument! Its eight machine guns had an incredibly crushing fire power.

All the pilots but one had had their share in the success. The sixth man, Pilot Officer Dzidek, the leader of the second section, had a victorious private adventure of his own a little later. Seeing the break-up of the flight in which his two companions were engaged behind him, he waggled his wings, signalling them to follow, and flew off to where in the distance he saw four other *Messerschmitts*. They were about two thousand yards away and seemed strangely nervous. They were all making manoeuvres to avoid attack. Dzidek caught them up easily, and only then realised that he was alone, without his companions.

He did not retreat. Whatever happened, he was determined to get his Jerry too. An old hand at the game, he did not rush into a headlong, suicidal attack. He took up a good position a few hundred yard above and behind the four *Messerschmitts*, shadowing them patiently, mile after mile. A hungry wolf following a flock.

They crossed a major part of Kent and approached the coast. The Germans, although they had superiority in numbers, had no desire to fight. They seemed rather to be fleeing in terror. After a while they showed signs of confusion, and one of them broke away from the others.

This is what Dzidek has been waiting for. He dives at full speed into the breach. Before the German has time to rejoin his formation, Dzidek catches him on the beam with two short bursts. The German turns sharply and dives. Dzidek dives after him. Two more short bursts. A trace of smoke from the *Messerschmitt*. Now they are over the coast. Yet another burst. The *Messerschmitt* drops like a stone. A great fountain of water, and then a long, white streak under the surface like a huge torpedo.

* * * *

There was an indescribable joy at the station. The pilots, the mechanics and everybody else already knew or guessed the news.They all rushed out of doors. The *Hurricanes* came in one after another, each doing a victory roll, fighter fashion, before landing. The enthusiasm knew no end.

After the fifth *Hurricane*, a pause. Then minutes passed, fifteen minutes. Where was the sixth? Anxiety grew. All eyes scanned the sky in vain. Flight Lieutenant Z., the Adjutant of the Squadron, the Squadron's "daddy" the guardian angel, was the most worried of all.

Then a tiny dot appeared in the evening sky. It grew into a *Hurricane*. It was the missing sixth pilot Officer Dzidek, safe and sound. As he made his victory roll over his colleagues' heads. He felt glad and proud.

The British have a fine sense of fairness. Squadron Leader K. knew now that he had misjudged his men, and he squeezed the pilots' hands long and fervently. Now he knew their value, and like a revelation it came upon him that these men were fighters of the finest breed. They were capable of fighting as a disciplined team, but they could also snatch a victim right out of a nest of hornets with fantastic impudence.

"I am delighted." the British chief of the group telegraphed to Squadron 303 that same day.

And a few days later, when they had performed fresh exploits, all Britain was saying it with him, astonished and enthusiastic, while two weeks later it was all the world's phrase.

Fighter Squadron 303 had entered the Battle of Britain with a victorious start.

Zbigniew Kustrzyński, Mieczysław Popka, Mirosław Ferić, Jan Kazimierz Daszewski and Jan Zumbach. All mascot dogs were English and fluent in both languages

Mechanics worked hard to keep the squadron ready for combat

Witold Łokuciewski

Waiting to scramble: John Kent, Walerian Żak and Witold Łokuciewski

Chapter 20

"We are beginning to Understand the Poles"

The second half of September proved conclusively that the 15th of that month had brought the climax of the Battle of Britain and had decisively broken the German offensive. After that day the Luftwaffe could not muster any considerable strength. Its attacks lost their former vigour, and weakened. Even when at times they flared up in a final desperate fury, the British fighters invariably smashed them and exacted a heavy toll. For instance, on September 27th the R.A.F. destroyed 116 German aircraft, and Squadron 303 shot down fifteen. But this attack was the last flash in the pan.

Britain and the Empire were saved. Only the initiated knew how close Britain had been in that month to utter disaster: on land she had hardly any defence.

The battle was won by fighter pilots. They frustrated the German plan of invasion. On the decisive day twenty-one fighter squadrons shouldered the whole weight of the Teutonic offensive and defended the entire might of the empire. Even today months afterwards, the very memory is breathtaking: it seems a terrifying fluke of history, an absurd paradox: the destinies of the 450,000,000 inhabitants of the British Empire depending on the valour and energy of about 250 pilots.

Thin was the thread which bound the British Empire together during those days, yet it did not break. By standing the strain, it aroused the conscience of the world. Only when, by an almost superhuman effort, these "few" achieved their task, were the rest of the Empire and the United States of North America awakened to the true meaning of this war.

It was a narrow front that two hundred and fifty men defended, but how far-reaching in its consequences. It rendered possible the the formation of a wider world front, stretching from Washington, through London and Moscow to Chungking. And only an armed force drawn from all over the world would destroy the German hydra. But in those months of August and September there were only a handful of defenders.

Amongst those few were Poles. And the Poles included Squadron 303. Its contribution to the Battle of Britain, in its most vital stage, during September, was undoubtedly magnificent. Its bag of Germans shot down was three times as high as the average of all the other squadrons. Yet its losses were only one-third of the average.

Expressed in figures, the achievements of the Polish fighting machines in all squadrons, and those in the R.A.F. during September 1940 were as follows:

Squadron 303: 77 Germans shot down by Poles, 17 by the Czech, Frantisek, and 14 by 3 British members of the Squadron. A total of 108 shot down in September. For the entire period of the Battle of Britain the Squadron had a total bag of 126.

Squadron 302 19 1/2 Germans shot down in September, and 26 1/2 during the Battle of Britain. (The Squadron came into action rather later than "303".)

Other Polish fighter pilots, assigned to British units, shot down 21 Germans in September, and 89 during the Battle of Britain.

Total Polish successes in September: 117 1/2 Germans shot down. The rest of the Royal Air Force accounted for 846 1/2 Germans (Ronald Walker: *Flight to Victory.*) Thus the ratio of Polish successes to the rest was 1:7.2 It must be added, to complete the picture, that anti-aircraft artillery accounted for 131 machines in September.

A comparison of achievements on the vital day of September 15th is still more favourable to the Polish pilots. For on that day two squadrons, i.e., "303" (14 Polish successes, 1 British, 1 Czech) and "302" (11 successes), together had 25 Polish successes, while other pilots had 153 Germans to their credit. Thus the ratio of Polish to other successes on that day was 1: 6.1.

So it is not surprising that the Polish fighter pilots are known by their achievements all over Britain. It is not surprising that the Polish Commander in Chief visited Squadron 303 to decorate its members, and the King himself came to shake hands with them. British writers also have appreciated their merit, George Saunders, the author of a best-seller of 1941, The Battle of Britain, wrote:

"...Conspicuous among them are the Poles. Their valour is tremendous: their skill bordering on the inhuman. They have done great service. They are still doing it, and they will go on doing it until victory, triumphant and complete, lights up their wings. We are beginning to understand the Poles..."

What, you may ask, are the famous pilots of Squadron 303 really like? Are they Supermen? Are they a team picked for exhibition purposes, a national symbol? Are they prodigies, freak performers? That is just what they are not. They are ordinary, healthy, simple boys. They have the same temperament and mentality, the same smile the same cares as most other Poles; they are just like thousands of other people living along the Vistula, the Warta, the Bug or the Dniester; they are neither better nor worse than the rest. They simply learned their job thoroughly in the old Polish school and are now conscientiously doing their duty—and that is all their secret.

That the efficiency and achievements of Squadron 303 are not exceptional is confirmed by the performance of other Polish pilots in British R.A.F. squadrons and by the results obtained by the Polish Squadron 302. The pilots of "302"even have a record of their own for they managed to bring down another 26 1/2 German machines, although they were stationed far from the main field of battle. When they got a chance of meeting the enemy in force, as on September 15th, they showed up well, destroying 11 Germans.

The story of the Polish men in Britain had its element of tragedy, itself a reflection of Poland's tragedy. Even the most fair-minded foreign nations are inclined to form very peculiar, sometimes fantastic, views about the Poles. The position of Poland is about the worst in the world, with restless neighbours, employing the most ruthless propaganda machines. For this reason information about Poland is often inaccurate and biased. (One small example is the use in the British atlas of German names and terms for Polish towns and places, as for example Posen, Lemberg, "Polish Corridor", etc)

In the summer of 1940 some circles of the R.A.F. Command, conscious of their tremendous responsibility, were doubtful about the employment of Polish pilots in the defence of Britain. They took the view that after two defeats the Poles would lack the morale necessary for fighting on such a vital sector. When the Poles were brought into active service they quickly proved that this view was not exactly correct.

Later the opinion was common that the Poles gained such great success because they are mad dare-devils, heedless of their own life. That also was hardly correct, for during the Battle of Britain the Polish casualties were relatively much lower than those of other pilots.

"The Poles are only good as fighter pilots, because they have such a mercurial temperament!" This widespread judgement also had to be modified when more and more Polish bomber crews distinguished themselves by their efficiency and whole-hearted support of their British colleagues.

"The Poles are only landsmen" This also was said at one time, but the achievements of the Polish submarines and other naval vessels, such as the "Orzel", the "Błyskawica" and "Grom", and the effective daily work of the Polish merchant navy, have disposed of that misconception.

The Germans have always declared and still declare (and the world has always been inclined to believe them) that the Poles are an unruly nation, incapable of creative work and organised effort. But within ten years of the recovery of Polish independence the small fishing hamlet of Gdynia grew into the largest port on the Baltic, with a turnover surpassing that of Stettin,

Stockholm or Leningrad, and in the south of Poland a new Central Industrial Region was developing at a remarkable rate, until the Germans laid their hands on it.

Poland's near neighbour has for years been telling the world that the Poles are a nation of reactionary landlords and romantic, arrogant aristocrats. Yet Poland's social and labour legislation was perhaps the most liberal and comprehensive in Europe.

A nation of aristocrats. Nearly all the Polish airmen fighting in Britain are sons of the middle and labouring classes.

If the Polish airmen were asked what Great Britain owes them for their services in this country and how the debt is to be paid—perhaps a tactless, but still a very human question—they would look surprised and would probably retort that they were carrying out their duty as loyal allies, and expect no reward.

On second thoughts, however, they might ask for a reward. They would ask for the British people to get to know the Poles better. To know them honestly, intimately, through and through, putting aside prejudices and preconceptions; to know the Poles as they really are and not as their neighbours represent them.

Then the British would no doubt discover that the nation living on the banks of the Vistula is just like all the other healthy and civilised nations, neither better nor worse. They would find the average Pole is not very different from the average Mr. Brown of London, Mr. Bruce of Edinburgh or Mr. Taylor of Chicago. He believes the same immutable moral standards as they do, will keep his word and never become a quisling.

And since the Poles are no different from any other decent nations, after the war they can be of great service to humanity, not by making exalted declarations and expressing high-flown aspirations, but through practical achievement. Just as the Polish airmen have served Britain during the most vital month of her existence. Provided always that their fate is not decided by people who do not know and understand them.

That is the reward which the Polish airmen desire: a fair intelligent view of their nation.

Extracts republished from the original by kind permission of Aquila Polonica Ltd. A new translation and expanded edition of '303 Squadron' published by Aquila Polonica is due out in 2010 to commemorate the 70th anniversary of the Battle of Britain, 1940.

Leading Polish Generals in the West
during World War Two

When Poland regained her independence after the First World War she got down with a will to building her own armed forces in very difficult conditions. Not only had the country suffered severe damage during the War, but all her experienced soldiers had grown up in Partitioned Poland and most of them had served in either the Austrian, German, or Russian Armies, depending on where they had lived before the War. Indeed, many had fought on opposite sides. They brought different traditions, training and linguistic backgrounds to the new force and these were the very men who would lead the Polish Armed Forces during the dark days of the Second World War.

Within a year the Polish Army received its baptism by fire in its unexpectedly successful war with Bolshevik Russia between 1919 and 1920. However, much work still remained to done, the main issue being that Poland was a poor agricultural country which would never be able to match her German and Soviet neighbours in terms of military expenditure. Even the emerging Soviet Union was, by sheer weight of numbers, able to produce more military hardware than Poland ever could.

The defeat and resultant occupation of Poland in 1939 led to a highly unusual situation with the country's armed forces operating as two separate entities. Those regular forces and commanders who had managed to avoid capture or internment in 1939 made their way to France to join the Polish regular armed forces re-forming there, moving on again to Great Britain after the Fall of France. It is easy with the passage of time to forget that these changes were no easy matter for men who had been raised to believe in French military prowess and to follow French doctrines and practices and who had little knowledge of England or its language. Furthermore, most of their families were still in Poland, now under joint occupation by Nazi Germany and the Soviet Union.

At the same time in Poland herself new clandestine forces were forming, the initial impetus for which had come from the Supreme Commander, and which the Poles saw as an integral part of their Armed Forces. Its senior commanders were former professional soldiers whose pre-war training had not encompassed guerrilla warfare, although a number of them had some experience of irregular operations from the days of Partition. The Western Allies, however, were unwilling to see what ultimately became the Home Army, the Armia Krajowa (AK), as a real field force and formally recognised it as part of the Polish Armed Forces only in August 1944. For political reasons of its own, the Soviet Union never did.

The situation then became even more complex and fraught when in 1943 a Communist Polish Army was formed in the USSR to fight with the Red Army and which would later become the nucleus of the post-war Communist Polish Army. Many of its senior officers had served before the war alongside those who were now fighting with the Western Allies. An even more anomalous situation now arose with the Western Allies recognising only the Polish Armed Forces in the West, while their ostensible ally, the Soviet Union, recognised only the competitor Communist Polish Army.

* * *

General Władysław Sikorski

Perhaps unsurprisingly, given the extensive influence of the military in inter-war Polish political life, Poland's first Prime Minister-in-Exile was a soldier, **General Władysław Sikorski** (1881-1943), who had not, however, belonged to the pre-war ruling *Sanacja* faction. Fortunately for Poland, it was decided that he should also hold the position of wartime Supreme Commander (*Naczelny Wódz*), which was something of a constitutional anomaly in that the holder reported to the President of the Republic and not to the government of the day—a product of Piłsudski's 'strong man' theory of government. Despite its unconventional birth, the Government-in-Exile, maintaining valid constitutional continuity, was a legitimate government and indeed it was recognised as such by foreign governments, including that of the Soviet Union between 1941 and 1943.

Sikorski was born in the Austrian Partition and served as Supreme Commander and Prime Minister from November 1939 until his untimely death in July 1943. An exceptionally able man, during the First World War he served with Piłsudski's Polish Legions and distinguished himself during the Russo-Polish War of 1919-1920. He had subsequently gone on to hold high political office, including for six months in 1922-1923 the post of Prime Minister. Out of favour with Marshal Piłsudski, Poland's de facto leader until his death in 1935, Sikorski turned to writing on military strategy, becoming something of a pundit.

When war broke out in 1939 he was, despite repeated requests, denied a field command by the then Supreme Commander **Marshal Śmigły-Rydz** (1886-1941) a long-time intimate and favourite of Marshal Piłsudski. Ironically, Sikorski's lack of a formal post allowed him to pass through Romania without being interned, unlike the Supreme Commander, and to reach Paris where he swiftly formed a new Government-in-Exile based on the pre-war opposition parties.

Sikorski was Poland's only world-class statesman during the war. His pragmatic decision in 1941 to sign an agreement with the Soviet Union, the so-called Sikorski-Maisky Pact, led to damaging splits within his Government. Indeed, the issue of relations with the Soviet Union was to dominate Polish political affairs for the rest of the war, with no satisfactory modus vivendi ever established. The discovery in 1943 by the Germans of mass Polish graves at Katyń and elsewhere made a bad situation very much worse causing the Soviet Union to break off diplomatic relations with the Polish Government-in-Exile. They were never re-established.

Meanwhile in Poland Lieutenant **General Stefan Rowecki** (1895-1944), also born in the Austrian Partition and who had served in the Austrian Army in the First World War, was turning into an effective clandestine commander. A pre-war professional soldier who had commanded infantry, frontier defence forces and latterly one of Poland's two armoured brigades, he was appointed by Sikorski Commander of the underground SZP and ZWZ military organisations which in February 1942 became the AK, the Armia Krajowa. It fell to him to mould a great number of armed movements into the AK, which was an extraordinarily difficult assignment and on his watch the AK grew to become an effective underground force. Tragically, in June 1943, Rowecki was betrayed to the Gestapo and arrested. Held in Sachsenhausen concentration camp in Germany, he was executed there in August 1944 on the outbreak of the Warsaw Rising on the direct orders of the Head of the SS, Heinrich Himmler.

In July 1943, barely a few days after Rowecki's arrest, General Sikorski was killed in an air crash off Gibraltar returning from an inspection tour of Polish forces in the Middle East. He was buried with full military honours at the Polish Air Force Cemetery in Newark, England, after a requiem mass at Westminster Cathedral. In 1993, his remains were moved to the Royal Crypt at Wawel Castle in Kraków – the resting place of Polish monarchs and leaders. Sikorski's death has been fertile ground for conspiracy theorists, although a recent forensic examination in Poland of his specially exhumed remains has ruled out foul play.

General Władysław Anders

Thus 1943 was to see the end of two of Poland's finest military leaders, although neither had held what could be termed a fighting command. In fact, Poland's leading fighting general was **General Władysław Anders** (1892-1970) who was born in the Russian Partition of Poland and served in the Russian Army during World War I. A cavalryman, he climbed the ranks between the wars and commanded a cavalry brigade in 1939 defending the northern approaches to Warsaw. During four weeks of fighting and retreating he was wounded a number of times. Eventually captured by the Soviets, he was imprisoned in the infamous Lubyanka prison in Moscow.

After the signing of the Sikorski-Maisky agreement in 1941, Anders was released from prison and given the task of forming a Polish army from prisoners held in camps all over the USSR. He continued to command this force when it moved to the Middle East to come under overall British command, eventually becoming the Polish Second Corps which fought with distinction in the Italian Campaign. It was under Anders that the Poles achieved arguably their greatest conventional military success during the war: the storming and capture of the German position at Monte Cassino in Italy in May 1944. He later served as Acting Supreme Commander while General Bór-Komorowski was a POW. Anders lived to see the end of the war and settled in London becoming a powerful influence in the émigré community there.

General Sikorski's replacement as Supreme Commander, although not as Prime Minister, was the experienced **General Kazimierz Sosnkowski** (1885-1969) who was born in the Russian Partition. During the First World War he too served in Piłsudski's Legions and then held both military and political office during the 1919-1920 War, a pattern which he followed for most of the interwar period. He was an effective senior commander in September 1939 in south-eastern Poland and managed to reach Paris and join General Sikorski's Government, even though he outranked Sikorski. In 1941, he resigned from the Government over the Sikorski-Maisky Pact, since it did not specifically indicate that the USSR would relinquish those Polish territories which it had seized in 1939.

Recalled to office in 1943, he served until September 1944 when he was dismissed in the aftermath of the Warsaw Uprising and disagreements with the British. General Sosnkowski left shortly thereafter for Canada where he ended his days as a respected senior member of the Polish émigré community.

The crash which took General Sikorski's life also killed **Major General Tadeusz Klimecki** (1895-1943) born in the Austrian Partition, Sikorski's Chief of Staff. His replacement was **Lieutenant General Stanisław Kopański** (1895-1976) another fine fighting general. Born in Saint Petersburg, Kopański served in the Russian Army during the Great War. He lost an eye during the Russo-Polish War, but continued his career as a gunner in the Polish Army. The outbreak of war saw him serving on the Supreme Commander's staff and he too managed to make it to France. In April 1940, he was given command of the Carpathian Rifle Brigade forming on the border of French-held Syria and Lebanon. After the fall of France, the Brigade joined British forces in Palestine and in August 1941, it was moved to besieged Tobruk and subsequently fought in the Battle of Gazala. After his summons to London, Kopański was to remain there until the end of the War after which he headed the Polish Resettlement Corps for most of its existence. He stayed in England for the rest of his life.

Another fine fighting general, this time an armour specialist, was **General Stanisław Maczek** (1892-1994), who was born in the Austrian Partition and who

General Stanisław Maczek

served in the Austrian Army during the First War. Originally an infantryman, he assumed command in 1938 of the 10th Motorised Cavalry Brigade, the first armoured formation in the Polish Army. Thereafter, he was to remain with armoured forces, since his unit gave a very good account of itself during the September Campaign.

He re-formed the Brigade in France and then raised the 1st Polish Armoured Division in Scotland. Landing in Normandy in August 1944, Maczek's Division was attached to First Canadian Army where it achieved a crucial success in closing the so-called 'Falaise Pocket'. Maczek ended the war in command of Polish First Corps. After the war he settled in Edinburgh where he worked as a barman. To this day there is a General Maczek Museum in the Dutch city of Breda, which the Division liberated in 1944.

After General Rowecki's arrest, his deputy, Lieutenant General Tadeusz Bór-Komorowski (1895-1966) assumed command of the Home Army. Born in the Austrian Partition of Poland, Bór-Komorowski fought in the Austrian Army on the Russian and Italian fronts. Another cavalryman, he served in the cavalry during the 1919-1920 War, throughout the interwar years and in 1939. It was he who took the difficult and fateful decision to begin the Warsaw Uprising at the beginning of August 1944. On the 30th of September, rather unexpectedly, he was appointed Supreme Commander just before being imprisoned in Colditz Castle. After the war he settled in London and served as Prime Minister of the émigré Government-in-Exile between 1947 and 1949.

The Home Army did not disintegrate after the failure of the Warsaw Uprising and continued until January 1945 when it was disbanded by its last commander, **Major General Leopold Okulicki** (1898-1946). Okulicki was born in the Austrian Partition and during the Great War served with Piłsudski's Legions. He then served in the infantry and in staff positions which is where the outbreak of war in 1939 found him. Evading capture, Okulicki joined what later would become the Home Army.

Picked up and held by the NKVD in January 1941 he was released under the terms of the Sikorski-Maisky Pact becoming Chief of Staff to General Anders. He later trained in Britain and returned to Poland as a *cichociemny* SOE parachutist. Appointed C-in-C designate of the AK he spent most of the Warsaw Uprising in deep cover. After the collapse of the Uprising, he moved to Częstochowa and worked to rebuild what he could of the Home Army. After disbanding it, he was again arrested by the NKVD and imprisoned in Moscow. Sentenced to 10 years at a show trial he died, probably murdered, on Christmas Eve 1946 in the Butyrka prison.

The Warsaw Uprising publicly brought to a head two major issues: the Western Allies' commitment to Poland and the attitude of the Soviet Union to its

*Major General
Stanisław
Sosabowski*

western neighbour. It was technically out of the question to send the Polish Parachute Brigade to help Warsaw, an attempt which would have resulted in its wholesale slaughter. However, its experienced commander, **Major General Stanisław Sosabowski** (1892-1969), had in fact prepared and trained it for just such a contingency and it was hardly his fault that a lack of suitable transport aircraft and Soviet unwillingness to wrest control of the airspace over Warsaw from the Germans prevented the Brigade's use in the Polish capital.

Sosabowski was born in the Austrian Partition and served in the Austrian Army. An infantryman, he rose steadily through the ranks and in September 1939 he was commanding a crack infantry regiment. Taken prisoner, he escaped, joined the Underground, but was subsequently sent to France. In Britain he transformed the 4th Rifle Brigade into the 1st Independent Parachute Brigade. Assigned to the ill-fated Operation 'Market Garden' in September 1944, the Brigade was one of the few units to emerge with any credit. Sadly, Sosabowski himself was to fall victim to subsequent finger-pointing. He was never again to hold a major combat command and ended his days in London working as a factory storeman.

* * *

The Polish Navy was led before the war by men who had served on opposite sides during the Great War. **Vice Admiral Jerzy Świrski** (1882-1959) was born in the Russian Partition and served in the Russian Navy. Taking over as Head of the Polish Navy in 1925 he spent the next 14 years building it up; no easy feat in a poor country with a small coastline and no real nautical tradition. In this he was ably assisted by **Vice Admiral Józef Unrug** (1883-1974) who had been born in Germany and had served as a German U-boat captain and flotilla commander during the Great War. A competent naval officer he was quickly promoted to Rear Admiral, despite a poor command of Polish, becoming C-in-C Fleet in 1925. Captured in 1939 after a stout defence of the Hel Peninsula and the Polish coast, Unrug spent the war in German captivity.

After Poland's defeat, Świrski managed to make it to London where he continued as Head of the Navy and worked closely with the British throughout the war. Never a major naval force, Poland's small fleet was, however, able to provide the Royal Navy with valuable assistance. Both men remained in the West after the war.

A man who served both in the underground forces in Poland and then in the regular army in the West, **General Michał Tokarzewski-Karaszewicz** (1883-1964) was born in the Austrian Partition. A medical student who joined Piłsudski's Legions, Tokarzewski was by all accounts a fine soldier. By the time of the Russo-Polish War in 1919 he was already a colonel and by 1924 a major general at the age of 31. This led to command of a division and then a military district. In 1939, he commanded his own operational group in 'Pomorze' Army and, after the defeat, was one of the first to set about organising underground military organisations: the SZP and the ZWZ. Interestingly enough, Tokarzewski had gained some experience in conspiratorial work during the First World War and he recognised the need to develop a political structure as well as a military one. In 1940, he was picked up by the NKVD. Upon his release after the Sikorski-Maisky Pact he became GOC 6th Infantry Division and then Anders's 2 i/c in the Middle East. He settled in the West after the war.

Lieutenant General Bronisław Duch (1885-1980) was born in the Russian Partition and served in the Russian Army during the First World War, transferring to Piłsudski's Legions. An infantryman he was commanding a reserve division in 1939. Managing to get away to France, Duch was given command of the 1st Grenadier Division which was deployed as part of French XX Corps. Thereafter, Duch made his way to England, and between 1941 and 1942 was Chief of the Polish Military Mission to Canada where it was hoped to recruit volunteers. In 1943 he was assigned to command the 3rd Carpathian Rifle Division which took part in the Battle of Monte Cassino. After the war he settled in London.

Arguably the most celebrated branch of the Polish Armed Forces was the Air Force and its fighter pilots who contributed so mightily to victory in the Battle of Britain. Its first commander in the West was **Major General (Air Vice-Marshal) Stanisław Ujejski** (1891-1981), born in the Austrian Partition and who had served in an Austrian balloon detachment. Between 1932 and 1937 he was Commandant of the Air Force Officers' Training Academy in Dęblin and between 1937 and 1939 he was Air Force Chief of Staff. He served as Inspector General of the Polish Air Force in Britain from 1940 until 1943 when he was replaced by **Major General (Air Vice-Marshal) Mateusz Iżycki** (1898-1952) a younger man, born in Odessa in Russia, who had served in the Russian cavalry between 1917 and 1918. Ironically, in the Russo-Polish War he fought against the Bolsheviks as a Polish cavalry officer and in the 1920s he transferred to the Air Force. In 1939 he was senior Air Officer in 'Łódź' Army and then 'Warsaw' Army. Between 1940 and 1942 he commanded Polish ferry pilots in the Middle East becoming in 1942 the representative in the Middle East of the Polish Air Force Inspector General and liaison officer with RAF Middle East.

Lieutenant General Zygmunt Bohusz-Szyszko (1893-1982) was born in the Russian Partition and became a Russian infantry officer. During the Great War he was wounded and captured by the Austrians. After managing to escape, he joined Piłsudski's Legions and was a successful unit commander in the Russo-Polish War. Before 1939 he served in a number of field and staff positions and in 1939 fought as a divisional commander. He reached France where he took command of the Highland Brigade during the Norwegian Campaign in 1940. After service with First Corps in Scotland, Bohusz-Szyszko, a Russian speaker, was sent to head the Polish Military Mission in the USSR from 1941 to 1942. He then began to raise the 7th Division, served as Chief of Staff to Anders's army and subsequently commanded the 5th Division in the Middle East. He eventually became 2 i/c of Second Corps, taking over command in March of 1945. He settled in London after the war.

Lieutenant General Marian Kukiel (1885-1973) was born in the Austrian Partition and was an interesting mix of man of action and intellectual. He served in Piłsudski's Legions and during the Russo-Polish War commanded an infantry regiment followed by a brigade. He was promoted Major General at the age of thirty-eight having already served as Head of the General Staff's historical division. After the Piłsudski coup of 1926, Kukiel left the Army and settled down to teaching military history at the Jagiellonian University in Kraków.

When war broke out he was unsuccessful in obtaining a field command, but he was able to make it to France where he joined the Government as Deputy Minister of the Army. Between 1940 and 1942 he commanded First Corps in Scotland and from 1942 until the end of the war he served as Minister of National Defence. After the war he was very active in the Polish Institute and Sikorski Museum in London.

Major General Klemens Rudnicki (1897-1992) was born in the Austrian Partition and served in the Austrian Army in the Great War. A cavalryman he went to war in 1939 as CO of the 9th Lancers. Captured by the Germans, he escaped and helped to organise a resistance network. Nominated Chief of Staff of the Underground movement in the Soviet Zone of Occupation, he was arrested by the Soviets and imprisoned. His disguise as a peasant at the time of his arrest saved him from the fate of many of his fellow officers. After the signing of the Sikorski-Maisky Pact in 1941, he joined the Polish Army being formed in the USSR where he was appointed 2 i/c 6th Infantry Division. Later Rudnicki was 2 i/c 5th Infantry Division which took part in the Italian campaign. In May 1945, he took command of the 1st Polish Armoured Division where he had been serving as 2 i/c.

Lieutenant General, The Reverend Dr. Józef Gawlina (1892-1964) was born in the Prussian Partition and served unwillingly in the German Army during the Great War. He took Holy Orders in 1921 and from then until 1932 served as an assistant priest, Secretary General to the Catholic Apostolic League in Upper Silesia and as editor of a Catholic weekly magazine. He also found the time to take a law degree. In February 1933 he was appointed Bishop to the Polish Armed Forces with the rank of Lieutenant General and was consecrated bishop a month later. At the outbreak of war he left Warsaw and crossed the border into Romania to reach Rome and then move on to Paris

In 1942 the Soviets rather surprisingly allowed Gawlina to carry out a pastoral visit to Polish troops and civilians in the USSR. He then continued his visit in the Middle East and he also travelled to the USA to appeal for help for Polish orphans in the Soviet Union. Given the amount of flying undertaken by the Bishop, the Polish Air Force awarded him his 'wings' (the Poles actually had an eagle), which he wore with pride on his uniform. He then took part in the Italian Campaign with the Polish Second Corps being present at the Battle of Monte Cassino helping tend the wounded. After the war he was raised to Archbishop to the Polish émigré community and lived out his days in Rome.

* * *

During the Second World War Poland's Armed Forces in the West were composed of men who were uncertain whether the War would eventually end in their favour and whether they would even have a home to return to. While knowing that their country was brutally occupied undoubtedly spurred them to feats of valour, the personal uncertainties also sapped their morale making their officers' task that much harder. Their senior commanders were thus thrust into the political limelight much more than their Western counterparts and more than many of them would perhaps have liked. This was especially true as the Western Allies' acquiescence towards Soviet claims on Poland became generally known and when it came time to wind down the Polish Armed Forces at the end of the war. By then the generals knew that post-war Poland would not be free in any way that they understood and yet their ultimate loyalty to the Allied cause never wavered. That alone speaks volumes to their integrity. We were all fortunate to have such men.

Jarek Garliński

(Jacek Bernasiński also contributed
research and much material to this essay.)

Work of The Polish Association of The Order of the Knights of Malta during the Second World War

Wacław Hubert Zawadzki

The Polish Association of the Order of the Knights of Malta

The Sovereign Military Hospitaller Order of St.John of Jerusalem of Rhodes and of Malta had been active in Poland since the 12th century. The development of the Order's Polish chapters was disrupted by the Partitions of Poland in the late 18th century. The Polish Association of the Order of the Knights of Malta was reconstituted in 1920 following the restoration of Polish statehood in 1918. During the inter-war period the Polish Association ran several charities and three hospitals in Poland. Already in 1928 guidelines were drawn up for the care of the sick and wounded in the event of war. With the threat of war looming in 1939 these arrangements were formalised in the summer of that year. Under a separate agreement with the Polish Red Cross the medical section of the Association was to function as an autonomous unit of the Polish Red Cross. The Association's hospitals and ambulance service thereby secured inviolability and protection under the terms of the Hague and Geneva Conventions, and were authorised to fly the flag of the Red Cross next to that of the Maltese Order.

The outbreak of war on 1st September 1939 therefore found the Polish Knights of Malta ready to play their part in bringing help to the victims of the conflict. This chapter in their humanitarian work was to be extremely difficult and was to demand great courage. On 7th September the Association opened a 220-bed military hospital near Warsaw's Old Town in a former aristocratic residence on Senatorska Street which housed a merchants' guild (Resursa Kupiecka). Stanisław Milewski-Lipkowski, a Knight of Malta, was to be the hospital's director throughout the war; Professor Julian Szymański, a former Speaker of the Polish Senate, was the senior physician/surgeon; and Barbara Glińska was in charge of the nursing staff. As the Germans tightened their siege of the city, the work of the Maltese Hospital grew despite acute shortages of food, medicines, bandages and then of electricity. The hospital's ambulances managed to collect many wounded from highly dangerous and seemingly inaccessible places. The courage and dedication of the staff rapidly earned the admiration of the city's population. The Polish Knights also suffered casualties while performing their hospital duties: Roman Chłapowski and Dominik Łempicki were killed by German bombs, while the Association's honorary chaplain, Professor Canon Alfred Dobiecki, was wounded.

When Warsaw fell, the hospital's staff were treated as prisoners-of-war, although they were granted freedom of movement. The hospital was initially placed under the jurisdiction of the German military medical authorities, and later under the civilian authorities running the city. A clinic established by the hospital in an adjacent building for poor needy Jews was closed by the Germans after two months. The Maltese Hospital continued to treat wounded soldiers sent to or returning from German POW camps, and in the spring of 1940 set up a convalescent home for officers in Milanówek, west of Warsaw. In May 1941 the hospital secured the right to treat casualties of aerial bombardment, which meant that it could remain permanently open. This provided the hospital with the perfect cover to become the main clandestine centre for treating and hiding wounded members of the underground Polish Home Army (AK) involved in sabotage and other operations against the Germans. It also trained nurses and other auxiliary personnel for the Home Army. Worthy of note is the role of the hospital staff in saving Polish children expelled by the Germans during their 'ethnic cleansing' operation in the region of Zamość.

The commanders of the Home Army allocated an important role for the Maltese Hospital during the Warsaw Uprising which broke out on 1st August 1944, and the hospital additionally provided staff for four small field hospitals in the Old Town. During the first two weeks of fighting the hospital changed hands repeatedly, and treated the wounded of both sides. On 14th August it was finally taken by the Germans who ordered its immediate evacuation; it was then relocated to the building of the Public Credit Bank on Zgoda Street in that part of the centre of Warsaw which was still held by the insurgents. The heavy bombardment of central Warsaw on 4th September inflicted grave losses among the hospital's patients and staff. The hospital had to be moved further south to a building on Śniadeckich Street which had previously served as a German military hospital.

Following the capitulation of Warsaw on 3rd October, the Germans moved most of the remaining civilian population out of the devastated city. And so on 15th October the hospital was evacuated yet again, this time to a former factory building in the district of Piastów, west of the city centre, where it continued to serve the population until the arrival of Soviet-sponsored Polish forces on 17th January 1945. In the face of the new political realities the Home Army was formally dissolved by its commander two days later. The hospital's director Stanislaw Milewski-Lipkowski was replaced by Dr. Jerzy Dreyza who had served as the hospital's chief physician since 1940. The hospital itself was taken over by the Polish Red Cross. During its more than five-year-long existence the Maltese

Hospital had treated over 15,000 patients. Still retaining its historic name, the Maltese Hospital was then moved out of Warsaw to the city of Częstochowa in south-central Poland. In September 1949 it was permanently closed down by the communist authorities; its assets and equipment were divided among local hospitals and other institutions.

On 7th September 1979, on the fortieth anniversary of the creation of the Maltese Hospital, a commemorative plaque was placed in the Garrison Church on Długa Street in Warsaw, in the presence of Cardinal Stefan Wyszyński, the Primate of Poland, in honour of the hospital's personnel and patients.

Stanisław Milewski-Lipkowski
Director of the Knights of
Malta Hospital

The Knights of Malta Hospital,
Mniszech Palace, Warsaw

Wilanów—A Palace at War

Anna Branicka-Wolska by Teresa Stella-Sawicka

Anna Branicka Wolska, last resident of The Royal Palace at Wilanów in Warsaw talks of her WW2 experience in 1939.

"I and my friends, there were 6 of us including Lula Jaroszyńska, Iza Czajkowska, Lala Brenstern and me, Anna Branicka, were undergoing Home Army (AK) training at the Knights of Malta Hospital in Warsaw, where we later stayed on to work. We were still living in the Palace of Wilanów and walked daily to the Hospital in Aleje Ujazdowskie. We were taught by the doctors in the hospital but given all the worst jobs such as feeding and cleaning. For me, the worst duty was feeding ward patients with facial injuries.

The Knights of Malta Hospital was the best organised hospital in Warsaw during the war. It still had some electricity, although oil lamps were mostly used to conserve energy, but as with other hospitals, it had a poor supply of drugs and no ether for operations. We often had to bandage up gunshot arms with patients screaming, 'don't touch, don't touch'... I was only 14 at the time.

In 1939 the Polish Army and the army hospital were stationed in Wilanów Palace, but when German forces arrived, the Polish Army had to move out, leaving some of its wounded behind in the hands of the remaining Polish staff. I was still living there with my sisters and aunt and often helped out at the army hospital. On one occasion, I had to bandage such a wounded screaming man, then I had to feed him with a thick broth and vegetable soup called 'eintopf', mostly, the patients had to be tube-fed, they couldn't talk so could only give written instructions. I was very affected by the human suffering—'*ludzkie cierpnienie*'—but the hospital really saved so many lives.

Another duty was to bury the dead and we had to dig graves with my sisters and the remaining servants, as all the men had gone to war. One day, we had a badly wounded man, he turned out to be related to the famous Polish actor, Węgrzyn. He was covered in blood, begging desperately and repeatedly for his confession to be heard and asking for a priest.

We all felt he had some great sin to confess but there were no priests and we didn't know what to do. My mother's sister, Mrs Dynowska, under terrible pressure from the mortally wounded man, decided to hear the man's confession, but covered her ears as she didn't wish to listen to the confession of a dying man. She felt she had to given him his last wish, and then made the sign of the cross over him. He died shortly afterwards and we buried him in a shallow grave behind the stables. Several months later, his wife came to us and asked to collect the body. He had only been buried in a sheet. He had to be exhumed and the body was taken away.

Later when the Germans overran Warsaw in autumn 1939, they occupied Wilanów Palace and my family had to go down to live in the cellars where we continued to look after the sick; eventually the Germans took the remaining wounded to another military hospital.

In 1944,when the Warsaw Uprising ended after 63 days, Stanislaw Milewski-Lipkowski, the Director of the Knights of Malta Hospital evacuated the whole hospital himself, and in a final act of defiance against the Germans, dressed in a Maltese Knights' choir gown, holding the Knights of Malta flag, led out his team right in front of the waiting German Army. The Germans had great respect for the order of the Knights of Malta and consequently he was unharmed. Stanislaw Milewski-Lipkowski was one of the bravest men I ever knew.

After the Warsaw Uprising collapsed, Home Army soldiers were taken to a camp at Pruszków which had barracks and was surrounded by barbed wire. I was with my mother and sister, and desperately trying to find my father and fiancé in other camps.

The Germans' policy was to take the strong ones to the camps and let the weak ones go to Milanówek, just outside Warsaw.

Before the war my family only occupied the right wing of the Palace as living quarters, since the rest of the Palace was already a gallery and museum.

Years later, at a wedding, Adam Zamoyski and Tadeusz de Virion suggested that I become a Dame of the Order of Malta, as there was only one other Dame in Poland, the Princess Hapsburg who lived in Zywiec. I was only the second Dame for 5 years, now there are 5 of us."

War Memories

Teresa Kleniewska-Karska

Right from the beginning of the German attack, Varsovians were conspiring against the German invaders and those women who were willing and able joined the Home Army as recruits and were given military training. Even before the Warsaw Uprising we all stared death in the face on a daily basis. One of my girlfriends was supposed to carry a rifle over to one of the training centres, and there was no other way of transporting it except by tram. It was spring time, so she dressed up the rifle as a sapling—sticking a twig down the barrel with some rough leaves poking out of the top, wrapping the whole thing up in paper. The tram was very crowded. A young man standing next to her did not look very happy about the space she was taking and commented: 'Are you carrying a rifle, Madam, or what?' She turned pale and nearly fainted, her hands shaking all the way until the tram arrived at the training centre. A discovery would have meant certain death.

Luck of the draw—the Uprising

In 1940 I was accepted into The School of Agriculture and it was during these studies I joined the AK (Home Army). Initially, I attended some first-aid courses and lectures on politics and history. On completion of our training we all took an oath to our group, which we called 'Our Strange Group'. After Red Cross training, I worked as a nurse in the Knights of Malta Hospital but my medical knowledge was rather limited. One particular night whilst on duty, I can never forget. A patient with appendicitis arrived and Doctor Zebrowski ordered: 'Straight to the operating theatre, nurse'. My job was to keep the patient under anaesthesia during the operation. 'My God—I thought—I have never administered anaesthetics before'. In those days you had to keep dripping the anaesthetic liquid directly into the patient's nose while holding his jaws open to prevent him from suffocating. My hands were rather weak and I struggled seriously but managed in the end. An experience not to be forgotten.'

At the same time, with my girlfriends, we ran a refuge for children. At the main train station in Warsaw, we would snatch Polish children being transported by the Germans from the Zamość district to camps or other parts of Poland or the Third Reich, as part of their policy of ethnic cleansing. We would approach the carriages and take some of the children as though they were our own and then hide them temporarily in a factory in Wola. Later, fake documents would be issued for them. We all took turns to take care for the children and just before the Uprising we drew lots – who would go to fight in the Uprising and who would stay with them. Luckily, Mr and Mrs Mazaraki lent us a small abode on their country estate near Skierniewice. Some of us stayed there with the children—but my lot was to join the Uprising .

Nursing staff at The Knights of Malta Hospital, Warsaw 1941

Bombardment of the hospital

In Okopowa Street in Wola, we organised a little hospital but only used it for a few days as we moved on to the Old Town. There was another little hospital there too, but we soon moved to Miodowa–Długa Passage, where a large hospital already existed in a basement. We had a few rooms—naturally we also had to look after some wounded German soldiers. We lived through bombardments, fire and even the crash of a South-African plane. And then the end came.

You could feel that the Old Town was falling and would taken by the Germans any day. We stayed on at the hospital to prepare for evacuation and as a precaution placed the wounded Germans close to the entrance. I turned to my friend, Helenka Brzozowska and said 'Listen, Helenka, next door a priest is conducting a mass for the sick,' as we walked out, a bomb hit the room! Twelve of our colleagues died. Only the two of us survived. Clearly we could not go back but we tried to remove the rubble but it was all too heavy. We talked to our trapped colleagues; we gave them water through a little hole. My cousin among them, Jolanta Miroslawska. I remember, she cried: 'I am burning from my feet up'. It was horrible! Through a small hole, she managed to hand me a signet-ring which I was to give to her mother.

What should we do next? We had to carry those who were alive out of the hospital. So we started moving them one by one—we would put one on the ground and come back to get the next one: step by step till we reached the Knights of Malta Hospital, in Senatorska Street—it was quite a long way away. The wounded were received there but I was transferred to the hospital in Wola. However, because there were enough medical personnel there, the nurses newly arrived from the Old Town were sent out of Warsaw, transported in horse carriages covered with cloth to the nearest train station. I left Warsaw by the next train. Till the end of my life, I will not forget the conversation I heard in the carriage: Two ladies sitting next to me were talking about the wonderful time they had had playing bridge the day before. It was a shock to me! Through such tragedy and ordeal... we thought the whole of Poland was involved and yet here life was going on normally!

In the summer of 1945 we organised the exhumation of our colleagues' bodies. A meeting with Helenka Brzozowska was arranged in Warsaw. We hired a funeral company who promised to help us. Life was very hard then, our financial situation was horrible. We had hardly anything to eat. We retrieved the burned corpses and buried them in Powązkowski Cemetery in Warsaw. There is an inscription on the grave-stone: 'Remember us in your prayers. One does not live to fight, but fights to live. And when life is scarce, look death in the eyes and brave it'.

I was in God's care during the occupation. I lived in Żoliborz at my sisters' and commuted to school. There were round-ups every day. One day the tram I was travelling in was stopped, everyone was taken out of the tram and sent to hard-labour camps. I managed to sit down on the floor in-between the carriages. The tram moved on with me inside, completely alone. Either the Germans did not notice or they just could not be bothered about me. One was always in danger, always under pressure.

There could be a round-up at any time. From the Uprising, I remember an event when, feeling tired, I sat down by a small basement window to get some rest. Sniping and firing was going on. One of my friends shouted: 'Teresa, back off from the window!'. I moved and seconds later a bullet whizzed through the window. I was so lucky! I was never wounded, but so many close to me died—during the war I lost 80 members of my family

When things became quieter I decided to go to see my aunt in Wloclawek to give her the ring from the daughter who had been killed by the bomb blast. At the station the train was seriously overcrowded. People shouted to me 'Get on the roof'. Can you imagine? I tried but because I was small I had problems. Suddenly I heard a voice: 'Teresa, Teresa, can I help you get up here?' I looked up and saw one of the nuns from the Niepokalanki Sisters' Convent in Szymanów where I had boarded before the war. I answered: 'Yes, please, Sister'. There were already people on the roof. I joined them. Between Warsaw and Włocławek there are quite a few tunnels. When approaching them somebody would shout: 'Heads down'. And all of us would duck. I don't know how I survived all of this? Perhaps it's the prerogative of youth.

* * *

Teresa Kleniewska-Karska (nee Kobylecka) was born in 1921 in Radomszczański district in Poland. She was a nurse and a member of 'Our Strange Group' ZWZ/AK during the Uprising; her *pseudonym* was 'Grazyna'. She is a recipient of the Cross of Valour. Mrs Kleniewska-Karska came to Great Britain in 1946. For over 30 years she lived in Canada. She resides now in London.

Translated by Ewa Cieplińska-Bertini

Teresa Kleniewska-Karska,
June 2009

The Pen is mightier than the Sword

Zbigniew Jasiński (Rudy) —Poet of the Warsaw Uprising

We demand ammunition!

Here we fight with wolves' teeth, our caps skewed to the side.
Here no-one weeps in this Warsaw of war.
Here we crush the Germans astride on their backs
and strangle our enemies with fists that are raw.

But you keep on singing: that with the ashes of brotherly blood
Warsaw is being destroyed in the smoke of the flames.
Yet here, we with bare breasts take the force of the flood
to your amazement and awe, your praise and acclaim.

Why do you in London still intone the funereal lament
when we finally have reason to await the feast.
Girls fight in the streets alongside their young men
Children fight too, blood pours against the beast.

Listen. Poland's heart is beating here. Here is Warsaw calling:
Get those dirges off the air—they're an imposition.
We've spirit enough for ourselves—and there's enough for you.
We really don't need your applause. **We demand ammunition!**

ŻĄDAMY AMUNICJI

Tu zęby mamy wilcze, a czapki na bakier,
Tu u nas nikt nie płacze w walczącej Warszawie,
Tu się Prusakom siada na karku okrakiem
I wrogów gołą pięścią za gardło się dławi.

A wy tam wciąż śpiewacie, że z kurzem krwi bratniej,
Że w dymie pożarów niszczeje Warszawa,
A my tu — nagą piersią na strzały armatnie,
Na podziw wasz, na śpiewy i na wasze brawa.

Czemu żałobny chorał śpiewacie wciąż w Londynie
Gdy tu nadeszło wreszcie oczekiwane święto?
U boku swoich chłopców tu walczą dziewczęta
I małe dzieci walczą i krew radośnie płynie.

Hallo!... Tu serce Polski... Tu mówi Warszawa!
Niech pogrzebowe śpiewy wyrzucą z audycji.
Nam ducha starczy dla nas i starczy go dla was.
Oklasków też nie trzeba. Żądamy amunicji!

SIERPIEŃ

Tobie — i wszystkim innym
Dziewczętom-Żołnierzom.

Gdzie sierpień?... Gdzie nasz złoty sierpień?...
Kłosy żytnie, brzęk pszczoły i cichy szept liści?...
— Nic, prócz trupów i ruin, spustoszeń i cierpień.
Mord. Pożoga. Szaleństwo. Sierpień nienawiści.

W oczach twoich, Kochana, w oczach twoich
                                    zmęczonych
trwanie chłodne. Stwardniały ręce twe dziewczęce.
I nie pytasz: co z bratem?... A dom — już spalony.
I tak już trzy tygodnie. I będzie ich więcej.

Więcej będzie zabitych, kalekich, bezdomnych.
Kto wie, czy ujrzymy, jak złocą się kłosy?...
Mord. Pożoga. Szaleństwo. Brat. Dom. Słońce.
                                    Bomby.
Trzy tygodnie. Trzy wieki! To dosyć. To dosyć.

Dosyć — lecz nie dla ciebie. Oczy twe dziewczęce
chłodem płoną i żołnierz otuchę z nich czerpie.
— Tysiące takich dziewcząt, skamieniałych w męce,
razem z tobą budują — inny, lepszy Sierpień!

August

—Dedicated to you and to all
the other soldier girls.

Where is August? Our golden August?
Corn stacks, buzzing bees and the quiet whisper of leaves?
—Nothing, but corpses, ruins, devastation and suffering.
Murder. Destruction. Madness. An August of hatred

In your eyes, my darling, in your exhausted eyes,
Cool fortitude. Your young girl's hands have hardened,
And you don't even ask: your brother? The house—burnt down.
It's been like this for three weeks now. And there'll be more.

More will be killed, crippled and homeless.
Who knows if we'll live to see the corn turn gold?
Murder. Destruction. Madness. Brother. Home. Sunshine. Bombs.
Three weeks. Three centuries. It's enough. It's enough.

Enough—but not for you. Your young girl's eyes
flame coldly. The soldier takes courage from them;
—yet thousands of girls, petrified in their suffering
are with you now, building a different, better August.

Poems translated from the Polish
by Basia Korzeniowska

Zbigniew Jasiński with his
sister-in-law in Warsaw 1940,
a few weeks before the Germans
created the Warsaw Ghetto

Christmas 1942 in Warsaw. Zbigniew Jasiński is seated
second from the right. His sister-in-law is comforting
a young Jewish girl hiding in their apartment in the
centre of town

Letters of Support
for the Polish Forces War Memorial

HRH The Duke of Gloucester KG GVCO

KENSINGTON PALACE
LONDON W8 4PU

1 7 July 2009

I was so pleased to hear there was to be a Polish War Memorial to commemorate the many who played important roles in Germany's defeat, and also for the large number who stayed on in this country afterwards and the contribution they made consequently. Although I take an interest in the history of the Second World War my knowledge of the Polish contribution to its final outcome is patchy, but I do know it was considerable.

Perhaps its greatest contribution was the Polish understanding of the Germans' use of the Enigma code that was believed erroneously to be unbreakable. I understand that there were several naval vessels that aided the Royal Navy and that the Isle of Wight was very grateful for their presence when the Luftwaffe came to call one day.

I became aware of the role that the Polish Air Force played in enhancing the RAF when I visited the Polish Air Force Memorial at Northholt. I enjoy mentioning the statistic when I ask people to guess how many escaped from Poland to fight in the air. Very few guess more than a few hundred, when in fact the figure is 27,000, some 10% of the RAF numerically, although their strike rate was much higher.

As for the Polish Army, I am reminded of pictures I have seen of my father visiting the Polish soldiers, who arrived in Palestine in 1940 after being in Russian prisoner-of-war camps and were sent out without their officers (all murdered). It was not so much that they needed re training as feeding up, as they had been starved ever since their capture. I believe these were the same soldiers who suffered so long and hard at Monte Cassino.

Finally, I know of the deplorable decision, when it was felt unwise to irritate Stalin, and the Polish Armed Forces were not invited to take part in the Victory Parade after many years of loyal endeavour with little benefit by finally exchanging one invader for another.

Richard

Dr. Andrew Meeson-Kielanowski, KM

3rd June 2009

Dr Andrew Meeson-Kielanowski KM
Vice Chairman
Polish Forces Memorial Committee

Dear Dr Meeson-Kielanowski

I am delighted to contribute to this book as I have strong Polish connections through my father, then Captain R G Grosvenor RA, who on the 6th September 1943 was posted as Training Major to No 2 RA Training Team, Polish Forces for six months.

He often talked about the enormous courage and determination of the Polish soldier who, of course, had families and friends so far away. In a letter to his mother in September 1943, he said "They are quite wonderful as all their families and friends are still in occupied Poland and they have had no news of them for years". Imagine for a moment how terrible for them, not to know anything of the fate of their loved ones and yet they fought and died in a foreign land to ensure eventual victory.

The huge contribution and sacrifice of the polish forces is well documented, their bravery and loyalty is well known and it is only right and fitting that we should remember them. In a letter to my father from the Polish Commander in Chief in 1945, General W Anders said and I quote "your assistance in the training of 2 Polish Corps enabled us to go into battle in true fighting trim to wear down and finally to finish off the enemy, you have truly earned the deep gratitude of 2 Polish Corps".

My father was very proud to have received such a tribute from such remarkable soldiers and I know he felt humble to have served alongside such fine men.

Yours sincerely

Major General the Duke of Westminster KG CB OBE TD CD DL

General the Lord Guthrie of Craigiebank GCB LVO OBE DL

The Polish contribution to the eventual defeat of Germany and her allies in the Second World War should never be forgotten. Poland had the great misfortune to be situated between the Soviet Union and Nazi Germany, and suffered as a result. During the dark days of occupation many thousands of Polish men and women fought and supported the allied cause and many fled Poland to fight and serve alongside the British Forces.

They formed units which were entirely Polish and also enlisted in British formations serving on Royal Naval ships, with British Regiments, and with the Royal Air Force. The story of their participation in the Battle of Britain is well known but they also fought in all the main theatres of war. Many died for the allied cause and many never returned to the country of their birth, Poland.

We, the British, owe much to those Polish men and women who came to join us in the struggle. There was a time in World War II when the only allies the British Commonwealth had were Polish and large numbers died in battle many miles away from their own country. Their spirit was indominatable and never waivered even when Poland was overrun by the enemy. A secret army was formed within German occupied terrortory, which contributed greatly to the final victory.

We are right to remember the Polish Government in exile and those gallant Polish men and women who, at a very difficult time in both our countries' history, were our firm friends and allies.

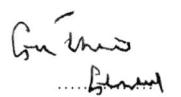

Biuro
b. Prezydenta
Rzeczypospolitej Polskiej
RYSZARDA KACZOROWSKIEGO

238–246 King Street, London W6 0RF
Tel/Fax 0181 563 7674

The Second World War is a historical event, which still touches Poland's present. The borders marked out by this conflict and its consequences, still remain an unhealed wound to many millions of people. There still are attempts to distort and falsify a true picture of events, often as part of a deliberate campaign to deform historical facts.

It is fitting that the proposed memorial aims to commemorate the Polish soldier and a timely reminder of his achievements in this horrendous war.

This book is published on the occasion of the unveiling of a memorial to the Polish Armed Forces at the National Memorial Arboretum. It is an important element emphasizing the steadfast and loyal commitment of the Polish Armed Forces alongside the Western Allies in defeating the enemy on all fronts of the Second World War.

Ryszard Kaczorowski
Last President
of the Polish Government-in-Exile

POLISH AIR FORCE ASSOCIATION
CHARITABLE TRUST 1995

Established 1953 - Charity Registration Number 1052651
Registered Office: 238-246 King Street, London W6 0RF
Telephone: General +44(0)20 8846 9487, Welfare +44(0)20 8741 4052,

Polish Memorial at the Aboretum, Staffordshire

During World War 2. was Poland fighting on the side of the Allies or on the side of the Germans? Such a surprising and provocative question was put to me several times within the last decade and always by a young adult, who certainly would have had the benefit of, at least, a secondary school education in this country.

In our circles of Polish ex-combatants and emigre's, we have repeatedly discussed the need for commemorating Poland's contribution to Allied victory.

We have spoken of erecting a memorial which would ensure that Poland's total engagement in the struggle against the Third Reich would not be erased from history and which would also convey to a younger generation the crucial role that Polish armed forces played throughout the conflict.

However, it is only now, thanks to the initiative and commitment of two of our fellow countrymen, Dr Marek Stella-Sawicki and Dr Andrzej Meeson-Kielanowski, the generous financial backing of the Polish ex-Combatants Association, the Polish Air Force Trust and of many other contributors, that the project has been realized.

The memorial which has been erected will fulfil, at least partially, the difficult task of perpetuating the memory of the effort, courage and sacrifice on the part of our nation in World War 2.

We all hoped that the memorial would prove worthy of its purpose and be erected on the best possible site. Each person held different views – it was impossible to please one and all.

However the memorial has found a home in an excellent position in the National Memorial Arboretum in Staffordshire, where it will attract the attention of visitors who in their thousands visit the site each year.

It will awaken the interest of many and, it is hoped, will cause some to find out more about Poland's participation and contribution to Allied victory, a victory which, though seemingly distant now, brought them the freedom and prosperity that they and their children are presently enjoying.

Acknowledging the effort and dedication of the planning Committee and those who supported the project, we would like to proffer our thanks to all who contributed to its successful completion.

Andrzej F.K. Jeziorski
Polish Air Force Association Trust

POLISH EX-COMBATANTS ASSOCIATION
GREAT BRITAIN

240 King Street London W6 ORF
Tel 0208 741 1911 Fax 0208 748 4558

Our Polish generation brought up in the spirit of patriotism, and now living in all corners of the world, pay tribute to the Polish Servicemen and Women, on this the 70th anniversary of the beginning of the Second World War.

The bravery of the Polish Military and Civilians who served and died during World War II 1939-1945 is well documented in many books and films but with the passing of years the memories start to fade. The Polish Forces War Monument with its granite surrounds will have this history engraved in stone, and will serve as an important focus for remembrance as well as an educational aid to young generations, for many years to come.

The concept of building The Polish Forces War Monument at the National Memorial Arboretum in Staffordshire was presented to our organisation two years ago, by a small enthusiastic group of Polish professionals who gained our full support for the project.

The worldwide support both for the building of the Monument and the donations towards its financing have exceeded expectations, whilst the publication of this book to commemorate the unveiling is made possible by a private donation.

Czesław Maryszczak
Chairman
Polish Ex Combatants Association
in Great Britain

THE POLISH INSTITUTE AND SIKORSKI MUSEUM

20 PRINCES GATE
LONDON SW7 1PT
TEL:020 7589 9249

Organising Committee
The Polish Forces War Memorial
 at the National Memorial Arboretum

30th July 2009

Dear Committee Members,

Until recently, it was considered that in the United Kingdom, the Polish Institute and Sikorski Museum was the visible "monument" to the struggle of the Polish Nation during the years 1939-1945, in particular her Armed Forces in the West and the Home Army in occupied Poland.

However there will now be two such "monuments"! The Polish Institute and Sikorski Museum continuing in its role as an archive and museum, conveying the events of the war years - and the Polish Forces War Memorial being the visible symbol of that struggle. It will of course also become a focus for national commemorations in future years.

Please accept my congratulations for your initiative for such a much needed project, as well as your perseverance in seeing it through in such a relatively short period of time, to the unveiling ceremony on 19th September 2009.

Yours sincerely

Krzysztof Barbarski CEng
Chairman

STUDIUM POLSKI PODZIEMNEJ
The Polish Underground Movement (1939–1945) Study Trust

11 Leopold Road, London W5 3PB
Tel & Fax: 020 8992 6057
E-mail: info@spp-pumst.org

Dr M. Stella-Sawicki
Committee Chairman

1 August 2009

Our ref. 132/09

Dear Dr Stella – Sawicki

  We wish to congratulate you and your team for the successful erection of the monument of the "Polish Armed Forces War Memorial" at the National Memorial Arboretum and for the very timely decision to publish a book entitled "First to Fight". It remains our sincere hope that this well researched work will be favourably received by the English speaking readership. We anticipate that after visiting the monument some of the interested British visitors will pick up copies at the Arboretum Bookshop.

  For many older volunteers who devote their time to work at our Archive, the newly erected monument and this book may bring back memories. Some long forgotten but triumphal events as well as tragedies, which befell the Polish Nation and its Armed Forces, during and after II World War.

  It remains our great joy to see that the history of the Secret Home Army, to which our Archive is devoted, is also commemorated at the Monument by a female soldier. The contribution of this force should be remembered, as it provided a 300,000 strong army, which fought the German and Soviet occupiers throughout the length of the war. The invaders, who both had coordinated plans to eliminate the Polish Nation from the map of Europe and to murder most of its citizens.

  With our grateful thanks and heartfelt congratulations to your team which worked so hard to bring this Monument to its final successful conclusion.

  We remain yours sincerely

Dr K. Stoliński
Chairman

Mr T. Melka
Vice-Chairman

Amalgamated with:
The Polish Institute and Sikorski Museum
Registered Charity No. 312168

MINISTRY OF NATIONAL DEFENCE
UNDERSECRETARY OF STATE
FOR DEFENSE POLICY

Stanisław J. KOMOROWSKI

Warsaw, 10th August 2009

It is a great honour to take part in the ceremony of the unveiling of the Polish Allied Forces War Memorial. The 70th Anniversary of the outbreak of World War II when Poland was attacked by both, Germany and the Soviet Union, is an exceptional occasion to pay tribute to the heroes of the WW II.

It is important that the past service and sacrifice of the Polish men and women who fought with the allies for freedom and world peace should not be forgotten.

This monument will serve as a reminder of the numerous campaigns in which the Polish Forces took part and of Poland's major contribution to allied intelligence, given with significant sacrifice of life. Only a small number of combatants now remain who fought in World War II. It is, therefore, pertinent that this monument should be erected at this time.

I am happy that Polish and British troops cooperate today in the spirit of traditional close relations of our countries. We are committed to continue developing our strong and successful relations.

Stanisław J. KOMOROWSKI

The Ambassador of the Republic of Poland to the Court of St James's

London

Polish Memorial at the Arboretum

It is more than fitting that exactly 70 years after the German and Soviet invasion of Poland, which marked the beginning of World War II in Europe, the Polish Armed Forces Memorial was finally unveiled within the grounds of The Arboretum. The contribution that Polish servicemen and women made towards the Allied victory over the Nazis has obviously been long acknowledged in the United Kingdom and elsewhere. It was a joint, national effort, involving soldiers across the globe: in Poland, the Home Army units led the way in the underground struggle against the occupation. Abroad, hundreds of thousands of uniformed Poles participated in active combat on land, high seas and in the air, defending the British skies in 1940, protecting the supply convoys in the North Atlantic, or liberating Dutch and Italian cities in the final phases of the war, to name but a few of the operations in which they distinguished themselves. Those actions have a rich historiography, which will undoubtedly grow in the years to come, increasing our understanding of that period and the scope of the Polish-British cooperation during the war. Following the World War Two, Great Britain became home to thousands of Polish soldiers and their heroic commanders. They found a welcome here and could rebuild their lives from the ravages of war, albeit far away from their homeland, which fell under the communist oppression for many years to come.

It is important, however, for the historical achievements and sacrifices of the wartime generation to live on beyond the sphere of specialist publications. And this is precisely where the role of such places, as The Arboretum, with its newly unveiled (long overdue, some would claim), Polish Armed Forces Memorial, comes into play. I believe that they have a crucial part in preserving our collective memory, thus linking the generations past, present and future in the common ethos of loyalty, solidarity and the unstinting belief that aggression may not be condoned. As such, those sites not only constitute tangible proofs of our respect for the heroism of the wartime generation, but also act as signposts towards the future to which we all aspire. I feel therefore reassured and truly grateful for the knowledge that from now on, young people in Britain – the British, the Polish and persons of other nationalities alike - will have an opportunity to walk around the beautiful grounds of The Arboretum, listen to the wind rustle in the trees, and perhaps – stopping in front of the Polish Forces Memorial - think respectfully of the fallen from an allied country, who sacrificed their lives in the hope that "Europe's darkest hours" would not happen again.

Barbara Tuge-Erecińska

Ambassade van het
Koninkrijk der Nederlanden

Dr Marek Stella-Sawicki

Embassy of the Kingdom of the
Netherlands
Defence Department
38 Hyde Park Gate
London SW7 5DP

Date   Friday 14 August 2009

Subject   Polish contribution in liberating the Netherlands

On September 16th 1944 the first units of the 1st Polish Armoured Division crossed the Dutch border, thus starting its invaluable contribution to the liberation of the Netherlands. Coming form Belgium, they entered the most south-western part of the Netherlands, a region called Zeeuws-Vlaanderen, of which they liberated the eastern half. This division, under the command of Major General Stanislaw Maczek, would fight on Dutch territory almost continuously until Nazi-Germany finally surrendered in May 1945. One of the most remarkable feats of the Poles was the seizure of the city of Breda on October 29th. The city was hardly damaged during the fighting, not only because the Germans retreated rather quickly, but also because the Poles refrained from using their artillery. The inhabitants of Breda greatly appreciated this cautious use of force. During the winter the front line in the Netherlands froze and came to lie alongside the great rivers, flowing from east to west. The 1st Polish Armoured Division stayed in the Breda area, the city becoming its main centre for rest and recreation. The already cordial relationship with the inhabitants intensified even further. During the final month of the war the division took part in the liberation of the managed to do so – they could not prevent the loss of the Oosterbeek bridgehead. On September 25th the British airbornes and the Polish paratroopers had to be evacuated to the south bank of the Lower Rhine. In 2006 the 1st Polish Independent Parachute Brigade was awarded the Military Order of William, the highest honour in the Netherlands, for the valour it displayed during operation Market Garden. At the same time general Sosabowski was posthumously honoured with the Bronze Lion.

The Polish Air Force also played a significant role in the struggle against Germany. Night after night Polish bomber crews crossed Dutch airspace on their way to and from Germany. During these flights over Holland several Polish bombers were shot down by nightfighters or anti-aircraft fire. In the closing months of the war Polish fighter aircraft operated over Dutch territory as well. In this period most Polish units were based on airfields in Belgium, but in March, the Polish 131 Wing operated from the Dutch aerodrome of Gilze-Rijen, in the south of the country. In April, after several attacks on railway junctions, all kinds of transport and troop movements, the Wing progressed to an airfield closer to the frontline. During this period several Polish fighter pilots lost their lives over Holland.

The Polish war cemetery in Breda, containing the graves of more than five hundred young men, is a silent witness of the sacrifice these men, far away from their own home country, paid for the liberation of the Netherlands. Other Polish soldiers and airmen, who died on or above Dutch soil, have found their final resting-place in cemeteries, elsewhere in the Netherlands. We thank them and we honour them.

Deputy Defence, Military & Air Attaché

J.P.E. van Tilburg
Lieutenant Colonel

The Sirmoor Rifles Association (The Sirmoor Club)

Brigadier B C Jackman OBE MC
Chairman

17 August 2009

Dr Marek Stella-Sawicki
Chairman of the Polish Forces War Memorial Project

Dear Dr Stella-Sawicki

I am writing as Chairman of the Sirmoor Rifles Association, the officers' association of the 2nd King Edward VII's Own Goorkhas (The Sirmoor Rifles).

I understand that on 19th September 2009 HRH The Duke of Kent will be unveiling a monument in the National Memorial Arboretum in Staffordshire to commemorate the Polish contribution to the defeat of Hitler in the Second World War 1939-1945. As Chairman of this project you must be enormously satisfied that the outstanding bravery of the Poles who fought alongside the British and other Allies will be remembered forever in this way. May I offer you my congratulations.

You will know that our 1st Battalion fought at Monte Casino, the very famous and one of the bloodiest battles of the World War II. Indeed we lost 80% of our battalion killed or wounded in the First Battle of Monte Casino, such was the intensity of the fighting. In May this year we conducted a battlefield tour of Monte Casino with a party of 25 ex-officers of the regiment and their dependents, two of whose fathers fought in the battle – one of whom was the Commanding Officer who was seriously wounded. It was a very moving occasion as we walked the ground, so different now but with photographs and maps of how it was at the time – truly awesome. We visited the splendid Polish War Memorial that honours those brave members of the Polish Division that distinguished itself so famously and gallantly at Monte Casino. It was with enormous pride that we stood on the ground where Gurkhas and Poles fought so courageously in indescribable conditions, on the most formidable terrain, and against such a tenacious enemy – and ultimately defeated them.

May I take this opportunity, on behalf of the Sirmoor Rifles Association, to salute you and the Members of the Polish Ex-Combatants Association, as brothers in arms. We will remember you on 19th September.

Jai Sirmoor and jai Polish comrades.

Yours sincerely.

Brigadier B C Jackman OBE MC
Chairman, Sirmoor Rifles Association (The Sirmoor Club)

EMBASSY OF THE UNITED STATES OF AMERICA

LONDON

June 3, 2009

Dr. Andrew Meeson-Kielanowski, KM
Polish Forces Memorial Committee

Dear Dr. Meeson-Kielanowski,

The U.S. Embassy in London commends the Polish Ex-Combatants Association
for its role in maintaining the memory of the brave men and women who served in
the defense of freedom during World War II.

As an early ally during the war, Poland fielded a proud army that courageously
defended Europe and the sovereignty of her nations. As Britons now remember
these fallen soldiers, Americans too will pause to remember Poland's contributions
to our shared efforts.

Sincerely,

Richard LeBaron
Chargé d'Affaires, a.i.

AUSTRALIA HOUSE
LONDON

THE HIGH COMMISSIONER

As we honour the Polish men and women who fought during the Second World War it is appropriate that we recall the close ties between our two nations. Indeed, the close relationship between Australia and the people of Poland is one of the least known facets of Australia's history.

Our entwined historical roots are deep, as the Poles were among the first explorers and settlers in Australia. In fact, according to *The Australian People: an Encyclopedia of the Nation, Its People and Their Origins* (2001), the earliest Polish visitors to Australia were "… ten citizens of the Polish-Lithuanian Commonwealth [who] stepped onto Australian soil in December, 1696, when Captain Willem de Vlamingh's Dutch expedition of three ships reached and explored the coast of Western Australia." Later, in the Nineteenth Century, Poles came to Australia as convicts and free settlers. Polish political refugees also made their way to Australia after the unsuccessful revolt against Austria in 1848. Many of these new Polish arrivals were engineers, teachers, artists and businessmen. They enriched Australia's society and were nation builders. One of the best-known Poles was Paul Edmond Strzelecki who, in the Nineteenth Century, explored the Snowy Mountains and named several Australian geographical features including Australia's highest mountain, Mount Kosciuszko, and the Strzelecki ranges, in Gippsland, Victoria.

While Polish settlers helped to build Australia as a free and democratic nation, they did not forget their homeland. In 1863, as a result of the January Uprising during the Polish-Russian Wars, the Polish gold diggers set up the "Polish Society" in Melbourne, aiming to assist Poland in its struggle for independence. This assistance to a needy homeland has remained a strong part of the Polish community to this very day. Prior to the First World War there were some eight thousand Poles, or Polish descendants in Australia, some of whom had arrived via Siberia and Manchuria. Between 1921 and 1939 thousands of Poles came to Australia, and the number of associations increased and the newspapers "Polonia Australijska" and "Dom Polski" were published. The Polish Consulate General was set up (prior to this there was only an Honorary Consul) and the Polish Australian Chamber of Commerce was established. In 1939, Polish Australians were also busy collecting war funds for Poland and the substantial sum, for those days, of 30 thousand pounds was forwarded to the Polish Government in Exile.

These domestic ties to Poland were reinforced in 1939 when Australia guaranteed to support Polish independence if threatened. Consequently, on 3 September, 1939, Australia was among the first countries, along with Britain, France and New Zealand, to declare war against Nazi Germany when Poland was invaded.

As allies, both Australia and Poland sustained a significant war effort. Polish forces continued to fight despite the fall of their country. The Poles never waivered in their commitment throughout the war and fought with gallantry in all theatres. They fought alongside Australians in the air over Europe, in both Fighter and Bomber Commands, and on the ground in North Africa, including the famous defence of Tobruk in 1941. Meanwhile on the homefront, Polish resistance fighters effectively, and with great sacrifice, distracted and hindered the Nazi war machine.

It is part of Australia's national character to proudly remember our citizens who fought and endured the hardships of war. It is therefore with honour we remember and commemorate the gallant deeds of the Polish forces, both regular and irregular, who fought so valiantly during the Second World War. We should remember this generation of Poles as a heroic one; they fought a war to defend and then liberate a country they loved and bequeathed to their descendants liberty and opportunity.

They also taught us much more. By their example, they showed us how allies can come together and triumph in a common cause. This spirit continues today with both Australia and Poland having made or continuing to make, significant contributions to coalition operations in Iraq and Afghanistan.

This book, and the Polish Allied Forces War Memorial at the National Arboretum in Alrewas, Staffordshire, will be a timeless memorial to the Polish men and women who gave their lives for our freedom. Australia will always remember and honour their sacrifice.

John Dauth

1 July 2009

NEW ZEALAND DEFENCE FORCE
Te Ope Kaatua o Aotearoa

New Zealand Defence Staff, London

New Zealand House, 80 Haymarket, London SW1Y 4TQ, United Kingdom
Telephone: (+44) 020 7930 8400 Ext 248, Facsimile: (+44) 020 7930 8401,
Email: john.boswell@nzdf.mil.nz

1108

19 August 2009

Dr Marek Stella-Sawicki
Polish Ex-Combatants Association

Dear Dr Stella - Sawicki

From the battles fought in your homeland, to the part played by your Armed Forces in North Africa, Europe and the defence of Great Britain; Poland's contribution to the fight against Nazi Germany was both considerable and significant. That there is now a memorial to the men and women of the four branches of the Polish Armed Forces who gave their lives in this fight for freedom is a fitting acknowledgement of their contribution to Germany's defeat.

New Zealand remembers with great fondness those occasions where we stood and fought together. In the deserts of North Africa and the Italian Campaign New Zealand and Polish soldiers were at the forefront of the fight. Tobruk and Monte Cassino are two battles that instantly come to mind. Similarly, our airman and sailors played key roles in the defence of Britain and then in support of Allied operations in Europe. Following the war these links were maintained as many Poles immigrated to New Zealand to rebuild their lives.

On this very special day, at this very special memorial to those many Polish men and women who died in the pursuit of freedom, New Zealand along with many other nations, will pause, reflect and remember.

Yours faithfully

W.J. WHITING
Brigadier
Defence Adviser

Colonel Robert VÁGNER
Defence Attaché
Embassy of the Czech Republic
26 Kensington Palace Gardens
W8 4QY London

19.8.2009

The Polish Ex-Combatants Association
Dr Marek Stella-Sawicki

Dear Chairman,

Thank you for the invitation of the Czech Defence Attaché to the unveiling of the monument in the National Memorial Arboretum in Alrewas, Staffordshire.

On behalf of the Czech Republic, I am really happy that I have the honour to take part in such a praiseworthy project reflecting on keeping in mind all the brave men and women served and fallen in defence of freedom during World War II. As acting Defence Attaché of the Czech Republic, one of Poland's Allies not only during WWII, I am also proud to acknowledge my definite support to this project.

Enclosed below I am sending you a text which I have obtained from the Czech Military History Institute in context to the upcoming book associated with your project. I hope you will make use of it.

*Despite relations between Poland and Czechoslovakia had not been as warm as both the neighbours would have been deserved, they have been entirely changed since the beginning of the World War II. In fact, Poland was the first country tolerating the dislocation of the Czechoslovak foreign troop in its own territory even before the Nazi invasion of Poland on 1*st *September 1939. On the other hand, the Czechoslovak troop taking part in the defence of Poland was the only allied troop fighting side by side with Polish at that time even it was too small and not well-appointed.*

*Both the countries found themselves in the same situation after Poland fell. After France was defeated in June 1940, it was Great Britain, where the main centre of both Czech and Polish foreign rising against Nazis enacted. On the British Islands, where the Czechoslovak government-in-exile constitution was accomplished, unprecedented rapprochement of the Polish and Czechoslovak political representations led in the declaration of a post-war confederation of both countries on 11*th *November 1940.*

1 of 2

The mentioned agreement was among other things reflected in increased partnership of both the Polish and Czech armies-in-exile wrestling with similar problems such as the perceptible reductions of numerical status of the armies. Whereas there were approximately 80 thousand Polish soldiers and 13 thousand Czechs dislocated in France, only about 27 thousand Polish and 5 thousand Czech soldiers were evacuated to the British Islands.

The soldiers of both armies departed to each other national troops for their internship. However, the Polish side offered significantly more, i.e. the proposal to establish Czechoslovak Navy, which was, unfortunately, never realized.

Furthermore, an entirely battle cooperation of both armies existed, i.e. among Polish and Czech pilots fighting side by side in RAF or in the Middle East, where the East part of the Czechoslovak Infantry Battalion No 11 East fighting in Libya and defending Tobruk was subordinated to Polish Independent Carpathian Rifle Brigade in 1941. It is also interesting, that dozens of Czech soldiers came with the Army of General Wladyslaw Anders to the Middle East, which meant, in fact, their salvation from the hell of the Soviet Gulag.

Much anticipated combat deployment of the Polish and Czechoslovak troops stationed in Great Britain became a reality after the Invasion of Allied forces in Normandy. Although the Polish soldiers had the honor to take part in the liberation of Western Europe and Italy, the participation on the siege of Dunkerque in North France was the task of the Czechoslovak Armoured Brigade until the end of the war. Neither Polish, nor Czechoslovak soldiers' dream to be involved in the liberation of their homelands came truth. Whereas more than a half of the Polish soldiers abroad stayed in the West after the World War II ended, the Czechoslovak soldiers returned back home. Unfortunatelly, many of them, either Czechoslovaks or Polish, were forced to flee abroad soon again after the communist putsch came to pass.

I do hope that the above will complement the narrative of the book 'First to Fight' you prepare for the occasion of the monument unveiling.

Sincerely yours,

Col Robert VÁGNER

Timeline—Poland in WWII

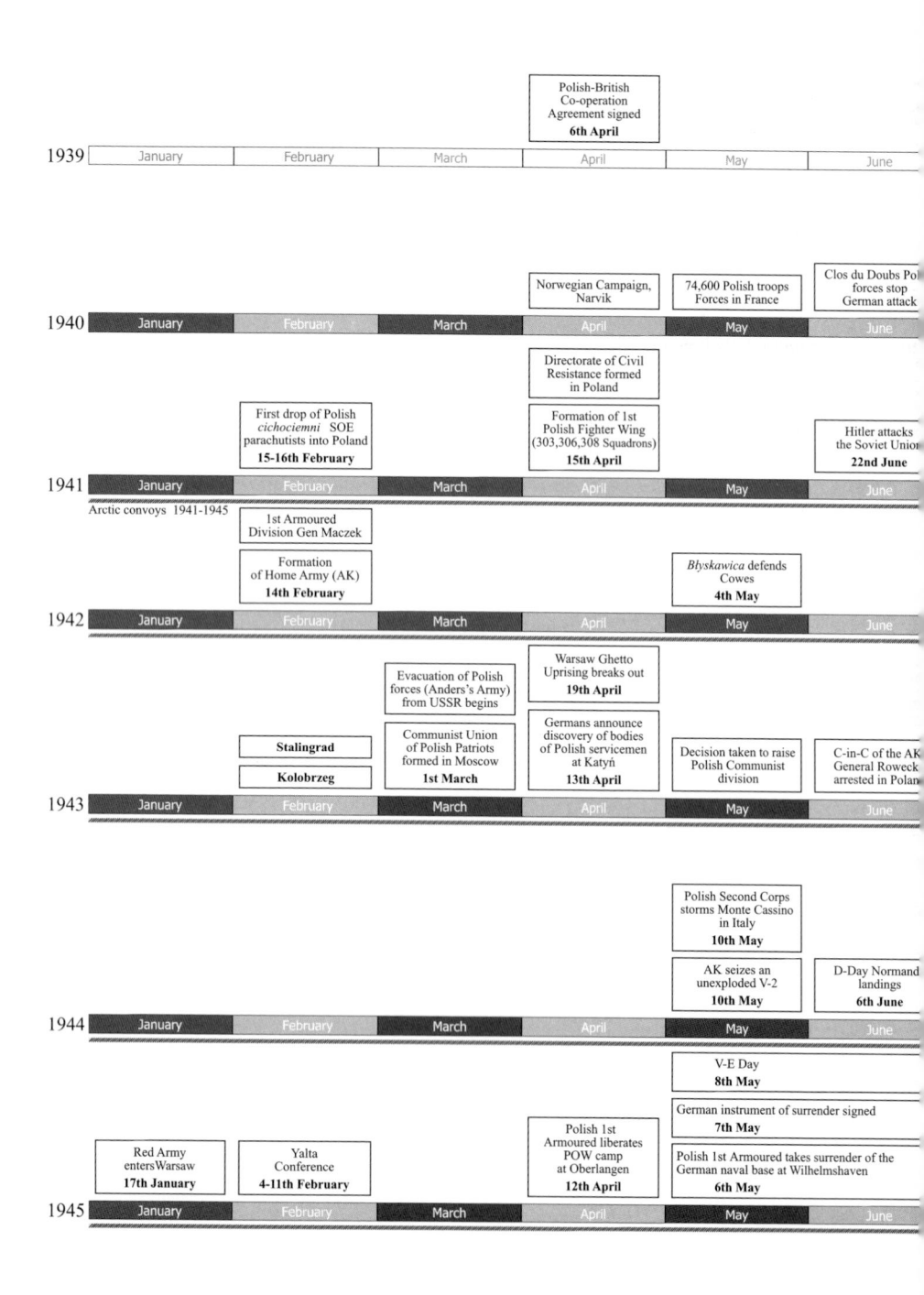

			Polish-British Co-operation Agreement signed **6th April**		
1939 January	February	March	April	May	June

			Norwegian Campaign, Narvik	74,600 Polish troops Forces in France	Clos du Doubs Pol forces stop German attack
1940 January	February	March	April	May	June

			Directorate of Civil Resistance formed in Poland		
	First drop of Polish *cichociemni* SOE parachutists into Poland **15-16th February**		Formation of 1st Polish Fighter Wing (303,306,308 Squadrons) **15th April**		Hitler attacks the Soviet Union **22nd June**
1941 January	February	March	April	May	June

Arctic convoys 1941-1945

	1st Armoured Division Gen Maczek				
	Formation of Home Army (AK) **14th February**			*Błyskawica* defends Cowes **4th May**	
1942 January	February	March	April	May	June

			Warsaw Ghetto Uprising breaks out **19th April**		
		Evacuation of Polish forces (Anders's Army) from USSR begins			
	Stalingrad	Communist Union of Polish Patriots formed in Moscow	Germans announce discovery of bodies of Polish servicemen at Katyń	Decision taken to raise Polish Communist division	C-in-C of the AK General Roweck arrested in Polan
	Kolobrzeg	**1st March**	**13th April**		
1943 January	February	March	April	May	June

				Polish Second Corps storms Monte Cassino in Italy **10th May**	
				AK seizes an unexploded V-2 **10th May**	D-Day Normand landings **6th June**
1944 January	February	March	April	May	June

				V-E Day **8th May**	
				German instrument of surrender signed **7th May**	
Red Army enters Warsaw **17th January**	Yalta Conference **4-11th February**		Polish 1st Armoured liberates POW camp at Oberlangen **12th April**	Polish 1st Armoured takes surrender of the German naval base at Wilhelmshaven **6th May**	
1945 January	February	March	April	May	June

250

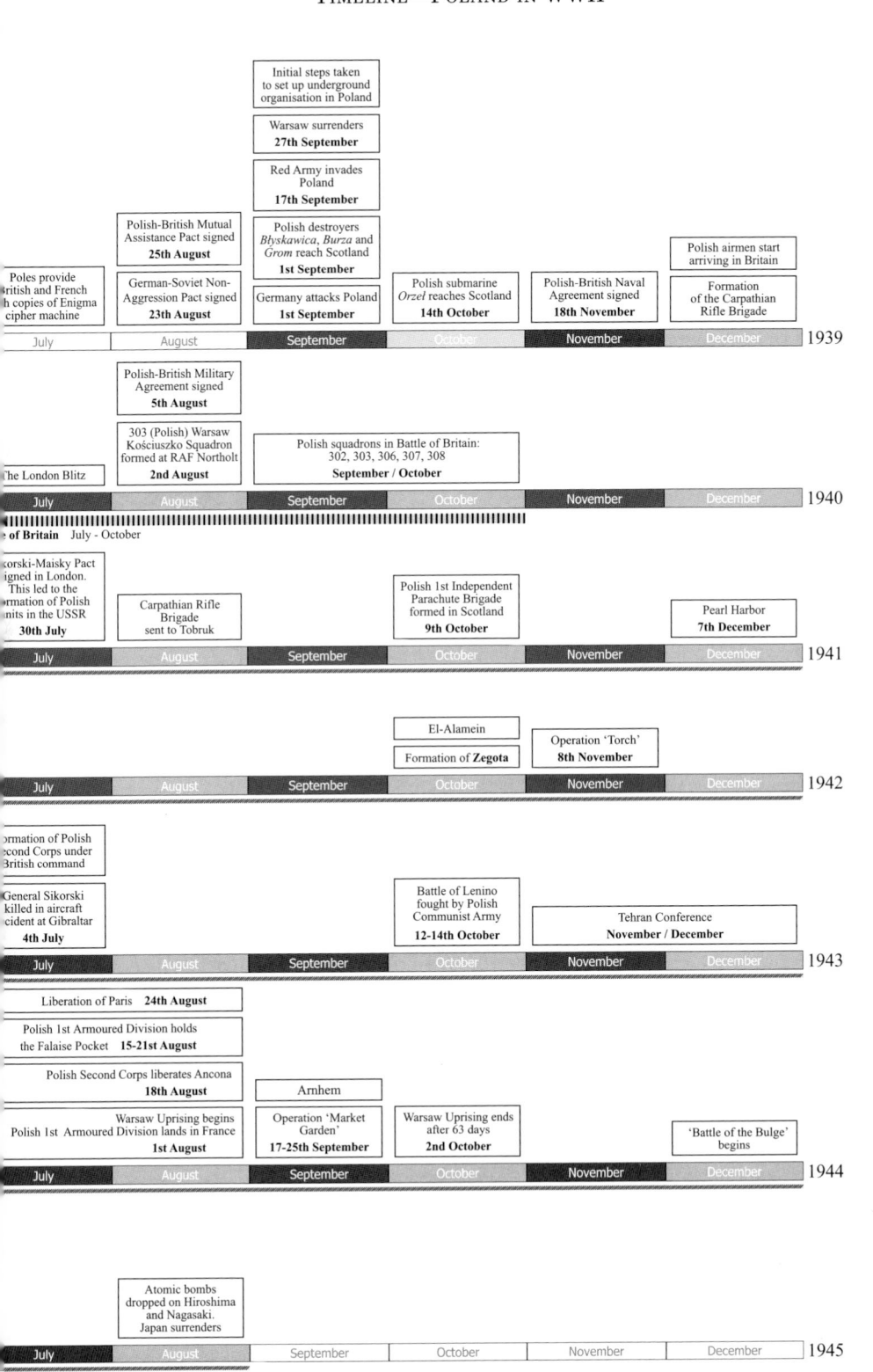

1939

Initial steps taken to set up underground organisation in Poland

Warsaw surrenders
27th September

Red Army invades Poland
17th September

Polish-British Mutual Assistance Pact signed
25th August

Polish destroyers *Błyskawica*, *Burza* and *Grom* reach Scotland
1st September

Polish airmen start arriving in Britain

Poles provide British and French with copies of Enigma cipher machine

German-Soviet Non-Aggression Pact signed
23rd August

Germany attacks Poland
1st September

Polish submarine *Orzel* reaches Scotland
14th October

Polish-British Naval Agreement signed
18th November

Formation of the Carpathian Rifle Brigade

July | August | September | October | November | December

1940

Polish-British Military Agreement signed
5th August

303 (Polish) Warsaw Kościuszko Squadron formed at RAF Northolt
2nd August

Polish squadrons in Battle of Britain: 302, 303, 305, 306, 307, 308
September / October

The London Blitz

July | August | September | October | November | December

Battle of Britain   July - October

1941

Sikorski-Maisky Pact signed in London. This led to the formation of Polish units in the USSR
30th July

Carpathian Rifle Brigade sent to Tobruk

Polish 1st Independent Parachute Brigade formed in Scotland
9th October

Pearl Harbor
7th December

July | August | September | October | November | December

1942

El-Alamein

Formation of **Zegota**

Operation 'Torch'
8th November

July | August | September | October | November | December

1943

Formation of Polish Second Corps under British command

General Sikorski killed in aircraft accident at Gibraltar
4th July

Battle of Lenino fought by Polish Communist Army
12-14th October

Tehran Conference
November / December

July | August | September | October | November | December

1944

Liberation of Paris   **24th August**

Polish 1st Armoured Division holds the Falaise Pocket   **15-21st August**

Polish Second Corps liberates Ancona
18th August

Arnhem

Warsaw Uprising begins
Polish 1st Armoured Division lands in France
1st August

Operation 'Market Garden'
17-25th September

Warsaw Uprising ends after 63 days
2nd October

'Battle of the Bulge' begins

July | August | September | October | November | December

1945

Atomic bombs dropped on Hiroshima and Nagasaki. Japan surrenders

July | August | September | October | November | December

251

Katyń: Mass murder at the stroke of a pen

On 13th April 1943 Berlin Radio announced to the world that the Germans had uncovered a series of mass graves in the Katyń woods near Smolensk in Western Russia. These graves contained the remains of Polish army officers, policemen, professional people and a number of other officials who had clearly been executed with a bullet to the back of the head. Initial German findings suggested that the men had been killed in early 1940 when the whole area had been in Soviet hands. Other such burial sites were subsequently found near Kalinin (Tver') and Kharkov and it is calculated that almost 20,000 Poles had been shot in cold blood. It was also later established that the victims had been murdered at a number of different locations

For the Poles, the news was confirmation of their worst fears. When the Soviet Union had invaded Poland in September 1939, the Red Army took more than 200,000 Polish soldiers prisoner. In addition, the NKVD had quickly set about combing the part of Poland the USSR now occupied for anyone who might constitute any kind of threat to the speedy imposition of Soviet political control. In practice this meant teachers, policemen, priests, businessmen, politicians and opinion-makers of any

stripe. While many of the private soldiers were released, the overwhelming majority of their officers and the professional people were held in camps in the Western part of the Soviet Union, primarily at Kozelsk, Ostashkov and Starobelsk or were transported deeper into the heartland of the USSR.

After the signing of the Polish-Soviet agreement in July 1941 and the resumption of diplomatic relations between the two countries, the Poles were troubled by the continuing absence of over 10,000 regular and reserve army officers who were urgently required for the forces now forming in the USSR and who had to all intents and purposes vanished in the spring of 1940. When taxed on the matter, Soviet officials were invariably evasive, Stalin even going so far as to make the extraordinary suggestion to the Polish leader General Sikorski that some of the missing men might have escaped to Manchuria!

As the Germans had intended, news of the discovery of the mass graves caused consternation amongst the Western Allies. For the British and the Americans it was critical that the Soviet Union continue to bear the lion's share of the ground fighting in Europe. They were not prepared to allow this issue, to drive a wedge between themselves and the Soviet Union, which is what the Germans were trying to achieve. The Poles, for their part, wanted to get to the truth of the matter, although few of them doubted that the Soviets were indeed the perpetrators.

When the Polish Government in London asked the International Red Cross to conduct an impartial investigation, the Soviet Union treated this as a pretext to sever diplomatic relations with the Poles accusing their government of being in league with the Nazis, who too had involved the Red Cross. Furthermore, the Soviet Government categorically denied involvement in the massacre. The British Government and Winston Churchill tried in vain on the one hand to convince Stalin to refrain from taking such a drastic step and, on the other, to get General Sikorski to downplay the whole issue, which was politically and emotionally quite impossible for him to do.

At the Nuremberg Trials after the War the Soviet Union tried to add what became known as the Katyń Massacre to the list of indictments, but significantly the Western Allies refused to agree to this. Indeed, as early as 1943 the British Ambassador to the Polish Government-in-Exile, Sir Own O'Malley, had written a detailed report showing that in fact the NKVD had carried out the murders. The report was given only limited circulation at the time. A similar conclusion was reached by a US Congressional Committee of Enquiry in the early 1950s.

The Soviets continued to deny all responsibility and too produced their own reports purporting to show that the murders were the work of the Germans. Sadly, but inevitably, the issue was to cloud Polish-Soviet relations until the 1990s when both Mikhail Gorbachev and later Boris Yeltsin admitted Soviet guilt. They produced the incriminating documents which we see here signed by the Head of the NKVD, Lavrenti Beria, and formally apologised to the Poles. No-one has ever been prosecuted for the crime.

СССР

**НАРОДНЫЙ КОМИССАРИАТ
ВНУТРЕННИХ ДЕЛ**

марта 1940 г.
№ 794/Б

г. МОСКВА

сов. секретно

Ц К   В К П (б)

товарищу С Т А Л И Н У

В лагерях для военнопленных НКВД СССР и в тюрьмах западных областей Украины и Белоруссии в настоящее время содержится большое количество бывших офицеров польской армии, бывших работников польской полиции и разведывательных органов, членов польских националистических к-р партий, участников вскрытых к-р повстанческих организаций, перебежчиков и др. Все они являются заклятыми врагами советской власти, преисполненными ненависти к советскому строю.

Военнопленные офицеры и полицейские, находясь в лагерях, пытаются продолжать к-р работу, ведут антисоветскую агитацию. Каждый из них только и ждет освобождения, чтобы иметь возможность активно включиться в борьбу против советской власти.

Органами НКВД в западных областях Украины и Белоруссии вскрыт ряд к-р повстанческих организаций. Во всех этих к-р организациях активную руководящую роль играли бывшие офицеры бывшей польской армии, бывшие полицейские и жандармы.

Среди задержанных перебежчиков и нарушителей гос-

т. Калинин -Я
т. Каганович -к

С подлинным верно
Главный государственный архив
Российской Федерации

Р.Г.Пихоя

Memorandum from the Head of the NKVD

of the USSR L.Beria for Stalin

(March 1940)

USSR
People's Commissariat
For Internal Affairs
March 1940
No. 794/5
Moscow

Top Secret
5 iii 1940

Committee Of the All-Union Communist Party (Bolshevik)

To Comrade Stalin

At the present time a great number of former officers of the Polish Army, former employees of the Polish police and intelligence services, members of Polish nationalist (counter-revolutionary) parties, members of declared (counter-revolutionary) insurgent organisations, fugitives and others are being held in NKVD POW camps in the USSR and in prisons in the western districts of the Ukraine and Belorussia. They are all fervent enemies of Soviet power and filled with hatred for the Soviet system.

The POWs, the officers and the policemen in the camps are trying to continue counter-revolutionary activities. Every one of them is only waiting to be freed in order to take an active role in the struggle against Soviet power.

In the Western districts of the Ukraine and Belorussia operatives of the NKVD have uncovered a number of insurrectionary organisations. Former officers of the former Polish Army, former policemen and gendarmes have been playing a leading role in these organisations.

Amongst the detained deserters and other persons who have violated state borders a considerable number of people have been discovered who are members of counter- revolutionary

_____ *Continued overleaf*

Diagonally across the page are Stalin's, Voroshilov's, Molotov's and Mikoyan's signatures. In the margin of the official document are Comrade Kalinin's and Comrade Kaganovich's signatures.

2. -

границы также выявлено значительное количество лиц,
которые являются участниками к-р шпионских и повстанческих организаций.

В лагерях для военнопленных содержится всего
(не считая солдат и унтерофицерского состава) -
14.736 бывших офицеров, чиновников, помещиков, поли-
цейских, жандармов, тюремщиков, осадников и разведчиков - по национальности свыше 97% поляки.

Из них:

Генералов, полковников и под-полковников	- 295
Майоров и капитанов	- 2.080
Поручиков, подпоручиков и хо-рунжих	- 6.049
Офицеров и младших командиров полиции, пограничной охраны и жандармерии	- 1.030
Рядовых полицейских, жандармов, тюремщиков и разведчиков	- 5.138
Чиновников, помещиков, ксендзов и осадников	- 144

В тюрьмах западных областей Украины и Белоруссии
всего содержится 18.632 арестованных (из них 10.685
поляки), в том числе:

бывших офицеров	- 1.207
бывших полицейских разведчиков и жандармов	- 5.141
Шпионов и диверсантов	- 347
Бывших помещиков, фабрикантов и чиновников	- 465
Членов различных к-р и повстан-ческих организаций и разного к-р элемента	- 5.345
Перебежчиков	- 6.127

С подлинным

Главный госу[...]
архивист Рос[...]
Федерации

Continued from previous ───────────────────────────────

espionage and insurrectionary organisations.

Altogether 14,736 former officers, civil servants, landowners, policemen, gendarmes, prison guards, settlers and intelligence agents (not counting private soldiers and NCOs), over 97% of them Polish, are being held in the POW camps.

They include:
Generals, colonels and lieutenant colonels	– 295
Majors and captains	– 2,080
Lieutenants, second lieutenants and officer cadets	– 6,049
Officers and junior leaders in the police, frontier guards and gendarmerie	– 1,030
Policemen, gendarmes, prison guards and intelligence agents	– 5,138
Civil servants, landowners, Roman Catholic priests and military settlers	– 144

Altogether 18,632 people (including 10,685 Poles) are being held in prisons in the western districts of the Ukraine and Belorussia.

They include:
Former officers	– 1,207
Former policemen, intelligence agents and gendarmes	– 5,141
Spies and saboteurs	– 347
Former landowners, factory owners and civil servants	– 465
Members of various counter-revolutionary and insurrectionary organisations and various counter-revolutionary elements	– 5,345
Deserters	– 6,127

─────────────────────────────────── *Continued overleaf*

3.-

Исходя из того, что все они являются закорене-
лыми, неисправимыми врагами советской власти, НКВД
СССР считает необходимым:

О.П.

Вопрос НКВД СССР

I. Предложить НКВД СССР:

1) Дела о находящихся в лагерях для
военнопленных 14.700 человек бывших польских офицеров, чиновников, помещиков, поли-
цейских, разведчиков, жандармов, осадников
и тюремщиков,

2) а также дела об арестованных и находящихся в тюрьмах западных областей Украины и Белоруссии в количестве 11.000 человек
членов различных к-р шпионских и диверсион-
ных организаций, бывших помещиков, фабри-
кантов, бывших польских офицеров, чиновников и перебежчиков —

— рассмотреть в особом порядке, с при-
менением к ним высшей меры наказания —
расстрела.

II. Рассмотрение дел провести без вызова арестованных и без предъявления обвинения, постановления
об окончании следствия и обвинительного заключения —
в следующем порядке:

а) на лиц, находящихся в лагерях воен-
нопленных — по справкам, представляемым
Управлением по делам военнопленных НКВД
СССР,

С подлинным
Главный
архивист
Федерации
...Пихоя

Continued from previous _____

Taking into account that they are all hardened opponents of Soviet power showing no signs of changing, the NKVD of the USSR considers it essential to:

I. Recommend to the NKVD of the USSR:

1). That the cases of the 14,700 people held in POW camps, the former Polish officers, civil servants, landowners, policemen, intelligence officers, gendarmes, settlers and prison guards,

2). As well as the cases of all those 11,000 people held in prisons in western Ukraine and Belorussia, members of various counter-revolutionary, espionage and sabotage organisations, former landowners, factory owners, former Polish officers, civil servants and deserters

- be reviewed as a matter of urgency and that the supreme penalty-death by shooting-be imposed.

II. That the cases be reviewed, without calling the accused, without presenting accusations, or the decisions to end interrogations or guilty verdicts for the following:

(a) those held in POW camps based on the information provided by the NKVD Committee for POW Affairs of the USSR.

_____ *Continued overleaf*

NOTE: In the margin there is a hand-written annotation:
'O.P. Matter for NKVD USSR'

4. -

б) на лиц, арестованных - по справкам из
дел, представляемым НКВД УССР и НКВД БССР.

Ш. Рассмотрение дел и вынесение решения возложить
на тройку, в составе т.т. ~~МЕРКУЛОВА~~ МЕРКУЛОВА и БАШТАКОВА
(Начальник 1-го Спецотдела НКВД СССР).

НАРОДНЫЙ КОМИССАР ВНУТРЕННИХ ДЕЛ
С о ю з а С С Р

(Л. БЕРИЯ)

Вн.
Берия

И 13/144
5.III.40г.

С подлинным верно
Главный государственный архивист
Российской Федерации   .Пихоя

Continued from previous ———————————————————————

(b) those held based on information provided by the NKVD of the Ukrainian SSR and the Belorussian SSR.

III. To empower a three-person panel composed of comrades (*NN crossed out by hand*), Merkulov Kabulov *[?]* *(added by hand),* and Bashtakov *(Head of the NKVD of the USSR 1st Special Department).*

The People's Commissar
For Internal Affairs of the USSR

(signature)

L. Beria

P 13/144
5 iii 1940

Handwritten
For action ?
(signature: Beria)

———————————————————————

Note: Each document is signed and stamped as being a faithful copy of the original by the chief state archivist of the Russian Federation, R.G. Pikhoya

Translated from the Russian by Jarek Garliński

History of the Memorial to the Polish Armed Forces in the National Memorial Arboretum

Jacek Korzeniowski

In the spring of 2007 Tadeusz Juhre turned to Dr Marek Stella-Sawicki with the question: 'Why is there no Polish Memorial amongst the 150 war memorials in the National Arboretum in Alrewas?' Tadeusz Juhre, whose estate Aqualate Hall is close-by the Arboretum, had spent over a year fruitlessly knocking on the doors of various Polish émigré organisations. This time he received an immediate and enthusiastic reaction. Dr Stella-Sawicki briskly started work by joining forces with Dr Andrzej Meeson- Kielanowski. Together they gathered a group of people who were not only willing to help but who also possessed the necessary knowledge and skills to be able to do so. The way Dr Stella-Sawicki operates is beautifully illustrated by the way he approached the author for help:

March 2008. The telephone rings.

'Jacek, I need a drawing done for tomorrow!'

'What sort of drawing?'

'A monument—we're building a monument! I'll come round with a sketch! Bye!'

And he came. He had already been to the Arboretum for preliminary talks.

After many hours of hard work, detailed discussions involving many people, several versions of the drawing were made. A model was made up using toy lead soldiers; potential sculptors were considered; a suitable spot was negotiated free of charge at the Arboretum. As the ideas began to crystallise – from a misty vision to a dream to something positive and possible, in April 2008, the initiators were able to turn to the Polish Ex-Combatants Association (SPK), in the hope that it would support this initiative.

The chairman, Czesław Maryszczak, and the SPK Board were immediately in favour of the idea. Soon after, their AGM approved the decision and agreed funds to start the work. It could begin straightaway thanks to the fact that so much effort and skill had gone into the planning. Robert Sobociński, an artist living in Poznań was chosen as the sculptor. In September 2008 his model of the monument immediately gained the approval of the Committee. By October 2008 the contract had been signed.

In September 2008 the British Polish Appeal Committee was set up, which drew a great deal of support from many eminent people, both British and Polish. The last President-in-Exile, Ryszard Kaczorowski, agreed to head the honourary committee and thanks to this and the unstinting hard work of Dr Andrzej Meeson-Kielanowski a significant amount of vital funds were collected.

Robert Sobociński worked on the sculpture day and night. He was later to recount how on Christmas Eve he was still trying to correct some details and was not able to sit down to the family celebrations until he had got them absolutely right.

Thus the first stage of the sculpture—in clay—was completed in January 2009. The Memorial Committee accepted it with very few changes.

Immediately after the Committee's return from Poznań the following article was published in *The Polish Daily*.

Introduction in Clay

At Robert Sobociński's workshop in Poznań, four tons of clay have already taken shape as the Monument to the Polish Armed Forces, which will be erected in the National Memorial Arboretum in Alrewas, Staffordshire. Several details are still missing. The surface is rougher than the final version in bronze will be, but this is due to techniques and methods invented by Leonardo da Vinci.

The symbolism of this monument is easy to decipher. Four figures: a woman (maybe a girl), a sailor, an airman and a soldier. They are standing with their backs to each other, facing outwards to the four corners of the earth. They are parting, not out of their own desire, but because they have to defend and fight for their country. They believe they will return victorious from their battle; they are leaving behind everything which links them, which unites them—Poland. Above them, a crowned eagle prepares for flight. He too must abandon his nest. Does the eagle know that when he finally returns to his country, when the war has ended, he won't be able to wear his crown for many years to come?

If they could speak, what would these figures of clay be able to tell us? Whose wartime fates would they recount? Did the people they knew pay the ultimate price? Did they lose everything that they ever owned on this earth? What fate met their loved ones? Did they, years later, reach a free Poland? Where is the girl from, the one standing with a message in her hand? Was she in the Grey Ranks (Szare Szeregi) or part of another organisation? Did she go to a so-called trade school so that she could study undercover for her academic exams? And did she sew shirts for the German Army? Did she sew a pin into every possible seam so that those men who had stolen her beloved homeland would feel a little pain? Did

Four toy soldiers illustrate the concept for the Polish Armed Forces Memorial

Clay original—detail of the Polish Army figure

From clay to plaster—the figures are starting to come to life

The heroic story of Poland's contribution to the Allied victory
in World War II is carved onto granite plaques

96 tonnes of hand-cut granite from Poland
are delivered the National Memorial Arboretum site

she survive the Uprising, or did she share the fate of 5,000 female soldiers of the Home Army? Or perhaps she was taken to a camp, and the soldier standing next to her, maybe he was one of those who liberated her from POW camp in Oberlangen?

And why is this soldier wearing battle dress with a Poland badge? Which unit is he in? We can't read the number. Is it the soldier in the tank, the one that the girl remembered? Maybe he fought in the September Campaign, at the very start of the war, and although he may have been wounded, he survived and got out of Poland. Maybe he was the one who received a severe warning in Budapest: he had been in a tram with his friend, commenting on a woman; it transpired that she was a worker in the Polish Consulate and had understood every word! He was young and he was still, despite the war, behaving like a schoolboy! But he soon grew up, and made his way to France, so as not to stop fighting, never losing his faith. He survived the next disaster, but he never lost his belief in victory. Again he was successful and was one of the few who sailed to England from Dunkirk.

But no, he must have been too young to fight in September. He was the one who was arrested together with his mother and sister by the NKVD that night in Lwów, in April 1940. His mother became hysterical, so the Russian grabbed his sister by the throat threatening to strangle her if their mother didn't control herself. And so his sister, for the rest of her life, could never button up a blouse to the neck. Then, as the youngest in his family, in Kazakhstan, he would gather dried cow dung for fuel. And so he grew up, and eventually left that hell, with General Anders and his army. But maybe he didn't, although he walked as fast as he could and fought at the Battle of Lenino; he always believed in a free Poland. He was cruelly cheated by his Communist leaders, but he didn't give in and so he survived to see the eagle crowned again.

On the monument you can see the soldier's friends, the sailor and the airman. The sailor lived in Gdynia before the War, and sailed on the *Lightning* (*Błyskawica*). And he was so happy when they sank the German U-boat in September on the way to England. Then in Narvik, he shot at the Germans hidden on the shore. But maybe he never sailed on a destroyer. Maybe he was on a merchant ship and delivered provisions to England across the Atlantic. And the airman? Oh, how much he would have liked to tell the girl from the Uprising how he flew towards her. And he believed, when he took off from Brindisi, that he would get there, that he would manage to help just a little Warsaw, already in flames, yet they got him above Yugoslavia.

Did this airman fight in the Battle of Britain? We don't have to write about that —everyone knows about it. But do they? And does everyone really know what a great price the countrymen of these four paid for their freedom, for which they had to wait so long? And how did they fight for your freedom and ours? And who was the first to break the Enigma code? Who delivered the parts of the V2 to London?

We need a little more imagination, so let's have another look at these four figures. Let's not look at them literally. Let's imagine that they are standing high on their plinth in the Arboretum, surrounded by granite walls engraved with a short history lesson. Let's think of all those, living and dead, who fought for us and everything that we should be grateful for. Let us pay homage to them. This is a monument to them all.

* * *

The next stage in the making of the sculpture was done according to the age-old technique of first making a negative mould in plaster and then a positive one using the clay original which has been divided into fragments. These are then all joined together again, with any alterations that have been made, and prepared for the final mould into which the bronze is poured.

In February 2009 almost 100 tons of granite arrived in Poznań from the Languedoc region in France and the stonemasonry could commence. The 16 granite panels which were to surround the terrace round the monument began to be formed. The history of the contribution of the Polish Armed Forces to the Second World War had to be carved into these walls. The plinth and the granite flooring were also being prepared.

By April 2009 the plaster version of the monument was ready to be accepted by members of the Memorial Committee, when they visited Poznań towards the end of the month. While they were there, they visited the masonry workshops so that they could see the work in progress and to sign the contracts for erecting the stonework in the Arboretum.

Having received the Committee's approval, Robert Sobociński was ready to start the final process of preparing the moulds for the bronze castings.

The British firm The Special Team began work on the foundations of the memorial on 1st May 2009.

The casting, assembling, welding and patinating of the sculpture took place during May and June. The lorries containing the monument and the granite arrived in Alrewas on 6th July. The next stage after safely unloading the precious cargo in the Arboretum was to mount the granite panels, the plinth and to lay the granite terrace. As is usual in these cases, lifting the monument from the lorry and placing it vertically not far from its final position, was a critical operation and a very emotional one.

At the beginning of August 2009 the stonemasonry work was finished and the memorial was mounted on its pedestal. On the 15th August, a day commemorating the miracle on the River Vistula, Polish Army Day, this article appeared in *The Polish Daily*:

Steadfast

It's no longer the rough, brown clay nor the brittle plaster in which the figures were set in the Polish Armed Forces Memorial in the National Memorial Arboretum. Now it is in beautiful and permanent bronze, which is so close to gunmetal, the symbol of permanence; bronze, whose production was perfected by the Romans in Brindisi, a town from which Polish airmen flew their missions to the aid of the Warsaw Uprising.

Let's stand at a distance and look at the eagle as he prepares for flight. He has to leave his nest and take his crown with him, so that it doesn't fall into enemy hands. The symbol of Poland's sovereignty must one day proudly return to Poland, in the same way that the insignia of the Second Republic returned to their homeland after many years.

Beneath the eagle the stones of the pillar are disintegrating, in the same way that Poland began to collapse beneath the force of the Nazi war machine which was supported soon after by Soviet Russia. Yet the pillar, though crumbling in parts, is still able to unite those who are around it, those who are going into the world in order to continue fighting for their country.

Let's get closer and look first at the young woman who is standing in the foreground. On her breast is her Girl Guide's cross, on her head her cap with an eagle badge. This symbol must have been very significant for her, as it replaced the traditional *fleur-de-lis*. Maybe it was her father's badge, from his pre-war uniform, which by some miracle she had managed to save throughout the Occupation, especially as she hadn't heard from him since he went to fight in the September Campaign. And now this eagle and the memories of those wonderful moments spent with her father on that last pre-war holiday in Rabka are keeping her going in these first days of the Uprising. Tucked into her belt is her *VIS* pistol and she is holding a report in her hand. What is in the report? Probably not good news, as her face is pensive. Is she actually thinking about her fiancé, who was lost in action and did not survive to experience the Uprising and its first days of euphoria and feelings of triumph?

She is also here on this monument for another reason. She is here to remind us of all the women, both young and old, who fought for Poland's freedom, of those who fought in the Polish Underground and those who drove ammunition trucks, of those who delivered aeroplanes and of those who worked in intelligence and sought out immeasurably important information. All these women contributed in their own particular way to fight for the freedom of Poland.

Let's walk around the monument. These figures are linked with each other yet at the same time each one is a monument in its own right. Now we have before us the soldier in battle dress with his Poland badge and a flat English helmet on his head; a Sten gun in his hand. And we almost didn't notice the eagle on his helmet. That's because our attention was rivetted by his face full of determination, brought on by all those years spent far away from Poland, from his beloved Lwów. He, who left that 'infernal place', resolved never to rest until Poland is free again. Now he is set on the monument in the act of moving forward, firm against any vagaries of fate, with only one idea in his head – victory! The artist has made him step upwards,—maybe he is going towards Monte Cassino, or perhaps his pose is only a symbol of the fact that the road to freedom is a hard climb.

Walking round the memorial we come across the sailor. The dynamics of the movement created within the monument make us look upwards. The sailor is standing straight, looking into the distance, with his hand raised as if to shield himself from the glare of the flares. Is he searching out a U-boat on the horizon? There is no fear of the enemy to be seen in his eyes, because he has served on a well-equipped destroyer; he was only anxious to protect his shipmates. The artist did not record the name of this sailor's ship; he has just put Navy on the band of his cap. This was not by chance—he did it to honour all those sailors who gave their life for their country, those who died in the first days of the war defending the Polish coast, and all those who fought and died far from their homeland. And this sailor, together with those others immortalised on this monument, will always remind everyone that Poland was the only nation to fight from the very first day of the war to the very end.

Our next step takes us to the airman. We must lift our head yet further, to look at his face full of glory, his hand outstretched in a greeting full of triumph. This airman has just returned from yet another successful mission. Is he one of those aces whose glory was gained in the Battle of Britain? Or is he one of those who flew from Brindisi to help in the struggle for Warsaw? They had fewer opportunities for elation, but in spite of heavy losses, they never curtailed their mission. It would be pointless to try and place the airman just by looking at his flying suit and the rest of his clothing, because his uniform changed as frequently as technology developed, especially in times of the greatest need—in times of war. These details aren't important—what is important is to pay homage to all the airmen, yet not forgetting the hard-working ground crews who gave them the necessary means and equipment.

Now our thoughts turn to all those who can't be seen directly on the monument; let's go to the edge of the granite tiled floor towards the panels with the engravings that remind us of everything that the Poles did in World War II. Let's start with the panel 'September'. Someone seems to have laid a bronze Polish four-cornered military cap in the same way that wreaths are laid on the graves of loved ones. This symbol must stop every passer-by in his tracks; it makes him look at the writing, reminding him that on 1st September, 1939, the Second World War was started by the German invasion of Poland and whose outcome might have been quite different, if it hadn't been for the mighty efforts

The cast bronze monument arrives safely
at the National Memorial Arboretum

The Polish Armed Forces Memorial

**ZA WOLNOŚĆ
NASZA I WASZA**

W HOŁDZIE POLEGŁYM
ŻOŁNIERZOM WOJSKA
POLSKIEGO I POLSKIEGO
PODZIEMIA, LOTNIKOM
I MARYNARZOM, KTÓRZY
WALCZYLI O WOLNOŚĆ
POLSKI W KRAJU I POZA
JEGO GRANICAMI
1939-1945.

**FOR OUR FREEDOM
AND YOURS**

IN GLORIOUS MEMORY
OF THE POLISH MEN
AND WOMEN WHO
GAVE THEIR LIVES FOR
OUR FREEDOM
IN THE SECOND
WORLD WAR 1939-1945

of the Poles, which cost Hitler far more than he ever expected. These efforts gave our allies more time to prepare for war.

Let's go further. Let's stop in front of the next panel, or maybe only by the one where it speaks about something that is especially close to our hearts; there isn't a Pole who hasn't lost someone close during this war. Let's not hurry; we don't have to read everything—we can always come back. And if there is someone with us who perhaps knows less about what Poland and Poles did towards the final victory, let's point out just the most important things—the breaking of the Enigma code, the handing over of the technical details for the V2, and the whole of the enormous input of the Polish intelligence services. Let's be proud of what our countrymen did, because this isn't the time or place for false modesty. We have had to wait a long time in order to be able to tell the whole truth, as long as it took to wait for an independent Poland. Looking at this Memorial to the Polish Armed Forces, let us pay homage to those who have made it possible for the younger generations of Poles to live in a free country. This monument is to every Pole who fought '*For Your Freedom and Ours*'.

Translated by Basia Korzeniowska

Poland's Contribution to WWII:
Further Reading

Articles

— Harrison, E.D.R., '*The British Special Operations Executive and Poland*', The Historical Journal, 43, 4, Cambridge, 2000, pp. 1071-1091.

— Wroński, Bohdan, *Relations between Polish and British Government* (sic) *1939-1945*, presented at a conference on Governments in Exile in London During the Second World War, 25th of October 1977 at the Imperial War Museum, London.

Books

— Astley, Joan Bright, *The Inner Circle*, London, 1973.

— Bekker, Cajus, *Hitler's Naval War*, London, 1974.

— Bethell, Nicholas, *The War Hitler Won*, London, 1976.

— Calvocoressi, Peter and Wint, Guy, *Total War*, Harmondsworth, 1972.

— Carton de Wiart, Adrian, *Happy Odyssey*, London, 1955.

— Cazalet, V.A., *With Sikorski to Russia*, London, 1942.

— Chapman, Guy, *Why France Collapsed*, London, 1968.

— Ciechanowski, Jan, *The Warsaw Rising of 1944*, Cambridge, 2002.

— Cienciala, Anna M., Lebedeva. Natalia S., Materski, Wojciech, (editors), *Katyn A Crime Without Punishment*, New Haven, 2007.

— Coutovidis, John and Reynolds, Jaime, *Poland 1939-1947*, Leicester, 1986.

— Davies, Norman, *Europe At War 1939-1945, No Simple Victory*, London, 2006.

— Davies, Norman, *God's Playground, A History of Poland*, vol. II, New York,1982.

— Davies, Norman, *Rising '44 'The Battle for Warsaw'*, London, 2004.

— Erickson, John, *The Road to Stalingrad*, London, 1975.

— Fest, Joachim, *Hitler*, London, 1977.

— Foot, Michael R.D., *Resistance*, London, 1976.

— Garliński, Józef, *Fighting Auschwitz*, London, 1975.

— Garliński, Józef, *Hitler's Last Weapons*, London, 1978.

— Garliński, Józef, *Intercept*, London, 1979.

— Garliński, Józef, *Poland in the Second World War*, London, 1975.

— Garliński, Józef, *Poland, SOE and the Allies*, London, 1969.

— Garliński, Józef, *The Swiss Corridor*, London, 1981.

— Hawes, Stephen and White, Ralph (editors), *Resistance in Europe: 1939-1945,* London, 1975.

— Hinsley, F.H et al, *British Intelligence in the Second World War*, volumes I and II, London, 1979 -1981.

— Irving, David, *The Death of General Sikorski*, London, 1967.

— Judt, Tony, Postwar. *A History of Europe Since 1945*, London, 2005.

— Keegan, John, *The Second World War*, London, 1989.

— Kemp, Peter, *No Colours or Crest*, London, 1958.

— Korboński, Stefan, *Fighting Warsaw*, New York, 2004.

— Koskodan, Kenneth, K, *No Greater Ally. The Untold Story of Poland's Forces in WWII*, Botley, 2009.

— Leslie, R.F., Polonsky, Antony, Ciechanowski, Jan M., Pełczyński, Z.A., *The History of Poland since 1863*, Cambridge, 1980.

— Lukas, Richard C, *Forgotten Holocaust—the Poles under German Occupation 1939-1945*, New York, 2005.

— Lukowski, Jerzy and Zawadzki, Hubert, *A Concise History of Poland*, second edition, Cambridge 2006.

— MacDonogh, Giles, *After the Reich—The Brutal History of the Allied Occupation*, New York, 2007.

— Mawdsley, Evan, *Thunder in the East—the Nazi-Soviet War 1941-1945,* London, 2005.

— Mikołajczyk, Stanisław, T*he Pattern of Soviet Domination*, London, 1948.

— Ney-Krwawicz, Marek, *The Polish Home Army 1939-1945*, London, 2001.

— Olson, Lynne and Cloud, Stanley, *A Question of Honor*, New York, 2003.

— Peszke, Michael, *Poland's Navy*, New York, 1999.

— Peszke, Michael, *The Polish Underground Army, the Western Allies, and the Failure of Strategic Unity in World War II*, Jefferson North Carolina, 2005.

— Polonsky, Antony, Politics in Independent Poland, 1921-1939, Oxford, 1972.

— Polonsky, Antony (editor), *The Great Powers and the Polish Question 1941-45*, London, 1976.

— Polonsky, Antony and Drukier, Bolesław, *The Beginnings of Communist Rule in Poland, December 1943-June 1945*, London, 1980.

— Prażmowska, Anita, *Britain and Poland 1939-1943 — The Betrayed Ally*, Cambridge, 1995.

— Prażmowska, Anita, *Civil War in Poland, 1942-1948*, Basingstoke, 2004.

— Prażmowska, Anita, *Britain, Poland and the Eastern Front, 1939*, Cambridge, 1987.

— Raczyński, Edward, *The British-Polish Alliance*, London, 1948

— Rees, Laurence, *World War Two Behind Closed Doors*, London, 2008.

— Reitlinger, Gerard, *The Final Solution*, London, 1971.

— Salmonowicz, Stanisław, Ney-Krwawicz, Marek and Górski, Grzegorz, *Polskie Pańswto Podziemne, Polish Underground State*, Warsaw, 1999.

— Schellenberg, Walter, *The Schellenberg Memoirs*, London, 1956.

— Seale, Patrick and McConville, Maureen, Philby, *The Long Road to Moscow*, London, 1973.

— Slessor, John, *The Central Blue*, London, 1956.

— Speer, Albert, *Inside The Third Reich*, London, 1971.

— Sword, Keith (editor), *Sikorski: Soldier and Statesman—A Collection of Essays*, London, 1990.

— Walker, Jonathan, *Poland Alone: Britain, SOE and the Collapse of the Polish Resistance, 1944*, Stroud, 2008.

— Wilkinson, Peter, *Foreign Fields: The Story of an SOE Operative*, London, 2002.

— Williamson, David G., *Poland Betrayed. The Nazi-Soviet Invasions 1939*, Barnsley, 2009.

— Zaloga, Steven J, *Poland 1939 The Birth of Blitzkrieg*, Botley, 2002.

— Zawodny, Janusz, *Death in the Forest*, London, 1971.

— Zawodny, Janusz, *Nothing But Honor*, London, 1978.

Collective Works

— *Documents on Polish-Soviet Relations, 1939-1945*, volumes I and II, London, 1961-1967.

— *Intelligence Co-operation between Poland and Great Britain during World War II*, eds. Stirling, Tessa et al, volume 1, London, 2005.

— *The Unseen and Silent,* London 1954.

Internet links and on-line documents

— Maresch, Eugenia, '*The Secret Army (AK) Intelligence Operations during the Second World War*', a lecture given at the Polish Underground Movement Study Trust on 22.11.2004,

www.polishresistance-archive.org/articles_by_pumst/004_Symp_Post_Maresh.pdf

— Newcourt-Nowodworski, Stanisław, '*Black Propaganda during World War Two*', a lecture given at the Polish Underground Movement Study Trust on 22.11.2004,

www.polishresistance-archive.org/articles_by_pumst/003_Symp_Black Propaganda_Nowodworski.pdf

— Ostrowski, Mark, '*To Return to Poland or not to Return*' The Dilemma Facing the Polish Armed Forces at the End of the Second World War, thesis published on-line at — www.angelfire.com/ok2/polisharmy

Foretold...

Dedicated to General Anders

A Soldiers' footprints
in Europe's muddied lands

Forward, where others fell and fail
reaching the peak of his Holy Grail

Freedom cut from bloodied hands,
yet no homeland in which to rest his soul

Wisely, sanely, cold, he says
foreseen for a long long time ...
"no debt for pain" the soldier's told
"the price of blood compares not to gold"

Who counted soldiers in shallow graves
or angels' souls fighting devil's might?
Your eyes do see sorrow, now the truth be told

So tell me what virtue in the fight?

The Soldier paused a while,
memories and talk of coming home
now lost, fallen in distant lands,
vanquished in foreign graves
"we'll return" they cried,
words turned to stone

Riders in dusts of Apocalypse
strains of mazurkas faintly slip
Crowds baying—
*"Dabrowski to Warsaw returns
from Italian land"*

Was it worth the price they paid?

Unthinkable Doubt!

By Jan Lechoń,
translated by Teresa Stella-Sawicka

The Polish Armed Forces War Memorial project team
with HE Polish Ambassador Barbara Tuge-Erecińska
at the National Memorial Arboretum in Alrewas,
Staffordshire, 17th August 2009